ORGANIC
Vegetable Growing

Visit our How To website at www.howto.co.uk

At **www.howto.co.uk** you can engage in conversation with our authors – all of whom have 'been there and done that' in their specialist fields. You can get access to special offers and additional content but most importantly you will be able to engage with, and become a part of, a wide and growing community of people just like yourself.

At **www.howto.co.uk** you'll be able to talk and share tips with people who have similar interests and are facing similar challenges in their lives. People who, just like you, have the desire to change their lives for the better – be it through moving to a new country, starting a new business, growing their own vegetables, or writing a novel.

At **www.howto.co.uk** you'll find the support and encouragement you need to help make your aspirations a reality.

You can go direct to **www.organicvegetablegrowing.co.uk** which is part of the main How To site.

How To Books strives to present authentic, inspiring, practical information in their books. Now, when you buy a title from **How To Books,** you get even more than just words on a page.

ORGANIC
Vegetable Growing

A practical, authoritative guide
to producing nutritious and flavourful vegetables
from your garden or allotment

ROBERT MILNE

SPRING HILL

To Anna and Henry

Published by Spring Hill, an imprint of How To Books Ltd
Spring Hill House, Spring Hill Road,
Begbroke, Oxford OX5 1RX. United Kingdom.
Tel: (01865) 375794. Fax: (01865) 379162.
info@howtobooks.co.uk
www.howtobooks.co.uk

How To Books greatly reduce the carbon footprint of their books by sourcing their
typesetting and printing in the UK.

British Library Cataloguing in Publication Data
A catalogue record for this book is available from the British Library

ISBN 978 1 905862 38 2

Illustrations by the author
Front cover photograph by Joe Hashman/Dirty Nails
Produced for How To Books by Deer Park Productions, Tavistock, Devon
Typeset by PDQ Typesetting, Newcastle-under-Lyme, Staffs.
Printed and bound by Bell & Bain Ltd, Glasgow

NOTE: The material contained in this book is set out in good faith for general
guidance and no liability can be accepted for loss or expense incurred as a result of
relying in particular circumstances on statements made in the book. The laws and
regulations are complex and liable to change, and readers should check the current
position with the relevant authorities before making personal arrangements.

Contents

Introduction

This book is based on 30 years of experience of growing
vegetables. The 20 years during which I grew all the vegetables
for a family were particularly instructive. Self-sufficiency was
time-consuming and unpaid. There was, therefore, a big
incentive to find the most efficient way of doing everything and
to maximize yield per square metre. In writing this book I have
thought through all the things one needs to know and do to get
good results and have tried to present this information logically
and clearly. It is also important to know when to do what
needs doing. Whatever your location and situation – latitude,
altitude, aspect and soil type – there will be a best time. I have
tried, therefore, to relate timing, not to calendar dates, but to
seasonal conditions.

Doing the right things at the right time, managing the soil to
conserve its structure and increase its fertility, knowing how to
deter or cope with pests and diseases, will not guarantee
success – there is always the unexpected – but most years most
crops will do well. Then the rewards are not just in terms of
having tasty, nutritious vegetables to eat but there is enormous
satisfaction from simply having grown them yourself.

Many think that gardening is hard work and not worth the
bother. Yes, it is hard work but good gardeners know that it is
enjoyable hard work; they would not do it if it were otherwise.

Nothing is irksome because every job is a necessary part of what has to be done to get the results one wants. Furthermore, even when not in the garden, at any time of day during the growing season you can indulge in the pleasurable awareness that crops are growing, increasing yield – every day more grams or kilos of potatoes, longer beans and carrots, and bigger cabbages.

Everyone who picks up this book will already have their own reasons for wanting to grow vegetables. Although based on the experience of the past 30 years I hope the book will be useful as various global processes make food gardening an increasingly relevant and necessary activity, perhaps more a matter of survival than mere lifestyle choice. Current global loss of agricultural land through urbanization (10 million hectares per year) and severe soil degradation (another 10m ha), over-exploitation and pollution of fresh water resources, peak oil, the possible catastrophic loss of productive land as a result of global warming, and the continued rise in population, could, together, result in food shortages on an unprecedented scale. Two generations have passed through the education system since food gardening was treated seriously in schools as part of the rural science course. It seems that those who should expect to live longest in this century are not being given the skills to adapt to it.

An increasing number of schools are taking up gardening, encouraged by the Royal Horticultural Society (RHS) and Garden Organic (the organic growing charity, formerly known as the Henry Doubleday Research Association www.gardenorganic.org.uk) but until gardening is treated as a serious and proper subject, with appropriately trained staff, it will continue to be regarded as peripheral to the curriculum and, therefore, vulnerable to other priorities. Nature and the seasons do not wait for us. Unless the right things are done at the right time results will be poor. Also, school gardens should be at least the size that families would need in order to feed themselves. Only then can a sufficiently wide range of crops be grown and all the techniques taught that are needed to manage a family-sized garden. Children are capable of managing gardens of this size; all they need is to be given the opportunity and the right level of tuition.

One of the motivations for writing this book was the hope that it would be useful to teachers and parents wishing to do gardening with children and young people. Adults in that situation will have a range of knowledge and experience. However, I have made no assumptions; anyone who considers themselves an absolute beginner will, I hope, find all the information they need, not only to create and manage a productive garden as they would for themselves but also included is information particular to the situation of working with children. I hope other readers will not find these brief sections too tedious or, indeed, irrelevant. The book is, essentially, a general vegetable gardening manual but with some extra bits relating to gardening with children, whether in schools or families.

My experience of gardening with upper primary age children has been very encouraging. I was pleasantly surprised by what they wanted to do and proved able to do. Two thoughts emerged. (1) Never underestimate what children can do. Give them challenging tasks. (2) Assume no previous knowledge of gardening; give clear instructions, then unintended disasters should be avoided.

Another observation was that children seem to enjoy quite strenuous physical work. We all need a balance between work which is sedentary and mentally demanding and work which is not just physical but materially productive. Our modern way of life offers few opportunities for many of us and no necessity for children to do productive physical work. Food gardening provides the opportunity for surely the most worthwhile exercise, not that gardening is just physical exercise. The more knowledge you have the better gardener you will be.

At the school gardens where I have worked the children were always very keen to take home bags of vegetables. I can only hope they were as keen to eat them. Having put in the effort to grow the produce I think children will be more interested in eating it than they might be to eat the same sort of food bought from a shop. Especially where green vegetables are concerned, shop-bought produce can never compete for freshness and flavour.

Young children seem to have an affinity with the natural world, before other distractions dominate their attention. All the children I have worked with seemed thoroughly to enjoy being in the garden, even if some were more keen than others on the gardening. However, I suggest that the association of happy experiences with a garden is good conditioning for later interest.

Playing with sand on a beach or in a sand pit at school or playgroup are recognized activities but children will just as happily play with soil, whether as dust or mud. Let them play with soil/dust/mud; let them climb trees and generally explore their surroundings. At the same time their attention may be drawn to the wonders of nature so that they come to appreciate and respect all forms of life.

Gardening may be thought of as 'vitamin G'. When you have the knowledge and skill to get good results, whether in food gardening or flower gardening, engaging in all the activities needed to allow plants to flourish produces a feeling of wellbeing that is hard to describe. The benefits of therapeutic horticulture are well recognized but you do not have to be ill to benefit from gardening. With food gardening, of course, there is a double benefit – provided you eat what you grow.

Tools and Back Care

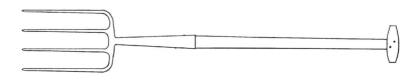

INTRODUCTION

There is much potential for improving gardening tools. Just as a
solo musician could not give a best performance on an inferior
instrument, so gardening cannot be done well with inferior
tools. One can manage but it will be much more laborious.
Tools need to suit the height and physical capability of the
gardener and should also vary according to the soil conditions
of the garden. The subject of tools and their use could fill
another book. This chapter, parts of Chapter 4 and Appendix I
merely provide a few basics.

FORKS AND SPADES

Most full-sized tools are too short for the average adult. This is
especially the case with spades and forks. I have found that the
most comfortable and efficient length of a spade or fork is one
that, while the lower tip is resting on the ground, the top of the
handle reaches the lowest rib. Or, to put it another way, when
the hand is resting on the top of the handle, the hand is slightly

higher than the elbow. Clearly, therefore, different lengths of tools are required to suit different heights of gardeners. I have made longer handles for my spade and forks (see illustration on back cover). Longer-handled tools have become available in recent years.

Standard-length spades and forks are about the right length for 10–12 year olds. Smaller forks and spades are available new. They might be called border forks or spades. These will suit younger children. It would probably be more harmful for children to use tools that are too small than ones that are a little big. I would caution against tools that have been made especially for children, as these might not be strong enough for real work in the garden. Enthusiasm makes up for a lot. Children manage very well with tools that are larger than the ideal size. So, do not worry if you cannot get tools of just the right length. Try to get hold of old tools. They are often a better design – they 'feel right' in your hands but they will also be worn, which means there will be less weight of metal.

When buying a spade look out for one with flanges on both sides. This design is more comfortable to use and causes less wear on shoes or boots. If you cannot find one with flanges it is worth finding a blacksmith and asking if he or she can weld a pair on. A blacksmith who is willing to do small jobs like this is well worth seeking out for mending tools and making alterations. See Appendix I for information on modification and maintenance of tools.

Fig. 1.1(a) Heavy duty fork, turfing iron, slasher, hedging hook, scythe.

Fig. 1.1(b) Spade, digging fork, five-pronged fork, border fork.

Fig. 1.1(d) Bronze trowel, pruning saw, secateurs, shears, sickle, leather gloves with gauntlets.

Fig. 1.1(c) Wooden set square, long-handled spade, long-handled muck fork, spring tined lawn rake.

CULTIVATOR

Fig. 1.2 The cultivator, elevation and end view.

This tool is the one I enjoy using more than any other and I regard it as essential. Unfortunately, I have never seen one for sale as new. Mine is old and was given to me. There is nothing available that does anything like as well the jobs that this tool may be used for. They were made for dragging farmyard manure off the back of carts, before mechanized muck spreaders were invented. Used as a cultivator, it is easy and satisfying to use and gets a very good tilth, ready for sowing seeds or planting anything. On well-used and light (i.e. not heavy clay) soils this tool will do all the preparation necessary. If you have dug the ground it may be left rather lumpy. By pushing the cultivator back and forth it is much easier to break up the lumps than using a sideways movement with a vertical fork. Also, the cultivator gets much deeper than a rake, which only tickles the surface – further down, the soil might still consist of hard lumps with large air pockets, neither of which are ideal for plant growth. (See Appendix I.)

HOE

I have always found the simple Dutch hoe the easiest and most effective type. This is the sort that works with a pushing action.

However, some people prefer the reciprocating or stirrup hoe. I recommend the narrowest one you can find. I buy the metal heads of the Dutch hoe separately and fit the shaft myself. I always saw off each side to make it still narrower, about 10cm. There are two advantages in having a narrow cutting edge: you can hoe in between plants more easily without damaging them and, for a given effort, there is more force being applied at the cutting edge, making it easier to use than a wider one, there being less resistance to a narrower blade. As with the spade, the hoe needs to be kept sharp. Sharpen on the upward-facing side only, using either of the methods described in Appendix I for the spade. It will wear mostly on the underside, from abrasion with stones and sand. As this happens, more pressure is needed to make it cut into the soil to slice the weeds off just under the surface. When sharpened properly it naturally cuts into the soil horizontally – neither tending to cut downwards nor slide out of the soil.

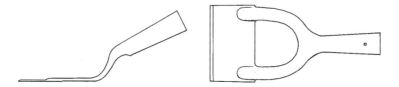

Fig. 1.3 Hoe. Note, each side has been sawn off to reduce width.

The shaft needs to be about the length of the height of the user. However, the angle of the cutting blade to the shaft is critical. The nearer to being in line the two are, the longer the shaft needs to be, or the lower you have to bend to use the tool. If the angle is too small, i.e. nearer to 45 degrees, between blade and shaft, you have to work hard with both arms as well as stomach and back muscles in order to make the hoe do its job. When the angle is right and the blade sharp you really only need to push the end of the shaft and steady it with the other hand for the tool to slice through the soil horizontally, just below the surface. When buying a hoe, test it in the shop by holding it as described, with the palm of one hand against the end of the shaft while standing upright. The blade of the hoe should be parallel with, i.e. resting flat on, the floor. If the blade is pointing down towards the floor, the shaft is too short for your height. Buy a separate head and make a shaft long enough to allow you to use it correctly while standing upright.

TROWEL

There are many shapes and sizes of trowel available. As with all tools it really is worth buying the best quality. There are two common problems with poor quality trowels: insufficient thickness of metal where it joins the handle, so that they bend at this point; and secondly, poorly fitted handles, resulting in the two parts of the trowel coming apart. My present one is made of bronze (www.implementations.co.uk) with a plain, unvarnished handle. It is rather big for children, although, again, children in the school gardens liked to borrow it. Previously I managed very well with small 'pointing' trowels, as used by builders and plasterers. When new the point is rather sharp, so they should be rounded off for garden use. Although they are not the traditional garden trowel design they are fine for digging out small weeds, planting small plants and firming the soil around them, and are a good size for children.

RAKE

I never use a rake for preparing seed beds – the cultivator does the job well enough. If your soil is dry, heavy or lacking in organic matter the cultivator might be inadequate. A rake is then useful to knock the lumps down using a vertical action. If used in the conventional way it merely pushes the lumps back and forth. Where the rake is useful is for preparing soil for sowing grass seed. Here, a combination of raking and knocking down is needed. On ordinary seed beds, if there are dry lumps and the soil is light, the back of the spade can be used to knock the lumps down and break them up. That leaves a very smooth surface suitable for fine seeds. A rake is useful, though, for raking up hoed weeds (although a spring tine/lawn rake is preferable in many circumstances) and for gathering up crop debris when clearing a bed after harvest.

Do not get one which looks as though it has been stamped out of a flat piece of metal. They are the worst for simply pushing the soil backwards and forwards and achieve little else. The best sort has teeth that look like nails. I have never seen one like it but, ideally, the teeth would be elliptical in section, set so that the narrow profile is pushed through the soil. There are many little improvements that could be made to gardening tools that would make them more efficient and easier to use.

SPRING TINE RAKE OR LAWN RAKE

These are light and easy to use and have a number of uses. A longer handle might need to be fitted, even for junior children and it will not make the rake unduly heavy. They are useful for raking small weeds off an empty bed after hoeing. They can also be used for raking light crop debris off beds after harvesting, although the more robust, ordinary rake might often be preferable. They are particularly useful for raking up hoed weeds from the paths between beds. Because the paths get trodden down they become slightly 'U' shaped in cross section. For this reason it is important to get a lawn rake where the ends of the tines form a curve so that, by getting the angle of the tool right with the ground, you can make the tines fit into the 'U' shape and gather everything up. An ordinary rake or a flat-ended tine rake would be useless for this job. The lawn rake needs to be narrower than the path, otherwise you will snag the outer rows of vegetables. One or two of the outer tines might need to be sawn off or just bent inwards.

WHEELBARROW

This is essential for many purposes in all but very small gardens. A standard building site barrow is best. Do not get a small, lightweight barrow – it will soon fall apart, will be too short to carry long tools in and will not carry enough of anything else either. It certainly will not stand up to children giving each other rides, which they love to do. Also, do not get one with splayed out legs, as they will keep catching and damaging crops, especially going round corners. The legs of the standard barrow might just fit on a path between beds, depending how wide you choose to make them. The wheelbarrow is a very good design and can be used by surprisingly small children. There is, however, one shortcoming with the design of the builder's barrow, which is that the handles are too short. This is more of a problem for adults, the more so the heavier the load being carried. The rear rim of the barrow is at the same level as one's kneecaps – very painful! Excruciating meetings of metal and knee can be prevented by a simple modification. Two short pieces of wood, shaved to fit, can be pushed into the barrow handles. The modification does not make it any harder for children to use. It probably makes it more stable, as hands and arms have to be slightly wider apart. Also, the leverage effect with respect to the wheel is slightly improved.

Other tools will be needed from time to time – secateurs, loppers, a pruning saw and lawn edging shears. Some are discussed in the next chapter.

THE BODY TOOL

The most important tool is your own body. Treat it with care and always think about the way you use it. Gardening can be good exercise but does not provide an all-round balanced activity. Most of the time one is standing, bending or squatting. If a job does necessitate bending it is important, periodically, to stand up (slowly, to avoid any possibility of strain or feeling faint), straighten the back, then, with both hands pushing on the back at waist level, bend backwards to compensate for the bending forwards. It is important to relax the back muscles as much as possible while doing this. This exercise can be done a few times, in a slow, relaxed way, each time bending a little further back. When cultivating, hoeing or raking you should hardly need to bend at all. This is where the right tools are important. When digging, try not to bend the spine around the level of the waist but instead bend the knees and at the hips.

Children will not necessarily work and use tools in the most efficient and safe way. They need instruction and constant supervision. It is important that children learn how to work efficiently and avoid hurting themselves. Damage to the back can be a long-term process and it is often difficult to persuade young people of the need to avoid doing something that might only affect them many years in the future.

Walking upright gives humans many advantages over other animals; we have hands free to hold and carry things. However, in evolutionary terms walking upright is quite recent. The spine, around the region of the waist, is a relatively weak point. Much is demanded of it: load carrying and movements that it was not really 'designed' or rather, evolved for. Sitting down is the most dangerous common-activity as far as the back is concerned, unless one maintains correct posture all the time, i.e. an inward curve of the spine at the waist. Whenever I have a spell of back pain, gardening deals with the problem more quickly than sitting down, even if I do maintain the correct posture and, for me, walking is the best remedy of all. In gardening let your arms and legs do the work. Ignore the old saying, 'put your back into it'. A more useful adage would be 'putting your back into it will put your back out of it'. Also, always use your head, to think of the easiest and most efficient ways of doing things.

Gardening does necessitate bending down. After working in the garden it is important not to rest by slouching in a chair. Sit upright or lie face down. Propping yourself up on your elbows when lying down is good for counteracting the forward bending that has been done.

Clearing the Ground

INTRODUCTION

Every site will be different, with different problems. Most will fall into one of the following categories:

1 Grass that has been maintained as a lawn or playing field. This is probably the easiest and most straightforward situation to deal with.

2 A neglected plot. There is a wide range of possibilities here, from a former garden that has become covered in common garden weeds to a site with self-sown trees and bushes, deep-rooted perennial weeds and tall grasses growing in large tussocks.

3 A site that has had little or nothing done to it since being a building site. This could be the most problematic unless a garden area was specified before construction began and treated appropriately.

4   Another possible situation is one where there is no soil at all and you wish to bring some in.

Wherever there have been people there will be rubbish. Unless your site, or source of soil, is a remote field it will contain broken china and glass, metal objects, including foil from cigarette packets and chocolate bars, plus all manner of plastic objects. Some of the rubbish can be interesting. The most interesting piece of 'rubbish' I ever found was a barbed and tanged flint arrow head, probably Neolithic. That was in a rural cottage garden. Some of the china can be quite pretty. I would recommend removing any rubbish – it looks unsightly. Children might wish to collect pretty pieces of china to make a mosaic, or any other interesting items specific to the site. At a school site there could be marbles, toy soldiers, 'jewellery', coins, as well as less interesting stuff like pen tops and sweet wrappers. In an old garden there could be many pieces of clay pipe. You might be lucky enough to find a bowl of one. The smaller it is the older it is, as tobacco was very expensive when it was first imported into this country.

GRASS SITE

Except in very small gardens the tools needed are:

surveying tape	turf cutter
string	turfing iron
pointed sticks	digging forks
large set square	wheelbarrow

It is possible to cut and lift turf with a spade but it is hard work. Also, with a spade it is difficult to cut turfs of even thickness. So, at one end you will be taking away an unnecessary amount of soil and at the other, not enough, which means that growing points of grasses could be left in the ground. How thick the turfs need to be will depend on the types of grasses present, soil structure and how moist it is. With ordinary lawn or playing field grasses, 3 or 4cm is usually adequate. You will be taking away a little more soil than strictly necessary but if you cut the turfs any thinner they are likely to break up when you try to handle them. This will slow down the whole procedure. With even-thickness turfs that hold together you can make a very neat stack. Of course, you will be taking away perhaps 20 per cent of the top soil but after a few months the stacked turf will have rotted down and can be put back on the garden. In fact, stacking turf was the traditional method of making potting soil.

Should you cover the turf stack? If you leave it uncovered, grass will grow on the top and the sides, whichever way up you put the turfs. Covering it with a light-excluding material will prevent this but rats will be attracted to move in. They seem to like the dark, moist and secluded conditions provided by covering a heap of anything. So, I would recommend leaving it uncovered. It looks attractive once it has grassed over. It will merely need clipping, to prevent the grass and any other plants going to seed. No purpose is served by stacking the turfs upside down, except if the stack is there over the growing season and you wish to try growing something on it. Then the top two layers should be inverted and some extra soil added to prevent the grass growing between the gaps. If you are going to grow something and the turfs are rather dry, water each layer as the stack is built. This is much easier than trying to moisten the whole of a dry stack from the top. Dwarf beans or squash have the sort of roots that could find their way between the turfs.

The easiest way to cut the turf into rectangles is by using a half moon edging tool, or turf cutter. Cut rectangles rather than squares as they will make a better stack: like bricks, overlapping will keep the stack from falling apart. With a little experiment you will find the optimum dimensions for lifting, handling and stacking. The turfing iron is quite a heavy tool but well designed. Three 10/11 year old boys did an excellent job at one school, taking turns to lift a substantial area of turf. Between them they lifted, barrowed and stacked and really enjoyed the strenuous work. At another school a Year Six girl proved to be the best turf lifter. Cut the turf vertically, except where there is to be an edge left between grass path and cultivated plot. There, cut it with a slope so that the edge is less likely to be trodden down. One should try to avoid treading right on the edge of the grass anyway. If you are going to use edging boards or purpose-made metal edging strips then the cut can be vertical.

Wherever there is going to be a straight edge of grass around a plot, the line needs to be carefully marked out with string at ground level. This is best done by two people. Once the two ends of the string are secured to sticks, one person stands at one end to see that the string remains straight while the other goes along the string putting in pairs of sticks either side of the string at about four-metre intervals and almost touching it. This will prevent you ending up with a curved edge by inadvertently moving the string as you work along it with the turf cutter.

The turf cutter should be kept sharp to make the job easier. Sharpen on one side only. I find it preferable to have this sharpened side facing away from me while using the tool and to cut along my side of the string. The technique I find most effective is to keep one foot on the tool as I pull it out and move along for the next cut. The blade only just comes out of the ground. As with any repetitious job it is a good idea to use one foot for a while then change to the other. That way the job gets done more quickly and you avoid aches and strains. Cut in parallel lines across the area to be cleared, then do the same across in the other direction. I find it easier, when progressing to the left, to have the right foot on the tool to push it in and, when working to the right, to push in with the left foot.

Before cutting any turf you will need to have drawn a scale plan of the garden (see Chapter 3). In a school site where the garden is being cut out of part of the playing field, I strongly recommend a fence of some kind. This will help protect the garden from straying footballs and will mark off the site as separate and special, where children only go when authorized. If the start of the project is getting near to when the first seeds need to be sown, consult your plan and clear first the area needed for them. Wherever you make a start, it would be a good idea, if you have not got a fence yet, to delineate the outer limits of the garden with string and sticks. The sticks need to be taller than the tallest child, so that no one can fall on one and injure an eye. The string is merely a token barrier.

Winter is a good time to start a garden, provided the ground is not frozen. In spring and summer, the ground could be hard and dry and cutting and stacking turfs will be difficult and hot work. The turfs will fall apart and the stack will be too dry to rot down properly. If conditions are wet, though, care should be taken to minimise walking on the soil where the turf has been removed. Soil compaction is detrimental to its structure and the next job is to dig it and create a good tilth.

NEGLECTED SITE

There is a very wide range of possibilities with neglected sites. Some basic principles will, I hope, be applicable to most. The first thing to do is to have a good look at the site and find out what is there. Children could make a list of the plants – trees, bushes, grasses, other leafy or flowery things – as well as any rubbish visible above ground (there will be plenty under the ground). The next thing to do is sit down and think about the most efficient and logical order in which to do all that needs doing. For every site there will be a best way of doing things and a most efficient and practical order in which to do them; doing things a different way or in a different order could make the work more difficult, or it might make it easier but lead to problems later on. Make a list: it is very satisfying to tick off jobs as they get done. The following is a suggested sequence. Few sites will have all of these problems and some will have others I have not thought of. As with most aspects of gardening, thoroughness is important and especially in the clearing stage; taking short cuts could result in much avoidable work later.

1   In summer or autumn there could be a great many seed heads of weeds visible. Each one could comprise hundreds or even thousands of seeds. The soil will already contain millions of seeds but there is no point adding to it. It is worthwhile, and very satisfying, to go round with a pair of secateurs and carefully cut each one off and drop it into a bucket or paper sack. Store these in a dry place for burning later. Alternatively, weed seeds can be killed by immersing them in water for two months.

Nettles are best dealt with by pulling them up. Good leather gloves are needed. Grasp the stem fairly low down and they will break off at ground level or just below, where the stem meets the root. The stems can then be folded up and put in the bag or a wheelbarrow.

2   Deal with the rubbish. At this stage, 'rubbish' means anything that could interfere with the next process. So, anything metallic and visible, such as wire netting, is particularly important to remove. Try to avoid trampling down the vegetation.

3   Clear the soft vegetation down to ground level. That means everything except trees and bushes. The time of year and the nature of the vegetation will determine what tools are needed for this. Personally, I do not like power tools, because of noise, pollution and their contribution to climate change; but particularly in the creation of a garden for children because they would not be able to use such tools. So, they would be denied the opportunity of helping with one or more stages of the process.

If the vegetation is long and still mostly green, a scythe might be the best tool. I have never seen a scythe designed for a child. The traditional English scythe is too heavy for children to use but modern Austrian-made scythes are much lighter and easier to use. I would imagine that most 11 year olds could manage one. For years I used an old heavy scythe but since trying a modern Austrian one it seems that it is a myth that a scythe needs to have the momentum of weight to be effective. Scything is best done early in the morning when there is still some dew present, or after rain, as the vegetation is easier to cut when wet. Whether there is a softening effect on the fibres I do not know. Perhaps the weight of water helps, resulting in more resistance to the movement of the scythe, so that it cuts rather than just pushes the vegetation over. If no scythe is available, a sickle or hedging hook would do. If the vegetation is not too tough a grass hook (a lightweight sickle) would be hard work but at least a child could use one. If the vegetation is dry and coarse, a slasher will be needed.

When the vegetation is cut it needs to be raked up. The cultivator and strong garden rakes are both good for this job. If you intend to burn it and much of the stuff is still green, rake it into rows and leave until dry enough to burn. If you have been diligent about collecting weed seeds as suggested above, all this cut material could be composted. If it is very coarse and dry it can be used straight away, mixed/ layered with softer green stuff such as young weeds and kitchen waste, but if there is a large quantity of dry, coarse material it can be stacked and used, a small amount at a time, mixed in with fresh green stuff during the normal making of compost heaps.

A scythe is inappropriate for blackberries. The best way with these is slow but sure: progress steadily forward with a pair of loppers and simply cut every prickly stem you can see into short lengths. Then rake it up and go back and cut the bits you missed. It sounds laborious but as with all gardening a methodical approach and steady work gets the job done.

4   Any trees or bushes should be dealt with next (I am assuming there is nothing big enough to need a tree surgeon). Lop and saw off as many branches as can be reached from the ground. If you are able to have a bonfire stack all burnable stuff two or three metres on the upwind side of where the fire will be. Before any wood is added to

the stack it should be cut into lengths: anything thin enough to lop, cut to about 50cm and anything larger to about a metre. If cut to those lengths you will be able to make a more compact stack and it will be easier to burn too. Make two or more stacks according to the thickness of the material. Do not cut trees or bushes right to the ground. Leave an adequate length of stem to provide leverage when digging them out.

Digging out trees and bushes can be hard work and take a long time. This is where the quality of spades and forks is tested. A heavy duty fork is very useful for this and other occasional tasks. I was lucky to find one in a junk shop. The prongs are longer and thicker than an ordinary digging fork. Instead of a short socket for the shaft to fit into, the metal divides into two and is riveted to the front and back of the shaft right up to the handle. It is impossible to break and can be sat on when levering roots out of the ground. Surprisingly large tree stumps can be pulled out using a hand winch.

Digging out trees and bushes more than a few years old will probably result in different soil layers getting mixed up. It is quite important to make an effort to put soil back in the right order, as it was before being disturbed. In most situations there will be topsoil which is dark, and below that, lighter soil, possibly more orange in colour.

Dealing with bushes and trees could be one of the challenging tasks as recommended in the Introduction. Common self-sown trees like sycamore and ash of up to a few years old could be dug out by upper junior children. Children like using loppers and pruning saws. I believe they should be taught how to use potentially dangerous tools properly and safely. Some children will come across all sorts of tools out of school anyway and want to use them. If they have never been shown how to use them safely they are more likely to injure themselves and each other.

The larger the tree stumps, the more valuable they are, aesthetically and for wildlife. If there is space available, consider creating a stumpery. This is an arrangement of stumps with their roots left on. The shapes of the roots can be very sculptural. You could make a circular enclosure with the roots on the inside, creating a quiet sitting area. Or they could be stacked up into a pile. A surrounding bed with plants would add to the wildlife value. In time, various beetles will colonize the stumps. If the site is in a suitable area woodpeckers might be attracted to come and peck out the larvae of beetles. Various fungi will also colonize the stumps and, eventually, the stumps will disappear – a lesson in decomposition and recycling.

5　What to do next depends on the nature of the site. If the surface resembles a turf layer you could continue as with the grass site. If it consists of stumps of coarse vegetation or large tussocks of grass, different approaches are needed. Whatever the surface is like, I would recommend removing the surface layer, as if it were turf. Take off at least 4cm. By doing this, two things are achieved:

(I) The surface layer will contain a vast number of the most recently shed weed seeds. Depending on the types of weeds present and the way the site has been managed, there could be tens of thousands per square metre. The seeds of some species can remain dormant in the soil for decades. Seeds from the same plant can have a range of dormancy, so that, even if they are at an appropriate level to germinate, only a percentage will do so. This means that, even if you never allow any more weeds to go to seed, each year there will be a fresh crop of weeds coming up from the soil seed bank. However, also each year a proportion of these dormant seeds will die. By taking off the surface layer you do at least remove a considerable proportion of the soil weed seed bank for however long you leave the soil stacked before returning it, by which time a proportion of the weed seeds in it will have died. The stack should be no more than 50 or 60cm high, to avoid compaction. Wherever you stack that depth of soil, it will, effectively, kill off whatever is growing beneath. So, the stack can be sited where you want this to happen. It can be an effective way of clearing ground. However, some species of perennial weeds will survive being covered up for more than a year. Lesser, or field, bindweed survived two years of being covered in three layers of thick black plastic! It was actually growing, although lacking any green colour.

(II) The surface layer might contain the worst of the matted roots of many weeds and grasses. For example, most couch grass rhizomes are near the surface. Rather than trying to shake the soil out from this matted layer as you dig, by removing it and leaving it to rot down, what is then left to be dug is much easier. There will still be the greater part of the roots of deep-rooted perennials but you will not lose them; they will be visible enough when you start digging, or even before. For example, the severed roots of docks and dandelions exude liquid, producing a damp patch on the soil surface, or if left for a while will start to grow leaves again.

Pigs

An alternative way of beginning to clear a neglected site is to employ pigs! This would be appropriate from spring to early summer when there will be plenty of fresh green vegetation but before weeds have gone to seed. I once borrowed a litter of pigs for a few months, to graze weeds to prevent them seeding in a walled garden I was clearing. Docks were the only weeds they did not eat. The pigs were rotated around using an electric fence. At a school, proper fence posts and pig netting would be preferable. Pigs are fascinating and very entertaining creatures.

They love having their backs scratched and would be the quickest means of recycling apple cores or any fruit and vegetable trimmings. A litter of pigs is easy to look after, quite within children's capabilities. Apart from the fence, all you need is some kind of shelter and a container for water.

BUILDING SITE

Unfortunately, I have no experience of this situation. In an ideal world, whenever a new building is being designed a garden area would be drawn on the plans and remain off limits to building staff, machinery, bricks, cement, etc. As soon as possible the area could be managed with future gardening in mind. In practice this might mean no more than cutting, sufficiently frequently, whatever is growing there, to prevent it going to seed (but see page 260). This will be a problem with fast-growing annuals and dandelions but I would not advocate covering the ground with a light-excluding material.

An area of ground that has been part of a building site could be so compacted and polluted with alien materials and potentially dangerous rubbish that, in the school situation, there might be little scope for children to be involved in the early stages. As with the neglected site, make a list of what needs doing and work out the most logical order to do everything. There might be some items worth keeping: whole or even half bricks, slabs or planks of wood, pending some imaginative practical or ornamental use. If there is any vegetation growing, proceed as with the neglected site. If there is none, just start digging, provided conditions are reasonable. The ground needs to be moist. If it is so compacted that any rain sits on the surface it might be necessary to go over the site with a fork making holes to facilitate drainage.

The ground might be compacted to some depth. You will need to dig to the full length of the fork prongs and then also push down deeper from that depth and work the fork to loosen the soil below. This is known as bastard trenching. Double digging might be needed. For this, a trench is dug and the soil taken to the other end of the plot to fill in the trench at the end. As you work back, the soil at the base of the trench is actually dug rather than just loosened. Double digging is something I have never had to do. It would only be in exceptional circumstances of subsoil compaction that it would be necessary.

If the soil layers have been mixed up, that is a problem. If the subsoil is in large lumps it should be possible to re-bury them. Alternatively, it could be used for paths between beds, allowing some topsoil from the paths area to go on to the beds. If the topsoil has been taken away then you will need to bring in some more.

Before starting to dig, which might bring to the surface all manner of junk, you could ask the builders what sort of stuff you might have to deal with. Also ask if they would be willing to take it away for you! (Well, there is no harm in asking!)

No soil

At a school where there are only hard surfaces an area of tarmac could be taken up and some soil brought in. This job could be done by keen parents with pickaxes and shovels. The new edge of tarmac might need to be held in place by strong boards and stakes to prevent it being trodden on and broken off.

Be very wary about bringing in soil. You need to know where it is coming from and what the site has been used for. You need to be sure that the soil is not contaminated by any industrial pollution or sharp objects. It is extremely unlikely that any brought-in soil will be from a site that has been kept free of weeds. The soil will, therefore, contain a vast number of weed seeds and the roots of perennial weeds such as couch grass, docks, thistles, bindweed and nettles.

When making a school garden there are many ways that parents can help. In this situation it could be suggested that each child's family donate some soil. A couple of barrow loads for every 40 square metres of garden would not be missed, except that these days many gardens are mostly lawn; a problem there. If some parents are farmers, acquiring soil should be easy.

Planning the Garden

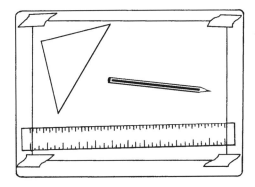

INTRODUCTION

Drawing a plan is a useful and enjoyable thing to do once the decision has been made to create a garden. Whether in a private garden or at a school, it is unlikely that there will be complete freedom to lay out whatever shape you want. The garden has to be fitted in with other areas and features. This can be an interesting challenge: to design an efficient and practical garden that also looks good. I believe there is a correlation between function and aesthetics; if a thing is well designed for its purpose, it will also look good. However, I suppose beauty is in the eye of the beholder (but the beholder might not have to be functional!). I was once shown round a private walled garden by the head gardener. It was a large, working kitchen garden but had been designed by a well-known 'professional garden designer'. The head gardener asked me what I thought of it. I said that it was a wonderful design – for a *carpet*, but for a garden it must be a nightmare to work in. He quietly agreed. To the owners, blissfully unaware of all the irritating inconveniences of actually working in the garden, it probably did look wonderful. To my eye, a tiny garden, if that is all the space available, of simple design, precisely laid out and filled with healthy vegetables is more beautiful than the grand, fussy carpet just mentioned. This chapter introduces some basic principles of laying out a garden for growing vegetables and fruit and suggests some simple designs.

I suggest keeping the design simple for children's gardens so that the children can become familiar with the basic principles. At secondary level and beyond, basic principles may be applied in more complex, decorative or fanciful ways – so long as practicalities are not forgotten. I believe the design of a school garden should be similar to a family garden, whatever size it might be, so that it is as relevant as possible to what children might wish to replicate at home or later in their own gardens. The only real difference necessary is slightly wider paths between beds and considerably wider access paths surrounding the plots.

Communal garden or individual plots?

Should a school garden be one unified design, as one might have in a private garden to feed a family, or should each child or pair of children have a separate plot for which they are totally responsible? Some children will be happy with a communal garden, others will want to have their own plot. While it is important to encourage an individual sense of caring for the earth, I believe that there are more benefits in the single design and working communally. The single design can demonstrate more easily the principles of design and rotation that are applicable on any scale and will serve as an example of the size of garden the children will, we hope, wish to create when they are grown up. With good management from the person in charge, the garden will produce quantities of each crop that will allow children to take home useful amounts of food each week. This will serve as an excellent example of just how productive a garden can be.

If children have their own individual plots, in most schools, because of space limitations the plots will be too small to grow a wide range of crops, especially of larger types such as broccoli and squash. Also, invariably, some children will obtain better results than others. Those with poor results will be discouraged. I am not anti-competition amongst children but I think that with the particular activity of gardening and certainly up to the end of primary age, competition would serve no useful purpose. In a communal garden, with good management, most crops will be successful and all the children can share in that success.

If and when gardening becomes a recognized subject in primary schools, if some sort of assessment is required, teachers are quite capable of recognizing the relative contributions of each child. At secondary level individual projects might be deemed necessary towards part of the assessment but they could be carried out within the overall system of one garden. At 'A' level, for example, each pupil could take complete responsibility for one crop, while at the same time recording what others were doing with their crops.

THE BED SYSTEM

Walking on the soil causes compaction and wherever you walk nothing can be grown. Therefore, while allowing *enough* space for walking, it seems sensible to minimize the area walked on and to make the location of walk areas permanent so that:

1   on the growing areas cultivation and applications of compost are always on areas used for growing and never wasted on soil which might only be walked on in the following year;

2   the growing areas never get walked on and compacted;

3   you never have to dig hard, compacted ground.

The arrangement which logically arises is that of narrow paths separated by growing areas, the width of which should be maximized but will be limited by how far you can comfortably reach to the middle, for sowing, weeding, etc., from the paths on either side. What has just been described is the bed system. It is the most logical and efficient way of using the ground and, over the garden as a whole, will produce a higher yield than could any other arrangement. It is not surprising, therefore, to learn that the bed system was probably universal in gardens and market gardens until the mid-eighteenth century (Campbell, 1996). Campbell also refers to classical Roman gardens being laid out in beds.

The practice of digging or rotavating the whole of the vegetable garden and then treading down again half the area by walking between single rows of vegetables is a relatively recent fashion and one that lingers, as a glance around any allotment site will confirm. When I started vegetable gardening I was unaware of the historical ubiquity of the bed system and had not heard of beds in the context of growing vegetables. I soon realised that it was a good idea to minimize walking on the soil as it was difficult getting weeds out of the compacted clay of my first garden. As a result of practical necessity, what I ended up with were beds. The advantages of the bed system may be summarized by the following eight points:

1 The area actually growing crops is maximized and that walked on minimized.

2 Growing areas never get walked on and compacted, thus minimizing the amount of cultivation required.

3 Cultivation and soil improvement are limited to areas always used for crops.

4 You never have to dig hard, compacted ground.

5 Within beds crops can be grown at optimum spacing for maximum yield.

6 Every part of the garden is accessible all year round.

7 Children easily learn where they may walk.

8 Work can be satisfyingly broken up into distinct units.

It does not matter how hard or puddled the paths become, as they never have to be cultivated or grow crops. They do, however, need to be kept free of weeds. Thorough ground preparation and the removal of perennial weeds before laying out paths is very important. There will always be a few perennial weeds, which must be dealt with at the earliest possible stage of their growth. The all year round access that beds allow is especially important in weed control as there are some species, annual meadow grass (*Poa annua*) being the prime example, that will flower and set seed at any time of year.

The bed system is particularly good for children because they can straight away have the confidence to go anywhere in the garden and know that they are not damaging anything. The point about easily definable units of work is good for the morale of any gardener but is especially useful in the school context. It makes it easy to allocate tasks; two or four children can do whatever needs doing on a bed – preparing the soil, sowing, weeding or harvesting. They can then stand back and see exactly what they have achieved.

Design for pleasure and practicality

To the individual onion or cabbage it does not matter where the next onion or cabbage is but what matters to us is that the spacing is equidistant at the optimum density to produce maximum yield; but there is something else that matters to us. Our eyes and minds crave order, pattern and symmetry – at least, mine do and I cannot believe I am unique in this. If all the requirements for practicality and maximum yield can be met, while at the same time creating order, pattern and symmetry at no extra cost of labour or anything else, who would choose to garden any other way? What can result is something that is not just pleasing to the eye of itself but is pleasing also because the mind knows that the design has been arrived at through considerations of practicality and efficiency. Seeds *could* be sown randomly at optimum density but sowing would be very slow and tedious. It is much quicker and the result looks much more attractive if sowing is done in rows with equidistant spacing within the rows to achieve the same optimum overall density.

Beds provide a unit for design. The dimensions of the beds will be determined by practicalities of working and the available space. Horticultural considerations then require another level of design, grouping beds together into plots to facilitate a rotation. While meeting these two basic practical requirements – beds and plots – there is much scope for pattern and symmetry. This takes gardening to a higher level and adds hugely to the pleasure of it. It urges on the work, like a child colouring in a pattern in a book – each bed prepared and sown is one more 'coloured in' with a different colour and texture provided by the crop. The result is never finished, never static. Each crop ripens and is harvested and then another sown in a continuing cycle within the outline pattern of beds and plots. Even at times of year when few crops are present, there is always the pattern of beds and plots, plus any perennial planting, such as fruit trees and bushes, herbs and some ornamental plants.

There is a time of year, the latter part of winter and before the spring work has got under way, when a vegetable garden can look untidy and neglected; weeds that managed to germinate in late summer have been slowly growing. However, with a bed system in place there is always the pattern of the beds and paths to attract the eye. Because the clearly defined paths are there, if they are slowly getting encroached upon and obscured by weeds (especially grasses) you feel obliged and inspired to go and do some clearing.

Provided they are not going to seed, most weeds are fine left in the beds over winter, as they will help to protect the soil. There are some exceptions, such as species that act as a 'bridge' for crop diseases from one year to the next. (See under 'pests and diseases' of individual vegetables and 'Some pros and cons of weeds' on p.274.) Weeds on the paths, though, should not be allowed to grow for long, as the trodden down soil there makes them harder to dig out than weeds in the beds.

Having the pattern of beds and paths gives the appearance of 'something going on' all year round. The paths make you want to walk on them and do something, or just take the opportunity to observe what *is* going on. There will always be something of interest – small wildlife, an unusual plant/weed or a tree seedling that you can transplant or give away. The bed system is definitely gardener-friendly.

The width of beds

How wide the beds are made should be determined by the height of the gardener. For an average man a convenient width is 120cm (or four feet) and the paths 35 or 40cm. Choose the dimensions that can be comfortably managed. If paving is being used for paths they need be no more than 30cm wide.

For children the beds need to be proportionately narrower and the paths wider. In a school garden the paths, if they are just bare soil, should be 45cm wide. This is because children are, shall we say, more exuberant gardeners and less knowledgeable about where their feet are going! Also, with a number of children in the garden, they will, at times, want to pass each other on a path. For upper juniors a bed width of 90cm is appropriate and for infants, 60cm. If all the infants cannot reach the middle of the bed that does not matter; they are going to need some adult help anyway but if the beds are any narrower it puts more limits on what can be grown in them.

The simplest designs

For reasons of appearance and practicality (see page 42) it is advisable to grow different crops separately. There are numerous occasions when different crops are mixed, as in intercropping and catch-cropping, but for the moment I wish to consider the basic idea of laying out a garden. However small the garden, it should be divided into a minimum of four plots.

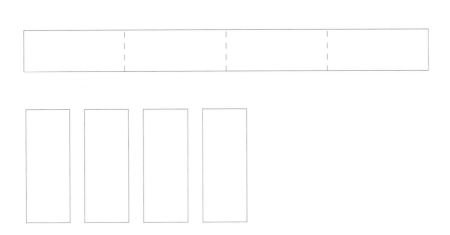

Fig. 3.1 Four bed/plot design showing two layouts.

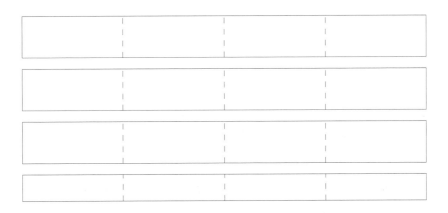

Fig. 3.2 Four plots of beds.

In a very small garden this might simply mean four beds, as shown in Figure 3.1. In larger gardens each plot is divided up into beds of whatever width is required. If you have the leeway to do so, make each bed the same width. If the available space is already circumscribed and it does not divide up evenly into beds of the size you want, there are three choices: you can be flexible with the widths of the paths, especially the periphery path, which is essential for access; you can alter the width of the beds so as to keep them all the same, even if they are narrower than you ideally would like; or, you can make the bed at one side of each plot narrower. These could be used for herbs, flowers or perennial crops (see Figure 3.2).

Orientation of beds

I tend to favour an east-west orientation but it does not matter which way they go; there are pros and cons for east-west and north-south. The chances are that your available rectangle will not allow you to align the beds precisely in either direction. One reason, given the freedom to do so, I would choose east-west is that if tall crops – runner beans, sweetcorn – are planted in the northern-most bed in a plot, there is no bed to the north of it over which shade would be cast. Even in a plan with crossing paths and four quarters there would be a wider path and possibly ornamental borders between a tall crop in either of the southern plots and the next cropping bed in the opposite plot to the north. Another, probably minor, advantage of east-west beds is that when crops are young and there is clear space between them, in early morning and late afternoon when the sun's angle is low, direct sunlight can get between the rows and warm the soil. Around midday, when the sun's angle is at maximum, the crops will have minimum shadows, again allowing the soil to be warmed. On the other hand, with a north-south orientation the crops get the sun on both sides. However, this last point is only of relevance to peas and climbing beans. My son's garden had north-south beds while our main garden had east-west beds and whilst no measurements were taken to compare results in the two gardens, no differences were noticed in growth rates or yield.

Raised beds

If you start with level, well-cultivated soil and then mark out beds and tread down paths between them, the beds, by comparison, become raised a little. I do not recommend raising them further. Unfortunately I have not had the experience of working in a garden which had raised beds retained by boards but I can only imagine that the disadvantages would outweigh the advantages. The advantages are that the beds are clearly defined, look neat and soil can be taken from the path area and used to deepen the soil in the beds. Also, slightly less bending is needed when sowing and weeding. Four disadvantages come to mind:

1   The cost of materials and the time involved constructing the retaining boards.

2   It is inevitable that perennial weeds will grow right next to the boards, from pieces you missed when clearing the ground as well as from blown-in seed. The boards will get in the way when digging them out.

3   When hoeing annual weeds it will be difficult to hoe properly right next to the boards and around the retaining stakes.

4 When cultivating, digging-in compost, digging up potatoes or the outer rows of leeks, parsnips or carrots, the boards would get in the way. On balance, I recommend keeping things simple: keep beds and paths more or less on the same level and avoid boards.

It might be tempting to have boards in a school garden to keep children off the beds but I think it is preferable to impress upon children the need to walk and not run and to watch where they are going and, what could be another golden rule, never walk backwards.

ROTATION AND THE PLOT SYSTEM

Consideration of the following three points determined the system of rotation described below. I have found the rotation to be practical and efficient:

1 Unavoidably, there are times when there will be bare soil or little cover of vegetation. This will tend to result in the soil becoming slowly more acid as a result of the leaching of lime. It should be stressed that this is a slow process, especially in clay soils. Acidity is expressed on a scale of 0–14, 7 being neutral, above 7 alkaline and below 7 acid. However, the chemist's concept of pH 7 being neutrality is not appropriate to soils; pH 6.5 is the value at which a soil normally exhibits neither acidic nor alkaline properties (Halley and Soffe, 1988). Acidity can be corrected (the pH raised) by adding lime.

2 It is advisable to grow each type of vegetable in a different area each year to reduce the problem of a build-up of certain soil-borne pests and diseases. It also evens out over the

garden what is taken from the soil, as each type of crop requires a slightly different ratio of nutrients. Furthermore, it allows for a pattern of compost application, as some crops benefit from recently enriched soil, while others produce better results in conditions not quite so rich, i.e. with a lower availability of nitrogen.

3   Different crops prefer, ideally, different values of pH in the soil.

All the vegetables you wish to grow may be divided into groups according to their pH preference (see table below). Divide the garden into an appropriate number of plots. Test one plot for its pH, and if below 6.4 (or 5.8 in a peat soil) apply lime to that plot, preferably in autumn. The following year the crops that prefer the highest pH are grown there. The year after that the crops preferring a slightly lower pH are grown, and so on. From the table you will see that if lime needs to be applied you should do so before leeks and onions are grown.

Ideal pH for a range of vegetables

Leek	7.0	Parsnip	6.6	Bean and pea	6.3
Carrot	7.0	Broccoli	6.5	Squash	6.2
Onion	6.8	Cabbage	6.5	Cucumber	6.1
Lettuce	6.7	Cauliflower	6.5	Potato	6.0
Swede	6.6	Beetroot	6.4		

Having explained a rotation on the basis of pH and lime application, beyond the recommendation that onions and leeks or brassicas (cabbages, etc.) should be at the beginning of the cycle and potatoes at the end, it does not matter much in which order the other crops are grown. In practice, however, it is advisable not to have potatoes at the end of the rotation because of the problem caused by those that, invariably, are not found when harvesting, remain in the ground over winter and then grow in the spring. These 'volunteer' potatoes will come up after alliums or brassicas have been sown, making it impossible to get them out without disturbing and destroying some of the new young plants. So, potatoes should be grown in the penultimate position in the rotation, to be followed by all the tender crops, which are not planted out until the danger of the last spring frost is over. 'Volunteer' potatoes come up shortly before this, allowing them to be dug out completely, before the tender crops are planted out.

When you test the soil for pH, as should always be done before applying lime, you will probably find that it varies very little from plot to plot and year to year. The leaching of lime is a very slow process in most soils. The pH figures shown above should not be thought of as precise values that must be achieved. They are in fact averages gathered from a number of research results, each of which gave different recommendations. A crop's pH preference is usually expressed in terms of a range within which it will grow without adverse effects caused by the soil being too acid or alkaline. A pH of between 6.0 and 6.8 will be acceptable to nearly all types of vegetable. At the higher pH there will be some scab on potatoes but this is a minor problem. The above figures are given for comparative purposes and should be regarded as an approximate guide. The figures refer to mineral soils. On peat soils they will be approximately 0.6 lower.

It is important to follow recommendations when adding lime to the soil. Too much lime can result in some essential elements being 'locked up'. Potassium, magnesium, manganese and boron will become unavailable to plants if too much lime is added.

The pH preferences of crops might seem too theoretical and not a sufficiently important criterion on which to base a rotation but the resulting system is similar to traditional rotations and, more importantly, it does work; there is a place for everything and every part of the garden can be made full use of. The different requirements of crops so far as compost application is concerned also fit in with this rotation.

The number of plots and crop rotation

Most gardening books recommend a four plot rotation. From the point of view of pests and diseases the greater the number of plots the better, as it will be longer before any particular vegetable is grown on the same ground. The size of garden, the range of crops and amount of each you wish to grow, will determine the number of plots most suitable. Earlier I recommended a minimum of four. In a symmetrical, rectangular garden it would be most convenient to have an even number of plots. So, six or eight are possibilities. In my odd-shaped self-sufficient garden, symmetry was not relevant, or achievable; a five plot rotation suited our needs (see Figure 3.3).

Unless everyone concerned with a garden has an aversion to a particular type of vegetable or, for whatever reason, chooses not to grow it, the range of crops that tend to be grown in temperate regions do seem to fall into five groups, as shown in Figure 3.4. A typical allotment, therefore, could be laid out entirely for practical purposes and for maximum efficiency, as shown in Figure 3.5.

Fitting the range into a four plot design requires some thought. Brassicas are, I would say, the most troublesome in terms of pests and diseases. At a school it might be decided to grow

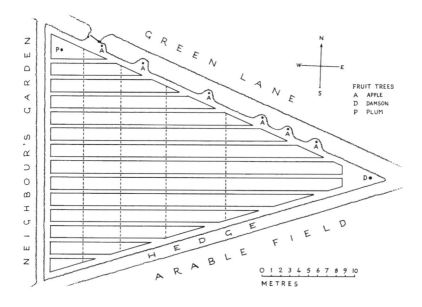

Fig. 3.3 Triangular garden divided into five plots.

none at all but then children would miss out on the wonderful purple sprouting broccoli and spring cauliflowers. One answer is to have half a plot each of alliums and brassicas. It would be a pity, though, not to have plenty of onions; they are easy to grow and harvest and children can have fun stringing them up. Leeks, too, are easy to grow and as they crop over a long period in winter, a large number can be used without any being wasted. I would always recommend a whole plot for potatoes and also the tender crops that follow, as there are many colourful and productive things to grow in that group. Some, like the squashes, need plenty of space. I would recommend, therefore, to fit five types of crop into four plots, brassicas and legumes could share a plot.

Garlic	Purple	Broad	Potatoes	Spring
Onions	sprouting	beans	Beetroot	cabbage
Leeks	broccoli	French and	Spring	Squash
Radish	Cauliflower	haricot	cabbage	Courgettes
Carrots	Brussels	beans		Sweetcorn
	sprouts	Runner		Tomatoes
	Cabbage	beans		Carrots
	Tomatoes	Peas		Lettuce
	Swedes	Carrots		?Jerusalem
	Turnips	Salads		artichokes
	Parsnips	?Jerusalem		
	Beetroot	artichokes		
	Lettuce			
Plot 1	Plot 2	Plot 3	Plot 4	Plot 5

Fig. 3.4 A five plot rotation. Crops move to the left. Onions etc. go to the far right.

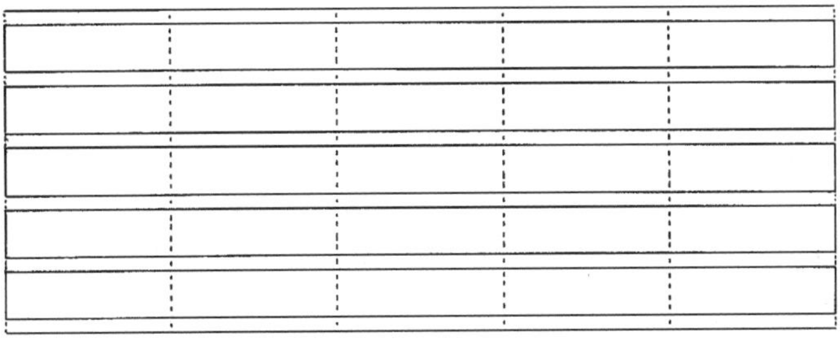

Fig. 3.5 Layout for an allotment, for maximum efficiency.

So as not to limit the range and quantity of brassicas and legumes too much, crops that would normally share a plot with brassicas, such as beetroot, carrots and parsnips, could be grown in the tender crops plot, i.e. where squashes, sweetcorn and tomatoes are grown. Figure 3.6 is a simplified version of the plan (see page 53). When, four years later, the brassicas and legumes return to the same plot, their relative positions can be reversed, giving, in effect, an eight year rotation for these two types of crop.

The following are the crops that would be grown on one plot over a five year period if you were actually to have five plots. In **year one**, following an autumn application of lime, *if needed,* alliums would be grown: onions, garlic and leeks. Leeks are supposed to deter carrot root fly. So, you could try alternate rows of leeks and carrots. However, I have not found this to be effective.

In **year two** brassicas are grown: cabbages, sprouts, broccoli, etc. Parsnips and beetroot can also be grown in this plot. In autumn, as beds are cleared of summer cabbage or beetroot, broad beans may be sown, if your climate will allow them to survive the winter. Otherwise, sow as early as possible in spring.

In **year three** legumes are grown: beans and peas. If your beds are aligned north-south, or nearly so, the following does not apply. Plant the tall legumes – climbing beans – at the northern end of the plot so that they do not cast shade on the other beds. Peas, especially, do not like being shaded and will lean towards the light and might, therefore, not cling on to whatever has been provided for them to climb up.

In **year four** potatoes are grown. Begin planting at the north end of the plot with early potatoes and if main crop potatoes are to be grown, plant them at the south end of the plot. This order is of some significance if there is any kind of shade-casting barrier – hedge or fence – at the southern boundary of the garden. Growing potatoes before the tender crops in the rotation allows a very valuable crop to be grown – spring cabbage. This is available at a time when there is little else fresh and green in the garden (in England this will be May to early July). The following describes how spring cabbage can be grown between two summer crops without displacing either.

When the first bed of early potatoes has been harvested the soil can be levelled with the cultivator and spring cabbage sown. Subsequently cleared beds of potatoes can be filled with transplanted cabbage later. The cabbage can stay in these beds until even after the tender crops are planted out the following year without interfering with the growth of the latter. If more beds of early potatoes are cleared, before the end of July, than you need for spring cabbage, beetroot and/or carrots may be sown. In most areas there will be time for quite good crops to grow before winter frosts begin.

The only other possible position in the rotation where spring cabbage could be grown without it displacing a main summer or winter crop is if it is sown after harvesting an early crop of garlic, and shallots as well if they have been planted in the autumn. When deciding where to plant garlic and shallots in autumn, you might want to consider where you want to sow beetroot and parsnips (and other non-brassica crops) 18 months later in what will then be the brassica plot. The timing and sequence of crops is as follows: garlic and shallots are planted in autumn, harvested in summer, spring cabbage is sown; most of the cabbage will not be used until after other brassicas are sown during the following spring; therefore, after spring cabbage is harvested (or while some are still there) non-brassica crops may be sown – beetroot, parsnips, carrots, or lettuce, for example. Good crops of beetroot can be grown when sown as late as July.

In **year five** the tender crops are grown: squash, courgette, sweetcorn, tomato, etc. One of the effects of global warming means that it is probably worthwhile growing melons in favourable areas. The chances are that in most years a reasonable crop will be produced. Again, if you have anything but north-south orientated beds, plant the sweetcorn in the northern-most bed so that it does not shade any other crop in the plot. Bear in mind, too, that squash plants are very 'adventurous' and can trail for several metres. They may trail between sweetcorn with little effect on the latter. If there are volunteer potatoes growing from the previous year, obviously they will need to be dug out from positions where you want to plant out squash, courgettes, melons etc., but in between these widely-spaced plants potatoes may be left a little longer, until the space they occupy is really needed by the new crops, by which time there will be some usable-sized new potatoes.

As beds are cleared of the tender crops, if you suspect that the pH is low, this is the time to test the soil in this plot. If it is below 6.4, or 5.8 on peat soils, a little lime may be added to the whole plot. The amount required will depend on the type of soil, rainfall, and the number of plots in your rotation. Soils with a high clay or organic matter content will require more lime to raise the pH by a given amount than soils low in clay or organic matter. So, on light, sandy soils, and especially in high rainfall areas, it is advisable to apply lime in smaller amounts but more frequently. In a garden rotation this might mean adding it before growing alliums and again the following year before growing brassicas. On heavy soils and those high in organic matter, you might go through more than one cycle in the rotation without needing to lime. On some soils it is possible that lime might never need to be applied, if plenty of compost is being added containing crushed egg shells and wood ash.

The rotation begins again when garlic is planted. The timing depends on your location. They should be planted early enough so that at least two or three cm of leaf shoot are showing before hard frost or snow sets in for the winter, if in areas where the ground is likely to remain frozen or snow-covered for most of the winter. In milder areas the timing is less important, the shoots may be taller before the first frost or if not up by then, they can continue growing whenever the weather is mild enough at any time during winter. Shallot sets can also be planted at the same time as garlic.

Dividing the garden into the plots

Not all gardens are a convenient rectangle. My self-sufficient garden was in two parts, either side of a lane; the main area was almost an isosceles triangle (See Figure 3.3 on page 46). When designing a garden there are two conflicting criteria, although most school gardens will be too small for this to be relevant. It is desirable to maximize the *length* of beds in order to minimize the number of times the garden line has to be moved when making seed drills, but it is also desirable to maximize the *number* of beds in order to give flexibility in arranging the crops, so that having more than one type of vegetable in a bed is avoided – it makes record keeping easier and looks neater. In a very small garden or a child's garden, there might only be four or five beds, which would be synonymous with plots. This arrangement might also be adequate for Year One children at a school. A suggested rotation for a four bed garden could be:

1   **Leeks**. In a school/child's garden onions grown from sets would be easier to grow and harvest.

2   **Runner beans**. In a school/child's garden early dwarf peas

would be easier to grow and harvest, and could be followed by beetroot and early carrots in alternate rows, or hardy lettuce.

3 **Early potatoes**, followed by beetroot and/or carrots.

4 **A bush type of winter squash**. Sweetcorn could be grown as well, with the squash in between.

In the example plan in Figure 3.6 the rotation moves round anti-clockwise. Crops printed in smaller type indicate that they follow or precede the main crop. The plan, therefore, shows how spring cabbage fits in, being sown after a bed of early potatoes are dug and remaining until the following year in the bed where squash will be planted.

Squeezing what is really a five plot rotation into four plots does cause a problem. Purple sprouting and spring cauliflower are not all harvested until late spring and, some cauliflowers will be at their best in early summer. If they were being followed by legumes (in a five plot garden) tender beans could be planted after this or even sown around remaining brassica plants. Potatoes, however, should be planted before this time and have a trench dug and some compost put in. So, if you do grow spring broccoli and cauliflower, the potatoes that follow them will be planted later than is ideal and will not be ready until late summer, too late to get a crop of carrots in afterwards. Instead, this would be a good place to sow winter salads such as land cress and rocket after the potatoes are harvested. Land cress needs to be sown earlier than rocket, as it is slower growing. In most of England land cress can go in some time in August and rocket in early September. Because of the short period (in the five plots in four plan) available for potatoes between spring

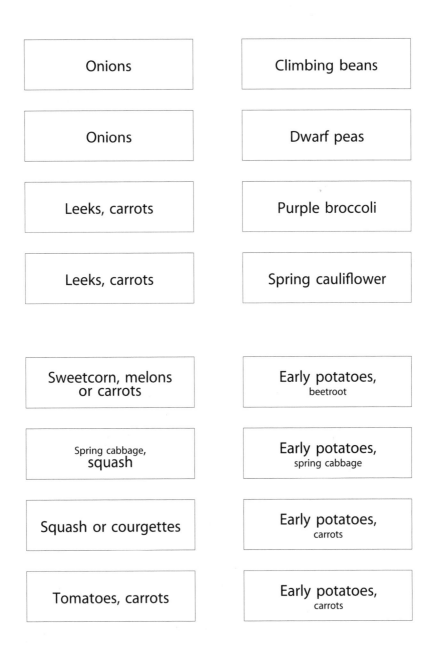

Fig. 3.6 Simplified version of a school garden, showing a five plot rotation fitted into four plots. Crops move anti-clockwise.

brassicas and sowing winter salads, only early varieties of potato should be grown. However, on the half of the plot where legumes were grown the previous year there would be time to grow main crop varieties. Some are described as late main crop. These should be avoided if you wish to sow winter salads afterwards, as the potatoes will not be mature before the salads need to be sown.

In my triangular garden I did not have paths between the plots as I considered it was not necessary and would waste space. In a school garden, partly for aesthetic or design reasons but mainly for practical reasons, there should be paths between plots, which means that every bed is surrounded by paths (Figure 3.7). If the paths between or surrounding the plots are of grass, they should be a minimum of 1.4m wide to avoid excessive wear or soil compaction and to allow room for wheelbarrows and for children to pass each other without needing to step on the beds.

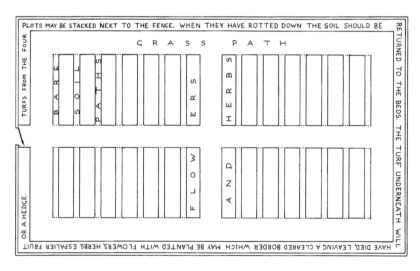

Fig. 3.7 A school garden.

It should be noted that, for those wishing to grow vegetables on a larger scale for commercial purposes, the same principles of beds and plots can be applied. Beds may be of any length and number in plots of any size.

MARKING THE BEDS ON THE GROUND

Creating raised beds retained by boards solves the problem of marking out the beds but if you are not doing that, another method is needed to mark where the beds and paths are. White-painted stakes protruding a few centimetres out of the ground is one solution but they can be tripped on, knocked out of place and will eventually need replacing. After the initial setting out of the beds and paths has been done, the only time you need to know exactly where they are is when sowing seeds, to know where to put the garden line when making seed drills. The rest of the time it is clear enough. So, no permanent markers are necessary. All you need is a length of cord along each side of the plot, with markings denoting the position of each path and bed. Thick grade nylon picture cord is the best material to use.

To prepare a marker cord, put a small stake or stick in the ground a few centimetres from the edge of a plot and in line with the adjacent boundary. For example, in Figure 3.6 at the top left hand corner, a few centimetres to the left of the onion bed and in line with its top edge. Make a non-slip loop in one end of the cord using a bowline knot (see Appendix III) and place it over the stick. The next step can either be a rather tedious one, which gives a better result, or a quick method. The quick method is to make another loop so that when the cord is reasonably taut it just reaches another stick at the other end of the plot, i.e. in Figure 3.6 at the lower left corner of the lower leek bed. Lay out a surveying tape alongside, between the two stakes. The end of the tape should be secured with a skewer or thin stick. If two people are available, one can hold the tape taut while the other person paints rings around the rope or cord at points to mark path, bed, path, bed, etc. Bright red is a good colour to contrast with the grass. (Figure 3.6 does not show it but there should be an access or working path of bare soil at each end of the plots so that you do not have to stand on the edge of the grass (if that is what surrounds the plots) in order to work on the outer beds, as in Figure 3.7.) Picture cord is rather thin and painted marks will not show up very well. The tedious but better method is to tie knots at the positions of beds and paths and then paint them. The result has the appearance of red beads on the cord. This is quite difficult to do. Starting at one end, you will need to apply the same tension to the cord when positioning each knot so that the previous knots are still in the correct place. It is much easier if two people, or more, work together to make sure that all the knots are at the right position as each new one is tied. Another solution is to thread, and tie in place, coloured buttons or beads at each required position. I have used small cuboids of hardwood.

To prepare cords to use where beds are 90cm wide and paths 45cm, start with one end looped over a stake and tie the first knot at the 45cm point to mark the first path, then at 1.35m for the first bed, then 1.80m for the second path and so on. When all the knots have been tied, tying the loop to fit over the stick at the other end of the plot might need a few attempts to make sure that all the knots along the length of the cord are still in the right positions. Thereafter, whether the cord becomes a little stretched and slack or is tight, does not matter. As long as the two ends are in the right positions, the knots will be also. Then, whenever you need to use the garden lines to mark the edges of a bed, to know where to cultivate, spread compost or sow seeds, put the marker cords in along each side of the plot (the same holes can be found each time if they are in turf) and position each end of the garden lines next to opposite knots/ buttons/beads on the marker cord. This might all seem rather complicated but in carrying out the procedure it will become clear and straightforward.

THE GARDEN PLAN

It is very useful to have an outline plan of the garden, showing the beds and paths and any permanent features – such as fruit trees, ornamentals, seats and tool shed. At a scale of 1:100 most gardens, including school gardens, will fit on to an A4 sheet of paper. If the garden is small enough it can be drawn at 1:50.

Outline copies of the plan may be used to record where crops are grown and their sowing and harvesting dates. In the formal, four plot plan each plot's crops can move round clockwise or anti-clockwise. In the example shown in Figure 3.6 they rotate anti-clockwise. Each plot and bed can have a permanent number, so that any bed can be referred to, e.g. 3.4 would be plot three, bed number four.

Using the system of plots and beds and working out a rotation to suit your needs avoids the problem of each year wondering what to sow where and possibly ending up with no room for some crops or unproductive empty space. The system structures the work and breaks it up into manageable units of beds. While it would be an exaggeration to say it does half the work, it certainly helps but is not inflexible; there is scope for change and experimentation.

FRUIT

Fruit trees and bushes may be grown in an area separate from the vegetable rotation plots. It might prove necessary to build a fruit cage over the soft fruit if blackbirds become a serious problem. This should be borne in mind when designing the fruit-growing area. Red seems to be the irresistible colour for blackbirds. Non-red fruits can, therefore, be integrated into the vegetable garden without too much loss and can give a three-dimensional structure to the garden to good effect. Tree and bush fruit can be trained in various forms, which makes them neat and ornamental as well as very productive for the area they take up. For example, in a formal, four plot garden the four beds next to the central path could be planted with espalier apples or pears. Espaliers are where tiers of branches are trained horizontally each way from the stem. If the garden is big enough, there could be a fruit border surrounding the whole vegetable garden, with a path on the inside for access to the plots.

All soft fruit, as well as trained apples and pears on dwarfing root stock, may be grown in the same width of beds as used for vegetables. This gives access at any time of year for whatever needs doing – pruning, weeding and harvesting. Depending on the variety, the same plants of strawberries should be grown for no longer than three or four years. In the four plot rotation, if one plot is being shared by brassicas and legumes, strawberries could be planted in one or two beds after beans or peas have been cleared and could remain for three years until the plot is again needed for brassicas and legumes. There are some excellent books on fruit cultivation. *The Fruit Garden Displayed* published by the Royal Horticultural Society is clear and comprehensive. *Fruit* by Harry Baker (former Fruit Officer,

RHS) has no photographs but very clear illustrations and includes a slightly wider range of fruit.

Where school fields have trees planted around them I have always thought that they might as well be fruit trees. Children, I would think from year six onwards, could be taught the art of pruning and training various types of fruit and, generally, be given responsibility for looking after the trees. *They* would then see to it that fruit was not picked before it was ripe, only to be used as footballs or thrown around.

Digging

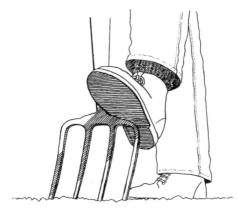

THE FORK

I recommend a fork rather than a spade for the following reasons:

1 It is easier to push a fork into the ground, especially in stony soil.

2 An ordinary digging fork is lighter than a comparable-sized spade. So, you are lifting less weight with every action.

3 A spade would cut through perennial weed roots, leaving more pieces to pick out, some of which would be very small and easily missed.

4 A spade does more damage to soil fauna, cutting through worms, for example.

5 A fork is more effective in breaking up lumps and can be used as a sort of sieve to separate the soil from roots, or whatever you wish to remove.

Other tools needed are buckets, a wheelbarrow and the cultivator. A minimum of two buckets are always useful when doing any sort of digging: one for rubbish and one for weeds; or three buckets if you wish to keep perennial weed roots and anything with seeds on separate from soft weeds to be composted if you are not confident of making a compost heap hot enough to kill seeds and perennial roots. If the soil is very stony, you might decide to have another bucket to collect large stones and take these off the garden. If there are some really large and deep roots to get out you might need the heavy duty fork and a spade as well to dig holes around the roots.

Before starting to dig it could be a useful exercise to dig a hole so that the soil profile can be seen. This would be particularly instructive for children, but it is valuable for anyone to know what the cross section of the soil is like. Prepare a south-facing side for viewing, so that it is well-lit and children will not have the sun in their eyes when looking at it. It need not be vertical. It could slope a little so that its angle is nearer to facing their viewpoint. Having dug the hole, with a flat, south-facing profile, the soil face needs to be prepared in a particular way to show soil characteristics. Rather than cutting or slicing the soil, use a sharp spade and, with a downwards, levering action, try to prize away the soil so that the texture and structure of the soil is more clearly seen. Soil texture refers to the sizes of the mineral grains in the soil: gravel, sand, silt and clay. Soil structure refers to the way the soil aggregates into various sizes and shapes of lumps, or peds, as they are known. If the soil were cut rather than being prized apart as described, the layers would be revealed but the structure would not be (see 'Soil layers' on p80).

Start at one edge of the site and work back in a line from that. Later the paths will be laid out on the dug soil, giving access to every part of the garden. If there is a slope, start at the higher end. There are two reasons for adults and one for children to face uphill and work down. If you are facing uphill your fork will seem longer and you will have less far to bend, when digging and picking up weeds, etc. As children will be using tools that are plenty long enough for them, i.e. adult tools, this is not a necessary consideration but what is, for adults and children, is that by facing uphill you will be moving the soil uphill slightly. This will counteract any tendency there will subsequently be for soil to move downhill as a result of garden cultivations.

It might seem too obvious to mention, but as I have seen children standing in the wrong place to dig, it might as well be explained to them that, when digging, you stand on ground yet to be dug and work backwards. If there are several children digging in a line, those who find they can dig faster will need to dig a wider piece of ground so that the digging progresses in a reasonably straight line.

Many gardening books have illustrations of double digging, as if this is a required thing to do, as a matter of course. I must have dug a few acres of new gardens and I have never done this and never felt the need to. I have long suspected that double digging was invented to keep Victorian gardeners busy over the winter. However, perhaps I have just been lucky in not having to deal with soils that needed double digging. If, before any work is started on the garden, there is no sign of poor drainage, double digging is probably not necessary. On the other hand, if water is occasionally seen lying on the surface it might be because of a high water table and double digging will not help.

It is always useful to dig a hole into the subsoil to see if there is any sign of poor drainage. This will be indicated by grey mottling in the subsoil. If grey mottling is present it indicates that the soil is waterlogged for part of the year. Over-wintering vegetables might not do well in it. If there is no mottling and if in winter, no water in the hole, the soil will be fine and double digging will not be necessary. It will be quite enough of a task to get single digging done.

Even if double digging is not being done, in some circumstances it might be worth digging out a trench where digging is started and dumping the soil in a spread-out ridge where the last few spits will be dug. Otherwise it will be difficult to avoid soil being scattered over whatever surface is beyond where the digging starts and, because it is natural to throw soil forwards when digging, at the end of the plot there will be a valley, a deficit of soil. On the area where soil from the top end has been spread, it will be necessary to dig deeper to reach the same level as on the rest of the plot but you should end up with a level surface, after some levelling out with the cultivator.

There are a number of possibilities of what actually forms the boundary where digging begins. There could be a wall, a fence, a hedge, a hard surface – playground or path of some kind or just a continuation of the ground that is not going to be dug up. A different approach is required depending on the situation.

1   **Wall**. Unfortunately, weed roots will grow right up against the wall, in spite of what might seem dry conditions. If digging against the prevailing wind/rain side of a wall, water will run down it. So, conditions will not be dry there. Anyway, weed roots have a nasty habit of growing into any gap they find. If couch grass, for example, has gone through

a hole in the wall it will be impossible to get it out. It will keep growing back. You just have to be vigilant and keep weeding every time it reappears.

2   **Fence**. Fences do not normally go into the ground, therefore, the situation is like open ground but the fence just makes the situation awkward. If the other side of the fence is a neighbour's garden, unless it is cultivated ground and the owner is diligent about weeding, there will be a constant problem with weeds encroaching into your side. When you have dug as far as you can, one option is to sink into the ground a barrier of some kind. I have used old roofing slates against a hedge within which there was couch grass which could not be dug out. This worked quite well. If you want to put down paving of some kind it is useful to leave a gap just wide enough to get a small fork into for weeding. Otherwise, couch grass and other root-creeping weeds will go right under the paving and come up in the garden. You then have to lift the paving stones to get them out, which is a nuisance after they have been carefully laid. If the other side of the fence is your property or another part of the school grounds, make the boundary of your dug area on the other side of the fence. It will be easier, working from that side, to cut an edge, as with the edge to a grass path, so that perennial roots do not keep growing back into your dug area.

3   **Hedge**. There could be many types of perennial weeds established in a hedge and it will be impossible to dig them all out. You just have to do the best you can. A barrier could then be inserted as described above. I have only tried slates but these are likely to get kicked and broken and could

cause injury if fallen on. Wooden boards would be effective. Whatever is used needs to go into the ground at least 20cm. However, that depth will not be enough to stop bindweed, lesser bindweed or creeping thistle.

4 **Hard surface**. Whether this is edged tarmac, paving or concrete, hard surfaces present similar problems to a wall. Perennial weed roots, ever the imperialist explorers, will go underneath. It will be impossible to dig them out. You just have to be diligent in dealing with them every time they reappear.

5 **Grass/playing field**. The edge of the area to be cultivated will already have been cut at an angle to turf depth. Before starting to dig, go round the edge of the plot with a sharp spade and deepen the angle of cut to a spade depth. When digging next to this, insert the fork at the same angle so as not to undermine the balk.

6 **Rough vegetation which is not to be used as a path.** There needs to be a bare soil path around the perimeter of the garden, for access, but it is very important to dig and clear the ground at least 30cm beyond whatever is the designated width of the path. This provides a *cordon sanitaire* that is easily weeded if perennials try to invade from the uncleared area. Invasion can be minimized by creating a mini equivalent of a ha-ha – a cut edge with the soil thrown forward on to the beds and leaving a border of loose soil between the cut edge and the path. It will not keep out the deep-rooted creeping thistle or bindweeds but grasses, including couch and some other small perennials will be stopped by this obstacle of open air. Once a year it will be necessary to go round the edge with a sharp spade to

sever any deep invading rhizomes and then dig them out on the garden side. The idea is to prevent them getting as far as the path, where it will be much harder to dig them out from the trodden down soil.

Digging technique

The way of holding a fork that comes naturally to a right-handed person is to have the right hand on the handle, the left somewhere along the shaft, when lifting, and to push the fork into the ground using the left foot on the left shoulder of the fork prongs. As with any repetitive job, aches and strains can develop and breaks will be needed more frequently than with more varied work. Try becoming ambidextrous at this most basic gardening activity. It feels awkward at first but it is worth persevering. You will be able to work for longer without breaks and be much less likely to develop aches and pains. I use hands and feet in the way described above only when progressing to the right along the line of digging. When progressing to the left I have my left hand on the handle, right hand on the shaft and push in with the right foot on the right side of the fork. It would be a good exercise of co-ordination for children to learn to dig both ways.

When digging a new site, two assumptions can be made about the soil: it will be compacted, and it will contain perennial weed roots. This will be the case, for example, with soil under the turf of a playing field. If the soil is what is known as 'heavy', i.e. contains much clay and feels sticky when moist, the block of soil just dug might need breaking up by spearing it or knocking it down a couple of times with the back of the fork. There is no need to invert the soil. Unless the soil is very light (sandy) and not compacted, it need not be broken down to a tilth at the first digging. Leave it roughly turned over in lumps. If any perennial roots can easily be taken out at this stage they may be but there is no need to be thorough. Wait until the lumps have dried sufficiently so that when trodden on they crumble rather than become compacted. Then, as you work backwards on the second dig your feet break up the big lumps, making the digging easier. The interval between first and second dig also allows the worms to get back down into moist soil so that fewer will be disturbed. It is only heavy, clay soils that are likely to need digging twice when making a new garden.

On the second dig it will be necessary to push the fork in deeper than the length of the prongs to reach the depth of the first dig which, by loosening the soil and introducing a large volume of air pores, will have raised the surface. It will also be necessary to dig a wider spit than on the first dig to allow you to lift it without much falling between the prongs. Throw the load forward, turning it over if you wish and break down the lumps with the back of the fork. A quicker and better method, though more energetic, is to bounce the soil on the fork, so that it serves as a sieve, allowing broken up soil to fall, loosely, to the ground. Although the soil will then consist of small lumps they are still lumps of compacted soil. They can be broken up further with the back of the fork. In a light soil, with low clay content, the bouncing/sieving technique can be used on the first and only dig.

The particular way of bouncing soil on the fork that seems to come naturally is not the most efficient way of doing it. When I suggested the technique to some volunteers working on a walled garden restoration they automatically did it the hard way. So did children. What seems to come naturally is for the

Fig. 4.1. Technique of shaking soil through a fork to separate weeds and break up lumps.

hand that is holding the shaft to do all the work while the hand on the handle stays still. The handle is, therefore the pivot point. If, however, you imagine the pivot to be mid way between the hands, which should be as far apart as is comfortable, and move both hands up and down alternately, like each end of a see-saw, the job is much easier.

The technique of soil bouncing on a fork when digging is appropriate for most situations, whether it is the second digging of de-turfed soil or when digging areas with weeds still growing. Depending on the nature of the weeds or roots, much or little will be left on the fork when the soil has fallen to the ground. This can then be thrown from the fork straight into the barrow or a bucket. Then, with one hand on the fork handle, which rests against your chest to support your back, bend down to pick up the weeds and roots that have fallen to the ground. This is where it becomes apparent that there is an optimum length of fork. If it were any longer than rib height it would be difficult to reach the ground to pick up weeds and still support your back by resting your chest on the handle.

ESTABLISHING THE BEDS

The second dig may be completed before any beds are laid out, or each bed may be laid out as the ground is cleared. There might be two reasons for choosing the latter. Laying out one bed at a time as you go along varies the work so that you are not just digging for long periods. Secondly, if the weather is dry it will be a better strategy for conserving soil moisture, as well as being easier, if all of the bed preparation work is done while there is moist soil at the surface. However, if the weather is cool and moist and you wish to complete the digging before laying out beds, after working back for a couple of metres, take a break from digging and use the cultivator to get a finer tilth and even out the surface, which might be left a little undulating from the digging.

If you decide to lay out beds as you go along, use the marker cords along each side of the plot. (See 'Marking the beds on the ground', on p.55.) When you have dug enough for a bed, plus a path, plus half way into the next bed, stop digging. Put in a garden line to mark each edge of the bed, using the marker cords to position the sticks at each side of the plot. Use the cultivator to level out the soil where the new paths will be along each side of where the bed will be. Try to pick out all the stones on the path areas. In the summer the paths will need hoeing several times and once the soil is compacted, stones make hoeing difficult. If the site is one where turf has been removed, resist the temptation to throw some soil from the path areas on to the bed. Treading on the paths will immediately lower their level and, eventually, all the soil from the turf stack will be put back on the garden and as it is top soil, high in organic matter, it should all be put on to the beds. The resulting rise in their level will be as much as can be managed without having retaining boards.

Unless the top soil is very shallow, I recommend keeping the levels of paths and beds about the same. So, if there is turf soil to be returned later, this may be anticipated by making the paths slightly higher. When cultivating the beds, if there are clayey lumps in the soil, these may be raked on to the paths and trodden down. Before doing this, if there are no turfs to be put back, then some soil should be taken off the path area and put on to the bed, to keep the level of path and bed about the same. The result is more of the better soil on the bed.

Cultivate the bed soil from the paths on each side, moving the cultivator mostly parallel to the paths. Then, use the back of the cultivator (or fork) to tamp down the surface to break up remaining lumps. If this is a new garden I would recommend, at this point, spreading some dried seaweed. It will provide a small amount of fine organic matter to feed soil bacteria but its main value is the trace elements it contains. Without a detailed soil analysis you will not know which element(s) are lacking but it would be difficult to apply an excess of seaweed as it is quite expensive. Scatter it evenly between the two lines marking the bed then rake it in; the cultivator is good for this. If farmyard manure is available it could be applied at this stage. The nearer the time is to when seeds will be sown, the more well rotted the manure should be, as unrotted straw will get in the way when making seed drills and will cause dry spots in the soil (but see 'Incorporating compost or manure' on p.110). It could even cause a temporary reduction in plant-available nitrogen, as the multiplying bacteria need nitrogen to break down the high carbon-content straw. Spread the manure and break it up with the fork, then take out the two lines either side of the bed, otherwise they will get in the way when turning the manure in with the spade. Use a sharp spade; a blunt one will be difficult to push in if there is much straw not fully rotted. Try to dig it in as deep as you can, although in practice it will be difficult even to get it all covered with soil. After turning in the manure use the back of the fork to level the surface, at the same time trying to cover the manure with soil. If the manure is sticky or the soil too damp, let the surface dry a little before tamping it down with the back of the cultivator or fork. If there is still straw on the surface it may be raked off to allow seed drills to be more easily made.

Transforming hard, bare, de-turfed, soil or weedy ground into precisely laid out paths, and slightly convex beds of beautifully cultivated friable soil is a very pleasurable experience.

DEALING WITH PERENNIAL WEEDS

When clearing ground for a new garden a considerable volume of coarse perennial weed roots could accumulate – docks, hogweed, nettles, couch grass, etc. There are three ways of dealing with this sort of material.

1   If the weather is hot and dry it can be spread out to dry and then composted.

2   It can be put into a pile and covered with a couple of layers of thick black plastic and left until the roots have died and rotted, which could take longer than the normal composting period.

3   It can be burnt. The organic matter will be lost but the minerals will be retained. Bonfire ash should be put on the compost heap, a little at a time in layers.

Each location will have a different range of weeds and its own particularly troublesome species. Below are some that are most likely to be encountered.

1 **Couch grass** *(Agropyron repens)*. This could be widespread in some sites and there will be few without any. However, it is one of the easiest perennials to get rid of, provided you are thorough about picking out every bit of root. It is easily recognised by its bootlace-like white rhizomes with nodes every two or three centimetres from where small, hair-like roots grow and from where shoots can grow too. The top growth is slow to go to seed; the plant spreads, mainly, by the underground growth of rhizomes. The growing tips of these are hardened, sharp points. They can grow straight through a potato! The rhizomes grow more or less horizontally and most are within 15cm of the surface. Occasionally, though, one will grow vertically downwards. These need to be followed and dug out. The rhizomes can be spread out to dry and when dead, composted. Or they can be composted straight away provided your heap is covered to exclude light. I have made large heaps of barrowloads of couch roots and covered them in thick black plastic until they rotted. The result was very attractive, light textured compost.

2 **Creeping buttercup** *(Ranunculus repens)*. This too is relatively easy to get rid of as it does not root very deeply and will not grow from a fragment of root. It is just very persistent and once you have crops growing, making digging out weeds more difficult, it can quickly cover the ground.

4 **Creeping thistle** *(Cirsium arvense)*. On mature plants the creeping roots are well below normal digging depth. They

send shoots up to the surface and as soon as they reach the light, develop their prickly leaves. Loosen the soil with a fork as deep as you can around the stems and grab them as low down as possible. They might break off at the base root if it is not too deep but usually at a point higher up the shoot. Wherever they snap they will grow again, probably two from each shoot – and again and again and again. As with the field bindweed you will not be able to dig out well-established plants, therefore it is a case of being persistent, pulling out every shoot as soon as they come up. Try to get out as much of the shoot as you can. In theory, eventually the deep roots will be exhausted but I have to admit I have not worked for long enough in any garden which has had this weed to know if this ploy will actually work. The flowers are small, purple and of a typical thistle shape. The plant takes quite a long time to grow to seed maturity. So, there is no excuse for ever letting them go to seed once you have started gardening but they certainly do not need to rely on seeding to spread.

4   **Dandelion** *(Taraxacum officinale)*. The flowers do provide an early feed for bees but there is no shortage of dandelions in the countryside. So, I would advocate trying to eliminate dandelions from the garden and anywhere near it. I recommend the same policy for every species which has wind-borne seeds. As with docks the whole root needs to be dug out, otherwise a piece will regrow and be more difficult to dig out as the new growth is weaker and liable to snap off. They can be dug out of grass by loosening, with a fork, the ground all around the plant and grabbing the root as low down as possible and pulling it out. The grass can be trodden down level again afterwards.

5   **Dock**, especially broad-leaved dock *(Rumex obtusifolius)*.
    This is the well-known antidote to stinging nettles. Dock
    roots are like long thin, brown parsnips. I once pulled one
    out with a tap root over 120cm long. It is not necessary to
    get the whole tap root out but you need to get out as far as
    the root is still tapering, otherwise it will grow back. If it
    does grow back from a piece left in, it is difficult to get out
    because the new growth is thinner and weaker than the
    piece it grew from and is likely to break, leaving the old
    piece of root to grow again. Meanwhile, the old root has
    gone still deeper and grown stronger. Unfortunately, some
    docks have multiple roots diverging off in all directions.
    These are more difficult to get out but it is just as important
    to remove every piece.

6   **Field or Lesser bindweed** *(Convolvulus arvensis)*. A single
    shoot will branch out and the shoots grow in several
    directions along the ground and then climb anything they
    encounter. It is quite a pretty plant with small, trumpet-
    shaped pink flowers. One school garden I worked in was
    infested with this weed and one day I thought I would see
    how far the roots went down. After 75cm I gave up. A single
    root, as thick as a pencil, was continuing down vertically.
    Such a root has so much in reserve, it will easily grow back
    if broken off at or just below normal digging depth. I
    suppose if you were to cover the ground with a completely
    light-excluding material for several years it would succumb,
    but if you want to get on with gardening there is no easy
    way, organically. Digging it out is not really an option. You
    would have to dig such enormous holes; it would be hard
    work and take a long time. The only suggestions I can make
    are that you loosen around the shoot as deep as you can

with a fork and grasp the root as low as possible and gently pull, so that it breaks off further down. This should be done every time you see the tiniest green shoot on the surface. Eventually this must exhaust the plant but I cannot say how long this will take.

7   **Ground elder** (*Aegopodium podagraria*). This is not a particularly difficult weed to deal with, just tedious. It is not deep rooting but the easily seen, wandering white roots are weak and break very easily. So, it is just time-consuming picking the little pieces out. Frequent mowing will eliminate it from a grass path.

8   **Hogweed** (*Heracleum sphondylium*). There are about 3000 species of plants in the family Umbelliferae. The flower heads are usually white or pink and the plant structures are really fascinating and beautiful. The roots of a large hogweed will be difficult to dig out. They are tapering and fleshy but spread out in a branched way, like some docks. As with docks and dandelions, every piece must be removed.

Before cutting off the seed heads, as was suggested doing during the early stages of clearing, it would be useful for children to have a closer look at this, or any similar species, to get an idea of how many seeds a weed can produce and how important, therefore, it is never to let them go to seed in a garden. They could count the number of seeds from a seed head or umbel. Or just count the number from a single cluster and multiply by the number of clusters in the umbel and then by the number of umbels on a whole plant. Then ask how long it might take to pull or dig out that number of new weeds, if all those seeds were allowed to grow.

9 **Stinging nettle** *(Urtica dioica)*. There is also a smaller version called small nettle, *Urtica urens*; small but just as vicious. Most children will have had personal experience of one or both of these. So, they should recognise it and also appreciate how important it is not to have them in a garden. Nettle seedlings are particularly annoying when you are weeding by hand between rows of vegetables. The good news is that even mature plants can be dug and pulled out, provided you have a good fork, leather gloves and get a bit angry! It is a case of brute force; not much finesse required. The roots are yellow and quite tough and tend to spread horizontally, with some going deeper, but they are not *very* deep rooted.

SUMMARY

It is inevitable that many pieces of perennial weed roots will have been missed and, of course, field bindweed and creeping thistle will come back as if nothing had happened. Wherever perennial weeds do reappear it is very important to be assiduous about getting them out, even if it means, in the process, digging up vegetable seedlings as well. Weeds always grow faster than crops. If you leave them in order to avoid disturbing the vegetables, before long the garden will look little different from before you started clearing it. Crops will have been smothered and weeds reinvigorated in the nice cultivated conditions that have been made for them. Where weeds come up in the paths they will be more of a problem because of the compacted soil but you need to be just as thorough in digging them out.

If clearing a private garden for a child, think ahead and clear the ground a year before the child is old enough to start gardening! Then leave it for a year and repeat the clearing process.

Maintaining Soil Fertility

INTRODUCTION

This subject could be summed up in five principles:

1 minimize soil disturbance;

2 maximize vegetation cover;

3 minimize periods of bare soil;

4 conserve and increase organic matter;

5 put back what is taken out.

Soil science is a vast and endlessly fascinating subject. Many books have been written on every specialized aspect of it and every year hundreds of papers are published in academic journals detailing recent research. Soil has been described as the poor man's rainforest – well, not so poor, when you consider that a gram of fertile soil can contain a few billion living organisms, most of them bacteria, perhaps 20,000 different species (Brady and Weil 2002, p481).

Gardening is far from being a natural activity. Rather, what we are doing is trying to optimize conditions to maximize production of a narrow range of plants that have been bred from wild ancestors to be more palatable and higher yielding. To achieve these ends it is necessary to disturb the soil, reduce its density and, at least once a year, clear it of all vegetation to provide the best possible chances for just one or two types of plant in a given area. Without our intervention soil remains covered in a diversity of protective vegetation, except in the most extreme regions of cold or hot and dry.

All terrestrial life depends upon soil. When we decide to become gardeners we take on a great responsibility. Fortunately for us, soil is surprisingly forgiving stuff. Undisturbed by humans it develops a complex stratigraphy of flora and fauna, with different species at different depths, yet after centuries of repeated inversion, mixing and compaction it still produces crops. Since tractors replaced horses the extent, depth, frequency and power of cultivation have increased. The effects on soil have been masked by increasing inputs of oil energy for cultivation and continued inputs of agrochemicals, which also depend on oil. In 1992 I watched as a ploughed field was rolled and cultivated six times to get an adequate tilth to sow swedes for sheep. The soil was too dry at the time but also it was pale in colour when wet and seemed to be low in organic matter – lost by repeated cultivation over many years. Another possible consequence of the way farmland is managed is that, while yields remain high, the nutritional content of crops has decreased (Thomas, 2003). All this provides added reasons to treat garden soil with great care, to maintain and even enhance its fertility so that it will grow the most nutritious crops possible.

SOME BASICS OF SOIL FORMATION, DEVELOPMENT AND PROPERTIES

Five major factors that control the formation of soils:

1   Parent material: rock, sediment or drift material on which soil develops.

2   Climate: especially temperature and precipitation.

3   Living organisms: vegetation, soil animals, micro-organisms and humans.

4   Topography: landscape position, slope, aspect.

5   Time: since the parent material became exposed to the forces of soil formation.

Vegetation in soil formation and maintenance, and the importance of humus

Vegetation is largely responsible for the creation of soil, from the first lichens that colonize bare rock, followed by mosses, grasses and trees. Exudates from plant roots and also weak carbonic acid in rain water act as agents that break down soil mineral particles, producing other materials, such as clays, and releasing into the soil solution minerals that can be taken up by plant roots.

Residues of vegetation are transformed by soil organisms into humus, that mostly dark coloured, amorphous material consisting of large complex molecules of varying resistance to further decay by micro-organisms. Humic acids erode the edges of soil mineral particles, releasing from them ions, which are then adsorbed on to more stable colloidal humus and particles of clay from where they can be released into the soil solution and taken up by plants. Earthworms are also important. By eating their way through soil, organic matter is thoroughly shredded and mixed with soil mineral particles. The increased bacterial activity in this material results in increased polysaccharide content in worm casts, which is beneficial for soil aggregation.

The most resistant type of humus is known as the passive fraction and is responsible for most of the nutrient and water holding capacity (Brady and Weil, 2002, p522). The passive fraction is extremely stable, with a half life (the time needed for half to decay) measured in centuries.

The active fraction of soil organic matter includes the living biomass, fine particles of plant and animal detritus and the less stable components of humus, the sugary organic acids or polysaccharides, and fulvic acids. The active fraction has very significant effects on a number of soil properties. It provides most of the readily available food for soil organisms and is the source of most of the readily available nitrogen. It also contributes to structural stability by promoting the aggregation of soil particles. The quality of aggregate structure has a big effect on the soil's resistance to erosion, its ability to absorb water and allow it to drain, and its ease of cultivation. However, it is the active fraction that is most rapidly lost as a result of cultivation. (See 'Cultivation' on p.86.)

Soil layers

As soil develops it differentiates into more or less distinct layers, broadly characterized by upper layers containing accumulating organic matter, from a surface layer of plant litter through to dark, amorphous humus mixed with the mineral component of the soil. The latter is what is referred to as topsoil. Below that are various layers characterized by deposition of clays formed by mineral weathering nearer the surface together with certain minerals leached from the soil above. This is commonly known as subsoil and in many areas has an orangey colour caused by the presence of iron. Below that the soil grades into what is eventually recognized as unaltered parent material.

The processes of soil formation are slowly but inexorably downwards. Parent material that is just beginning to crack will eventually be topsoil. An approximate figure for the rate of soil formation under natural vegetation is 0.1mm per year (Zachar, 1982). At the same time, of course, the natural processes of denudation are lowering the surface at a rate more or less than that. The fact that there *is* a soil profile demonstrates that, overall, soil formation has exceeded soil erosion. The rate of soil formation under well-managed cultivated land can be ten times the natural rate. This is fine as long as the rate of soil loss/ erosion does not exceed that, as can happen where excessive tillage is used on sloping land. It should not be difficult to manage a garden so that soil formation exceeds soil loss.

Soil texture

Soil texture refers to the proportion of different sizes of mineral particles – sand, silt and clay. The ratio of particle size determines many of the soil's properties, for example, speed of drainage, how easy it is to cultivate, and its capacity to retain moisture and nutrients. As already mentioned, humus content is also important in determining these properties. Particle size determines surface area within the soil and it is surface area that has a great effect on soil properties. A fine clay can have a surface area 10,000 times that of the same weight of a medium sandy loam. A spoonful of clay can have the surface area of a football field. A soil that is generally considered to have the best texture for cultivation and crop growth is referred to as a loam. This has 30–50% sand, 30–50% silt and 10–25% clay. Different ratios may be termed clay loams, silt loams, sandy loams and so on. At the extremes are clay soils, silts, and sands.

Soil aggregation

In a pile of gravel the stones do not fit together. There is pore space between them. A similar arrangement exists in soils between the much smaller mineral grains. However, only in pure sand or silt would the situation be strictly analogous. In soil the situation is much more complex. Within any given soil, particle size can vary from gravel to the finest clay particles. The presence of plant roots, fungal hyphae, humus, micro flora and fauna and their various sticky exudates results in the soil aggregating into lumps, or peds, as they are known. Take a lump of soil and it may easily be broken into crumbs of a few millimetres across. At that scale it might be plant roots and fungal hyphae that hold them together. Crumble those again into sub-millimetre peds and these might be held together by root hairs, hyphae and the sticky polysaccharides of humus. Two further hierarchies of aggregates take the ped size down to a few micrometres (thousandths of a millimetre). The way that soil aggregates into a range of hierarchies is referred to as its structure.

Soil porosity

A soil in good condition for plant/crop growth will consist of about 50% space, accounted for by worm and other animal burrows, old root channels and the gaps between soil aggregates and individual mineral grains. Different sizes of aggregates leave a range of sizes of pores between them. Pore sizes between aggregates are classified into three types according to their function. The ratio of these three is critical to soil quality.

Soil pore classification and function
Pores larger than 50 micrometres (m), or 0.05mm, are called transmission pores. After being saturated by rain these pores drain under gravity, provided there is sufficient vertical connectivity. Soil is then described as being at field capacity. Transmission pores are important for aeration. Plant roots and soil organisms use oxygen and produce carbon dioxide. This results in a gradient of O_2 and CO_2 concentrations between the soil and the atmosphere. This causes CO_2 to diffuse out of the soil and O_2 to diffuse in. Another mechanism of aeration occurs as water drains from the soil, drawing in the bulk movement of air. Transmission pores are also important for root penetration. Pores larger than 0.2mm are required for the roots of most crops, although pores can be enlarged, to some extent, by peds being pushed aside by the growing root.

Pores between 50 and 0.2μm (0.05–0.0002mm) are called storage pores. Transpiration of water from leaves causes suction within the plant. The force of this suction defines the lower size limit of storage pores. Plants are unable to draw water from pores smaller than about 0.2μm. When storage pores are empty the soil is at the permanent wilting point, which means that wilting has occurred but without recovery overnight.

Pores smaller than 0.2μm are called residual pores and are to be found mostly between clay-sized particles.

Porosity varies according to soil texture. Transmission pores form a relatively high proportion of the porosity in sandy soils and a low proportion of the porosity in clay soils. In a medium-textured soil (loam) the highest proportion of pore space is in the category of storage pores. This is good for plant growth. At field capacity a loam has more plant-available water than sandy or clay soils. The ratios of pore sizes in the three types of soil explain why sandy soils drain quickly and clay soils do not.

Properties related to surface area within soil

The surfaces of mineral particles carry electrical charge, mostly negative. Many mineral elements required by plants occur in the soil as positively charged ions, which are attracted to the negatively charged mineral particle surfaces. The finer the soil texture the greater the surface area and the greater the soil's capacity to adsorb plant nutrients. Weathering, by the action of the various acids in the soil solution, also takes place at the surface of mineral particles, releasing elements into the soil solution; the greater the surface area the greater the rate of release of plant nutrients. Micro-organisms grow on particle surfaces. The total surface area, therefore, affects the degree of microbial reactions within soils, given adequate organic matter.

The huge surface area within clay soils would suggest that they have the greatest potential for fertility. However, the physical problems of clay soil militate against this. The low volume of transmission pores and high volume of residual pores make clay soils slow to drain, sticky when wet and hard when dry, and have a comparatively brief period, between wet and dry, when cultivation is possible. The lack of transmission pores can also hinder root growth.

Mycorrhizae

The word is from Greek for mushroom and root. Literally it means fungus root but should really be thought of as root fungus. It describes the symbiotic relationship between soil fungi and plant roots. In non-tree plants the fungus actually penetrates the root cells and obtains sugars from the plant. There are nearly a hundred known species of this type of mycorrhizae. About 80% of plants have associations with mycorrhizal fungi. Examples of plants that do not form mycorrhizal associations are the Cruciferae family (brassicas, rocket) and the Chenopodiaceae family (beetroot, spinach, fat hen).

Mycorrhizae take from the host plant between 5 and 30% of the food produced from photosynthesis. In return mycorrhizae provide the plant with minerals from the soil solution. The fungal hyphae extend 5–15cm from the root and can penetrate smaller pores than can root hairs. In effect, the absorptive surface of the plant is extended by up to ten times. The result is that the plant is able to take up, typically, between one and a half and three times the amount of some nutrients than it could on its own. This is particularly important with minerals with low solubility which are less mobile in the soil solution. Of these, phosphorous is especially significant. The minerals are carried through the hyphae by water, which is also used by the plant, helping it to withstand drought.

Mycorrhizae play some part in protecting plants from infection by some soil-borne diseases, attack by nematodes and infestation by pathogenic fungi. They do this, respectively, by producing antibiotics, effecting certain changes to the outer cells of roots, and by competing for infection sites on roots.

Mycorrhizae also secrete a sticky protein called glomalin, which helps to bind soil aggregates.

In the vegetable garden, where one is endeavouring to build up a highly fertile soil, it is likely that mycorrhizal associations are of little relevance. It is in nutrient poor soils that mycorrhizae are significant in plant nutrition. Mycorrhizal preparations are now on sale to gardeners, supposedly to improve yields, but I have not tried any to test those claims.

Actinomycetes

These are fungus-like bacteria. Their numbers are usually less than bacteria but their total biomass can be greater, up to 5 tonnes per hectare. They are especially numerous in soils with a high humus content. The characteristic earthy smell of freshly turned soil comes from substances called geosmins, volatile derivatives of terpines, which are produced by actinomycetes. Actinomycetes are capable of decomposing the more resistant parts of organic matter such as cellulose, chitin and phospholipids. They are also important in the final stages of composting. The minor problem of potato scab is caused by an actinomycete.

Cultivation

When soil is dug, or mechanically cultivated, an unnaturally high level of oxygen is incorporated into the soil matrix. This results in a rapid increase in the oxidation of organic matter through the activity of soil bacteria, whose populations are given a boost by the sudden influx of oxygen. Carbon is lost from the soil in the form of carbon dioxide and nitrate is released into the soil. The rate of these processes is temperature dependent, with greater activity of bacteria in warm soils, provided there is adequate moisture. If a crop is grown straight afterwards, nitrate can be utilized, otherwise it is leached from the soil, as nitrate (NO_3^-) being negatively charged, is not held by the mostly negatively charged soil colloids of clay and humus. The oxidation of organic matter following cultivation explains why arable soils are generally lower in organic matter than permanent grassland.

Another effect of cultivation is that it destroys the burrows of soil organisms, most importantly, those of earthworms. Worm burrows can function as major drainage channels, rather like storm drains. Under heavy rainfall worm burrows can carry away water quickly; less water, therefore, passes through the bulk of the soil matrix where it could cause leaching of plant nutrients. This protective function of burrows is particularly important in winter, when there is little or no crop growth to take up nutrients and when the net movement of soil water is downwards because of low surface evaporation, little plant uptake and, possibly, higher rates of precipitation than at other times of year.

For reasons described in the above two paragraphs, cultivation in autumn or winter is particularly detrimental to soil. A further problem is that it leaves the soil without a protective covering of vegetation. Raindrops can wash fine soil particles to fill up soil pores, causing a high density layer at the surface, known as a surface seal or soil cap. When dry it becomes a hard crust. This impedes drainage of subsequent rain. If there is sufficient extent and degree of slope, soil erosion can occur.

'Although tillage may temporarily loosen the surface soil, in the long term intense tillage increases soil bulk density because it depletes soil organic matter and weakens soil structure.' (Brady and Weil, 2002, p141).

'Digging almost always destroys soil structure, and should rarely be done on clayey soils, where the frost in winter and drying in summer will regenerate the structure naturally. On sandy and silty soils some digging [might] be beneficial but, except for vegetable production, a light cultivation with a fork, hoe or rake will often suffice.' (Ingram et al., 2008, p93).

It is possible that the writer of the second quote is assuming that vegetable production entails walking on the soil between single rows, necessitating digging to prepare for the next crop. With the bed system, once the ground has been cleared of perennial weeds, dug, cultivated and the beds laid out, no more digging need be done except that which is necessary for the planting and harvesting of potatoes, lifting parsnips and leeks, and for the incorporation of compost. (See 'Incorporating compost or manure' on p.110.)

Conclusion

The above nine sections provide some idea of the complexity of soil and the enormous diversity of life to be found there. In order to safeguard the processes of soil formation and the complex physical, chemical and biological interactions that occur in soil, adoption and implementation of at least the first four principles suggested at the beginning of this chapter would seem to be a justifiable conclusion to come to. The fifth principle, putting back what is taken out, is what the rest of this chapter is about.

PUTTING BACK WHAT IS TAKEN OUT

Introduction

When crops are harvested, although a large part of the crop

weight is water, small amounts of minerals are also included. The question is, does the rate of soil formation, the weathering of elements from mineral particles and their release into the soil solution, keep pace with the loss brought about by crop removal? Without detailed soil analyses on cropped land over a long period of time it is impossible to say. If specific mineral deficiency symptoms begin to occur in certain crops, that would suggest that there is a net loss occurring, at least, in the elements concerned. However, 'Increasing evidence indicates that food grown on soils with low levels of trace elements [might] provide insufficient dietary levels of certain elements, even though the crop plants show no signs of deficiency themselves' (Brady and Weil, 2002, p638).

There are many variables that will determine the answer to the question. One important factor is soil texture. A sandy soil, with relatively low surface area, clay colloids and humus, might be expected to be the most vulnerable type of soil to become deficient. Yet sandy soil under natural vegetation seems able to maintain fertility, apparently indefinitely, but its management is different to that in a garden. The soil is never cultivated, it is always covered by vegetation, and nothing is removed. Where a sandy soil is cultivated (even though minimally) periodically without vegetation cover (unavoidably) and where crops are removed, it would seem reasonable to assume that it could become deficient in at least some minerals.

David Thomas (2003), analysing data published in five editions between 1940 and 1991, showed that the mineral content of all foods declined during that period. Considering vegetables, averages for five minerals were as follows:

Potassium:	down 49%	Iron:	down 27%
Magnesium:	down 24%	Copper:	down 76%
Calcium:	down 46%		

Declines for some individual vegetables were particularly high:

Magnesium in carrots:	down 75%	Iron in swedes:	down 71%
Calcium in broccoli:	down 75%	Copper in watercress:	down 93%

There are a number of possible causes for this decline in the mineral content of food. It would be pertinent to know where the sampled crops were grown. Were they all from the same area over the five decades of sampling? It could be that levels of some elements in 1940 were the result of fall-out, over many previous decades, from industrial pollution, which has since gradually reduced as a result of the decline in manufacturing and improved pollution legislation. Other explanations could include changes in crop variety, destruction of mycorrhizae, thus reducing the crop plant's effective root area and nutrient-gathering potential, or soil management which results in leaching of minerals due to lack of humus colloids to adsorb them. A detailed discussion of this subject and the implications for health are beyond the scope of this book. Thomas (2003) gives some interesting references. See also the recommended reading section on p.322.

While plants can and do exercise some discrimination in their take up of different nutrients in the soil solution, they cannot take up what is not there. Plants need 14 mineral elements to sustain healthy growth. Six of these are known as macronutrients: nitrogen (N), phosphorous (P), potassium (K), calcium (Ca), magnesium (Mg) and sulphur (S).

The other eight are termed micronutrients or trace elements: iron (Fe), manganese (Mn), copper (Cu), zinc (Zn), boron (B), chlorine (Cl), molybdenum (Mo) and nickel (Ni).

The difference is somewhat arbitrary, but the difference between the requirements of macro. and micro. is at least ten times. To give an idea of the tiny amounts required of some trace elements, analyses of plant material might reveal a million times more nitrogen than molybdenum. Molybdenum is essential for the functioning of nitrogen-fixing soil bacteria, as is cobalt; and molybdenum and manganese are needed for nitrate assimilation in plants. Interactions between elements are complex, for example various pairs of elements are needed for the optimum utilization of a third. Other elements are required by some plants and also, some are beneficial while not being essential. Sodium is beneficial to sugar beet and beetroot.

There are other elements that are required by humans but not by most plants. This means that it is possible to grow healthy crops that are not providing an adequate diet. These elements include chromium, iodine, selenium, cobalt, silicon, tin and vanadium. Some are required in ultra-trace amounts – parts per billion in the diet and are not likely to be deficient in most soils. However, iodine and selenium can be deficient even in some areas of Britain. When people's diets were limited much more to what was grown locally, specific chronic conditions related to soil deficiencies were more common. 'Derbyshire neck' – swollen thyroid due to lack of iodine in the soil – was one example. Selenium deficiency is more widespread in British soils but the desire of livestock farmers to maintain healthy animals means that the element is entering the food chain via feed supplements. However, this does not guarantee that everyone's diet will have adequate amounts of selenium or any other mineral element.

Rock dust is now being marketed to gardeners and farmers to 're-mineralize' the soil. Graham Harvey (2006) suggests that glaciation produced huge quantities of finely ground rock which produced deep, fertile soils. He argues that this store of minerals has, largely, been used up, washed out of soils, resulting in crops deficient in many essential elements. Examples of re-mineralizing given in his book certainly support the theory, but a combination of food refining, poor diet choices and cooking methods also make a major contribution to the prevalence of degenerative diseases that Harvey suggests is the result of 'worn out' soils (see Chapter 11). However, we should be alarmed that the mineral content of food has declined even in the short period since 1940. It might not be coincidence that the 1940s was when tractors replaced horses, enabling the extent, depth, frequency and power of cultivation to be greatly increased.

Is rock dust the answer to increasing and maintaining soil fertility? The recommended application rate is 2 tonnes per acre (about $0.5kg/m^2$) *every year.* To produce the amount needed to apply to all farmland and gardens would require an enormous amount of energy. Could renewable sources ever be enough? If not, the process of crushing all that rock would be a major contributor to global warming. Energy is also needed to transport it to where it will be used. The use of rock dust is claimed to replicate the benefits of glaciation but the energy input of tens of thousands of years of moving, mile-thick ice is surely beyond our capacity to provide. We must make do with soils as we find them but manage them so that soil forming processes are not outpaced by soil losses.

Completing the cycle of nutrients

Unless your garden is sited on what was recently arable land or has been subjected to years of winter cultivations, especially rotavating, it will probably have reasonable potential to form good, fertile soil. Then if the first four principles suggested at the beginning of this chapter are applied, that will promote the process. Earlier it was stated that in the natural environment nothing is taken away. Given that, in gardening, some soil disturbance (cultivation) is necessary and the soil will be without a protective cover of vegetation for some periods, it would seem to be essential to apply the fifth principle of returning to the soil what has been taken out, i.e. not taking anything away. In nature all creatures eat, digest and excrete and the excretion material returns, more or less randomly, to the soil that provides their food.

Throughout the history of western civilization human waste seems to have been regarded as more of a problem to be got rid of than a resource to be used (Small, 1974). Some use was made of it as a fertilizer in all periods but collection and application were never comprehensive. From the cities of ancient Sumeria, through the public toilets of Rome and the monasteries of medieval Europe to nineteenth century London, use was made of running water to take away the problem together with any possibility of making use of its fertilizer potential. For the majority, in urban areas, however, running water was not available. The streets, dumps and cess pits were used, resulting in appalling conditions and public health problems, including the contamination of wells. Eventually, comprehensive, water-borne sanitation succeeded in cutting off, as far as humans were concerned, the cycling of nutrients that obtains in the rest of nature.

For every tonne of nitrogen fertilizer produced, two tonnes of CO_2 is emitted. A tanker load of urine could be transported for 220km before as much energy would have been used as it takes to make the equivalent amount of nitrogen fertilizer using the Haber-Bosch process (Steinfeld, 2004). Sewage sludge is no longer dumped at sea and some is used as fertilizer but it is contaminated with industrial effluent. Peak oil, peak phosphorous, general losses from agricultural soils, concerns about global warming, all point to the simple solution of completing the cycle of nutrients in the food production system. Sweden is far ahead of us on this and through Ecological Sanitation Research (EcoSanRes) in the Stockholm Environment Institute, much research has been done and schemes implemented in various parts of the world, with great benefits to soil, food production and local economies. If every toilet were converted to the urine separation compost type, they could supply all fertilizer needs for agriculture and, from households, only grey water would go through the sewage system, reducing costs.

Peak phosphorous
The concept of peak oil is well known but another summit looming over the horizon is peak phosphorous. Microbes, plants and animals need phosphorous. Current relatively cheap and accessible reserves are predicted to be gone in 50 years and the rest in 100 to 130 years. There is already a problem of disposing of toxic waste produced in the refining process and phosphate fertilizer retains unacceptable levels of cadmium contamination. Sooner or later we are going to have to face up to the problem of phosphorous loss from the food-producing system. Not only is it lost from this system but it becomes a serious environmental problem through the enrichment (eutrophication) of rivers, lakes and coastal waters.

Seaweed

Alternatives to total recycling are to accept the slow decline in the availability of mineral nutrients, or to buy them in some form. Trace elements can be provided by products from the sea. Dried or concentrated liquid seaweed may be used and also calcified seaweed when a source of lime is needed. Calcified seaweed is composed of calcareous nodules accumulated by two species of seaweed. When the plants die the nodules are deposited on the sea bed in sufficient quantities, in some areas, for them to be dredged up. However, products of seaweed should not be thought of as adequate source of trace elements. The stimulating effects of seaweed extract are thought to result from amino acids called betaines. Maxicrop's web site gives some information on various beneficial effects of their products.

Buckets

When I moved to the country in 1977 I was pleased to find that the tiny cottage I rented had no WC but just a bucket in a shed, which seems to me a very civilized arrangement, keeping smells out of the house. Our next cottage had a WC but in an outbuilding with space for a bucket. To begin with, an ordinary garden bucket was used but later the sort sold as a toilet, with a tight-fitting lid and holes for ventilation but too small to let flies in.

Composting faeces, especially in urban areas, might be a practice most gardeners would choose not to do but using urine is very easy as well as effective and presents no real problems. Of the total N, P and K we excrete, urine contains 70–90% of the nitrogen, 45–80% of the phosphorous and 60–95% of the potassium. Only small proportions of other elements are excreted in urine.

I discovered for myself the great efficacy of urine and composted faeces but others have written in glowing terms about it long ago. Shirley Hibberd (1863) wrote:

> If a given quantity of land, sown without manure yields three times the seed employed, then the same quantity of land will produce five times the quantity sown when manured with old herbage, putrid grass or leaves, garden stuff, etc., seven times with cow dung, nine times with pigeon dung, ten times with horse dung, twelve times with human urine, twelve times with goat dung, twelve times with sheep dung, and fourteen times with human manure, or bullocks' blood.

Animal manures

Animal manures are another possibility. They might not be easy for urban gardeners to obtain, they cost money, and fossil fuel is used to transport them. If the manure comes from cattle fed a high proportion of concentrates rather than mostly grass, it is more likely to contain pathogenic forms of *E. coli* bacteria, which could present problems at a school. If the manure is well rotted there is little nitrogen left in it, although that is not a problem if urine is used as well. Wherever the organic matter has been grown, that is where it should be returned to. So, it represents a kind of theft. Some livestock farms have surpluses – pig and poultry units and stables – which means that much of the nutrients have come from elsewhere. Ultimately they will have come from the fertilizer industry. Any bought manure is unlikely to be from an organic farm as they are not allowed to sell it.

Composting

Many gardening books recommend making a compost heap in one operation but gardens produce compostable material throughout the year, albeit little in winter. Where do you store the stuff until there is enough to make a heap? Wherever it is it will start to rot. So, it might as well be on the compost heap. If a heap is built up as material becomes available, presumably what happens is that the heating process moves upwards, leaving behind partially decomposed compost which continues to be decomposed by bacteria which thrive at lower temperatures. The following sections contain information on dealing with toilet buckets but the rest applies to composting generally.

The first thing to decide is location. I would recommend that heaps be made on the beds rather than in a permanent position. The addition of urine is very beneficial and, therefore, there will be some drainage of liquid. This will enrich the soil and benefit whatever is grown there when the heap has gone. This effect could be borne in mind when choosing which plot to locate them on. Otherwise it is a case of selecting the plot on which there is least pressure for space to grow a crop.

The second decision is whether to have open or enclosed heaps. For many years I had open heaps. These needed turning two or three times and, on the second or third occasion, inside out, so that the outer material, which had not rotted, went to the middle where it could heat up. Much as I dislike plastic generally in the environment, it has two good uses in gardening, flower pots and compost containers. I like the bottomless, ridged sort with a lid and no opening in the side. Beauty is in the eye of the beholder: because they are performing a useful function they look attractive and everything is kept neat and tidy. The contents rot down much faster than in open heaps and, except for the winter heap (see below), they might not need turning.

There is no need to start a heap with a base of bricks or sticks to facilitate ventilation. I found this made no difference and the material gets in the way when moving the end product. Just loosen the soil with the cultivator or a fork to provide a little aeration, increased surface area and a greater exposure to soil bacteria, then start with whatever is available. For optimum conditions in a compost heap there should be a ratio of 24 of carbon to 1 of nitrogen but who knows what the C to N ratio is in the material one wants to put into the container? Just put in whatever is available – crop residues, kitchen trimmings, soft hedge clippings and a little lawn grass. If you have a large lawn (why aren't you growing vegetables there instead?!) do not put all the grass on the heap, as it will become soggy and airless, but some now and again is fine. It is better to leave it on the lawn for the worms to incorporate, to increase organic matter and avoid compaction. (I recommend leaving fallen leaves on lawns as well, spread around if too thick in places. Worms will deal with them.)

Add some urine occasionally using a watering can with a rose. If the compost is already moist dilute the urine 1:1, if it seems dry add more water. Wash in with a little more water. Worms react adversely to neat urine and can be killed by it. Use your judgement as to amounts and frequency. If you are adding shredded paper, cardboard, wood shavings, sawdust or straw, more nitrogen (urine) will be needed. The strength of colour in urine is an indication of its nitrogen content (unless you have been eating beetroot, which makes it red). During-the-night and early morning product tends to be more concentrated. So, more dilution is needed.

For those using a bucket, start with a layer of grass, weeds or leaves in the bucket to prevent faeces sticking. Add a layer of green stuff after each contribution. This is not just for aesthetic reasons but it means the bucket will fill up sooner and not become too heavy, and there will not be too much faeces going on to the heap at one time, which would make it more difficult to rot. If using a compost container the larger of the two common models is preferable, as (a) it will get hotter and (b) there is more surface area to use. With an open heap start with a minimum of 1.2m diameter. When emptying the contents of the bucket, keep them away from the edge of the heap, as the temperature there will be lower. Also avoid having too much at the centre, where conditions could become anaerobic. Use a fork to spread the contents evenly. The prongs can be wiped on the outside of the heap inside the container and then pushed in and out of the soil to clean them. Rinse out the bucket with a little water and pour it into the compost container. Add a good layer of whatever is available. It is very satisfying to take responsibility for this otherwise waste product and to reuse the valuable nutrients in the garden to grow more food.

The three heaps system
This system was worked out to achieve three aims:

1   to accommodate the large volumes of crop residues at particular times of year;

2   to produce three lots of compost for the three main uses;

3   to avoid adding residue of the same crop that the resulting

compost will be used for. This third aim is to reduce the opportunities of carry-over of disease from one crop to the same crop the next year. How scientifically sound this reasoning is I am not sure, but it can be done without inconvenience and it brings some order into composting and makes you think about what to put where and why.

The three main uses of compost are for potatoes, brassicas and some legumes, and the tender crops of squash, sweetcorn, tomatoes, etc. It does work out so that when the bulk of the residue of a main crop type needs to be composted, the heap currently being added to will be ready for use as compost when it is needed for a different type of crop. This might seem unnecessarily complicated but it does fit in with what needs to be done throughout the gardening year. There can be some overlap, with one heap still having material added while another is started, to avoid a particular crop residue going on an inappropriate heap. Each heap, therefore, can have material added to it over a period of at least four months.

It is practical to manage with just one compost bin. When you cease adding material to one heap, the bin can be moved to another position to start the next. However, it is preferable to have two bins so that the first heap can remain covered until the third heap needs to be started. Or a piece of thick black plastic will do to cover the first heap, but be sure to weigh the edges down well with bricks or stones. Best of all, however, is to have three bins so that all three heaps can be kept enclosed during the whole composting process. As the making and use of each heap is described, the system should become clear. First, though, the problems of flies and rats need to be mentioned.

When I had open heaps I do not recall flies or rats being a problem. Flies were there but I rarely noticed them, unlike later, when taking off the lid of a compost bin and having a cloud of them fly up. These will probably be the little brown fruit flies. It was noticeable that when I came to turn the winter heap, because it had not heated up while it was being added to, there were numerous larvae and pupae of flies amongst the faeces. This was a natural part of the process. The larvae were making their own faeces which had a much greater surface area that could more easily be used by fungi and bacteria in the next process of decomposition.

As soon as I began covering heaps, first with black plastic, then with bottomless bins, they suddenly became desirable residences for our little squeaky friends. Rats are everywhere: it is reckoned that everyone lives within a few metres of rats but you do notice them if you have compost bins. Rats are also attracted to meat, fish, cheese and any cooked food. The only way rats can get into a lidded bin is by tunnelling under the base. I have not tried this, but it has been suggested they could be kept out by standing the bin on some heavy duty wire netting of sufficiently small mesh. It might be necessary to secure this to the bin by drilling holes in the flange at the base and tying the two together with lengths of flexible wire.

The spring heap will all be used the following spring for potatoes, spread in the trenches when planting. The heap is begun in early spring and material added to it until about the end of June. Anything can go on to this heap except any part of the potato plant. It is a simple matter to avoid adding potato trimmings. Keep them separate in the kitchen; then scatter them on the lawn, under fruit bushes or put on to a separate heap to make compost for fruit bushes, etc. If you have access to a patch of rough ground the lush early summer growth of grass and nettles could be scythed for compost, unless you prefer to leave them for wildlife. All the residue of winter and spring brassicas can be added. Some lawn clippings and bonfire ash can also go on in thin layers. Some hedges might need a trim before the heap is complete but do not add coniferous species, as they take too long to rot down.

If the heap needs to be turned, this can be done in late summer or early autumn. To get the heap to heat up again add some green material in alternating layers: lawn clippings, soft weeds, crop residue of beans and peas but not broad bean stalks, as they will not rot before spring. They can go in the summer heap. However, if the compost seems rather dense and not to have rotted much, broad bean stalks will add air pockets that will help further decomposition. When the compost is used in the spring the unrotted bean stalks can be picked out and added to the new spring heap. Add some dilute urine after each layer or two. A good sized compost heap can absorb several litres plus a similar volume of water. To help the heating process, choose a warm spell of weather to turn the heap. If there is a bin available or some black plastic, covering will also help. As the compost will not be used until spring, it is preferable to keep it covered over the winter. When using in potato trenches, use extra in the beds where broad beans grew the previous year, as they will not have had compost applied.

The summer heap will be used the following spring on beds planted with tender crops: squash, courgette, sweetcorn, tomatoes and summer salads. So, avoid adding crop residue from cucurbits and sweetcorn – they can go into the winter heap which will be started in autumn. Tomato residue may be added, along with potato haulms, even if they have blight. The summer heap might need to be started before the spring heap ceases to have material added if you start digging early potatoes in June. A suitable site for the summer heap is on the first potato bed to be cleared. Non-coniferous hedge trimmings can also be included, as can grass and weeds. Broad bean stalks may be included and, as soon as cropping has finished, the haulms of other legumes.

In a warm period in autumn the summer heap may be turned. Try to find some fresh green material to layer with it. The lower, yellowing leaves of brassicas may be included. If not turned in autumn, it can be turned during the first warm spell in early spring. If it has been covered the whole time it might not need turning at all, even if it includes faeces, especially if it managed to heat up for a while after the last toilet bucket contents. However, the legume haulms, which will be on or near the top, will probably not be sufficiently rotted by the time the compost is needed. If this is the case they can be separated out with a fork and put on to the current spring heap where they will have another year to rot down. In spring apply the summer heap compost to the beds as soon as conditions allow – when the soil has not been frozen for at least a few days and is at field capacity or a little drier. (See 'Incorporating compost or manure' on p.110.) There might be time for a catch crop of radish, spring onion, turnip and certainly rocket before the tender crops need all the space in the beds.

The winter heap will be used for brassicas and legumes, except broad beans. The heap may be started as soon as sweetcorn has finished cropping. The stems should be chopped or cut up first. Later, the haulms of squash, etc., will be added. If garlic is to be planted, some of the squash/pumpkin haulms can be put to more immediate use. (See the section on garlic care on p.121.) All the trimmings of the onion crop should go on this heap; so too should the garlic trimmings, although these will be produced much earlier in the year. Garlic trimmings could be raked into a pile and form the start of the winter heap, as where the garlic was grown is on the plot where the compost will be used for brassicas. Throughout autumn, winter and early spring the trimmings of leeks make a substantial contribution to the heap. Bonfire ash, stored from summer weed fires, is also a useful ingredient.

The winter heap is unlikely to heat up, leaving most of its contents not fully decomposed at the end of the period it was being added to. As it will not be used for another year it could just be left to rot slowly with the help of mesophilic organisms. However, especially if it contains faeces, it is better to turn it in the spring to speed up decomposition. Use all the hoed off cover crop material to incorporate in layers and any other green stuff available. Add diluted urine as the new heap is built up and the result, if done in a warm period of early summer, will be a great deal of heat. If the heap is not covered it might need turning inside out in autumn. As soon as conditions are suitable in spring, incorporate the compost into beds for brassicas and legumes, except broad beans – they do not need it, and anyway, they should already be sown, either in autumn or late winter/early spring.

If a bucket toilet is being used and it is found that for periods in winter there is insufficient material to cover faeces on the compost heap, the bucket may be emptied into a trench in one of the beds. I have occasionally done this where squash, runner beans and sweetcorn were grown only a few months later. I have not done controlled trials but the effect seemed to be positive. If the material is well spread out in a wide trench in one half of a bed and covered by at least 10cm of soil it is surprising how quickly everything rots down.

Uses of urine

The uses of urine to grow particular crops are described under each crop in Chapter 7. Urine contains 70–90% of the nitrogen (N), 45–80% of the phosphorous (P) and 60–95% of the potassium (K) that is excreted from the body. Of the other elements, proportions vary, but for most, the greater part is excreted in the faeces. Plants need to absorb at least 14 elements from the soil (see the Introduction to this section on p.88). If any one of them is not sufficiently available, growth is affected. Nitrogen is the most commonly limiting element but gardeners need never be short of it if they use urine. It can be applied to any of the beds when they are not carrying crops and to a few high N-demanding crops while they are growing. It is also useful as a compost activator, balancing the high carbon content of dried legume and cucurbit haulms, any coarse herbage, shredded paper and card, or sawdust and shavings.

In one garden I had a particular problem with annual meadow grass on the paths between beds. These needed hoeing all year round and, unless the weather was hot and dry, the hoeings were raked up to prevent them re-growing. I made piles of this mixture of soil and weeds and used them as 'reservoir sponges' for urine. In the spring this enriched soil was spread on to one or two low lying beds. One year I riddled the heap of hoeings and used the soil in half of the pots to grow the squash plants.

At planting out time the plants grown in the enriched soil were two or three times the size of the others. I regret not recording whether there was any difference in the final crop.

It is advisable to collect urine separately from faeces, so far as is practical, so that it may be used as a liquid feed on crops without any risk of contamination by pathogens. The risk would be very small but it does mean that even salads grown in urine-fertilized soil are quite safe to eat. Also, separately collected urine is easier to apply evenly on the ground, as it can be done through a watering can with a rose.

Most of the nitrogen excreted in urine is urea, which degrades in the soil within hours to ammonium, which plants can absorb. Within a few days ammonium is transformed into nitrate, which many crops prefer. The phosphorous in urine is mostly in the form of plant-available inorganic phosphate ions. Potassium is also excreted as plant-available ions (Jönsson et al., 2004).

A garden that is big enough to supply all the vegetables for the household can absorb most of the urine produced. As a guideline rule of thumb, apply around 1.5 litres per square metre on each occasion on beds when they are not carrying crops. For the sake of the worms dilute 1:1 with water, more if the soil is dry. Then wash in with another litre or two of water, more if the soil is dry and the weather warm. Beds may be 'watered' in sequence throughout the winter. Although much of the nitrogen will be leached, other nutrients may be held by soil colloids (organic matter and clay) and become available to plants. Most crops benefit from an application a few days before sowing but broad beans show no response. The most impressive response I have known was with beetroot. In a trial in 2004 six beds were fertilized with urine in amounts ranging from zero to

1.35 litres per square metre, which equates to a modest 80kg of nitrogen per hectare. The yield was about six times that from the bed which had no urine applied. The trial plot (not my garden) was stony and possibly lacking in nitrogen.

Crops which will benefit most from fertilizing with urine during their growth are brassicas and leeks (see Chapter 7). Potatoes, perhaps, would also benefit but it is easier to apply urine to the soil directly after planting.

Preparing Beds and Sowing Seeds

PREPARING THE SOIL ON THE BEDS

Creating good conditions for seeds to germinate and grow is very important. It is worth putting in the necessary time and effort to achieve them. It is assumed, in this section, that the garden is already in cultivation or, if it is the first year of use, has been thoroughly cleared of perennial weeds, and cultivated to a reasonable tilth.

First, remove any weeds. Perennials should be dug out or pulled if small enough, e.g. seedling docks. Annuals can be pulled up or, if small enough, hoed off if the soil surface is dry and the weather warm. The hoe needs to be sharp to cut the weeds just below ground level. The softer the soil, the sharper the hoe needs to be to do this. If you are confident that the compost heap will get hot, any plant material may be added – roots of perennials and weeds with seed heads. Otherwise, it is advisable to separate perennial roots and seedy, even flowering, weeds for burning. If a bonfire is not an option, perennial roots can be left on the surface somewhere until they are dead from drying out. Seeding and flowering weeds can be buried in holes or a trench in a bed but they need to go below the level of future digging. Alternatively, they may be immersed in water for two months. This kills the seeds. If annual weeds are quite large with flowers and seeds on the top, it is worth going round with a bucket pulling the seed/flower heads off first (for burning, burial or drowning) and then pulling the whole plants up for composting.

How much cultivation is required will depend on the type and condition of the soil. Soil texture (how 'heavy' or 'light' it is, i.e. its clay, silt and sand content), organic matter content and moisture content will all have a bearing on how much cultivation is required. A moist, sandy loam with good organic matter content might only require the use of the cultivator, even if it has had nothing done to it for several months over the winter, especially if it has been protected (against compaction by rain) by a crop, cover crop, winter salad or carefully monitored weeds. If the soil is too hard, dry or compacted to allow the cultivator to get an adequate tilth, the digging fork will be needed. If the soil is so dry that it needs to be watered, holes might need to be made first with the fork to facilitate a more even moistening and to prevent run-off or pooling. You might need to wait several hours for the water to soak in properly. If compaction is the main problem, it might be necessary to dig with a fork. Or, if not too compacted, repeatedly pushing in the fork and moving it back and forth may break up the soil sufficiently to allow the cultivator to be used.

In dry conditions it is better to water the bed *before* sowing rather than after. It can be difficult to avoid compaction when watering artificially. The bed needs to be watered sufficiently so that the soil is continuously moist from the surface down. Again, it is a matter of judgement as to how much water is required. After watering you need to wait for the soil to drain to field capacity. A clay soil might take two or three days. There will also be evaporation from the surface, the rate depending on soil texture, structure (the size of the lumps), temperature, wind and humidity. Alternatively, instead of watering the whole bed you can trickle water into each drill. However, with slow germinating seeds in hot, dry weather, the drill could dry out before the seedlings' roots have reached naturally moist soil.

Watering a bed, whatever the soil texture, might result in the surface being a little too compacted for sowing seeds in. When the soil has drained to field capacity, going over it lightly with the cultivator, to just a few centimetres depth, will create the best conditions. If the soil is naturally too wet, using the cultivator is a good ploy to speed up the drying process, as it will greatly increase the surface area. If the soil is too dry and you do not want, have not time or are unable to water, provided it is not already too compacted, it may be patted down with the back of a spade to facilitate capillary action to draw moisture from below. The following day, early in the morning, will be the best time to sow. If the soil is sandy or silty, somewhat lumpy but sufficiently friable, patting it down can be a way of breaking up the lumps if a fine seed bed is required.

INCORPORATING COMPOST OR MANURE

When applying compost or manure it needs to be well mixed in with the soil where it is most needed, throughout the rooting zone of the crop. While some crops have long tap roots most have most of their feeding roots within 20cm of the surface. The top few centimetres of soil are likely to dry out at times during the summer. Therefore, it is advisable for all of the compost or manure to be incorporated below this level so that soil bacteria can feed on it, uninterrupted by periods of drought, and release nutrients in a plant-available form.

Put a line in along one side of the bed and the other line parallel down the middle. With the spade facing you, make a cut next to but on your side of the centre line, then turn the spade round and make another next to the edge of the bed. Then spade or shovel out a flat trench, four or five centimetres deep, throwing the soil on to the other half of the bed. Remove the centre line. Spread the compost/manure evenly in the trench and turn it into the soil below with a spade. Do not bury it deep; it just needs to be incorporated within the root zone. If dried seaweed is being applied it may be sprinkled on before turning in the compost. Even out the surface with the back of a fork. If urine is being applied, this can go on next. The dilution will depend on how moist the soil and compost are. If the soil is already moist, apply at 1:1 but if the ground is very dry, 4 or 5:1 water to urine would be appropriate. Finally, fill in the trench and level the surface with a rake or the back of a fork.

A quicker method is to spread the compost on the surface and turn it in with a spade, then level out with the back of a fork. This method will leave some of the compost very near to or at the surface. This might not matter much early in the season and if conditions are moist, as the worms will help take organic matter into the soil. If conditions are dry, however, the compost will dry out and be of little benefit. If manure is being used that is not well rotted, clumps of compressed straw at the soil surface will be a nuisance when making seed drills.

Never apply lime and compost or manure at the same time. They will react, resulting in a loss of nitrogen. If lime is to be applied this should be done in the autumn. The following spring will be the soonest time afterwards that any compost should be added to the soil.

Stale beds

Whenever possible, sow into a 'stale' seedbed. This means doing all the bed preparation at least ten days before sowing. Of course, this is not always possible or practical but there are two advantages in doing so. Preparation includes patting the soil down to draw moisture to the surface so as to encourage the germination of weeds. Then, just before you wish to sow seeds the weeds are hoed. There are then fewer weed seeds sufficiently near the surface to germinate during the time the crop is present. However, the advantages of the technique are limited because many weed species tend to germinate in similar conditions that suit vegetable seeds, so that if a stale bed is prepared weeks before sowing seeds there might be little germination of weeds until after the vegetable seeds are sown. Fat hen (*Chenopodium album*) is especially late in germinating; it comes up throughout the summer, when crops are already established. However, stale beds are still worth using. There will be *some* germination of weeds. Even if none are apparent, they could be just about to emerge from the surface and hoeing will kill them at this very vulnerable stage. The later in the season that seeds are to be sown, the more effective the stale bed procedure will be. Main crop carrots are best sown in early summer to avoid carrot fly; beetroot likewise to get good germination and steady growth and all the non hardy crops – French and runner beans, cucurbits and sweet corn – will benefit from being sown or planted into a stale bed.

The best example of the importance of sowing into a stale bed concerns the bean seed fly (see 'Pests and diseases of French and haricot beans' on p.163).

Row spacing

The recommendations suggested in the next chapter are intended to provide the maximum yield per unit of area rather than particularly large or small vegetables. Some of the spacing suggestions are based on rough trials while others are more intuitive after many years of growing. It would be fascinating to carry out exhaustive scientific trials to determine the optimum spacing for each vegetable but the results would only be applicable for the soil and location where the trials were done. The best spacing for a very fertile, good quality soil would be over generous for a poor soil, because the potential for growth for each plant is less in the poor soil. So, a closer spacing would give the best yield, per square metre, in the poorer soil. Each gardener needs to be observant and get a feel for the soil condition and whether the crops look crowded or too sparse.

Many seed packets recommend row spacing that seems to come from a bygone age when horse-drawn hoes were used to weed between rows! In many cases, therefore, row spacing recommended on seed packets and, I have to say, in many books, can be halved. It is probably the case that within a range of row spacing, yield would not vary very much. If yield per unit area were plotted on the vertical axis of a graph and spacing on the horizontal axis, a bell-shaped curve would result; yield would be low at the overcrowded end and although individual specimens might be large at the widely-spaced end of the curve, overall yield would also be low. So, a fairly close spacing could result in the same total yield of small vegetables as twice the spacing would of large ones and both could be very close to the maximum, grown at the optimum spacing. There is, then, some flexibility concerning the size of vegetables you want – *fairly* small or *fairly* large – while still attaining close to maximum overall yields. What I would recommend, however, is that whatever row spacing you decide upon make the rows equidistant within the bed and leave a gap of no more than half that between the outer two rows and the edge of the bed, whether there is a physical edge (board) or not. If you have more than one bed of the same crop, sown on the same day, experiment with different row spacing and/or space between plants along the rows.

MARKING OUT, MAKING DRILLS AND SOWING SEEDS

There are a number of ways of doing these operations. With experience, only the outer two rows need to be set out using string while the other rows can be accurately enough done by eye. The string, or garden line, as it is usually referred to, need be simply a thin, strong cord, each end of which is tied to a pointed stick. White nylon picture cord is ideal for this. With children it is probably better to have two garden lines so that one can be stretched out along each side of the bed at the start of sowing seeds there. This allows the extent of the bed to be seen at a glance.

Books usually have pictures of drills being made by drawing one corner of a draw hoe through the soil alongside the garden line.

This works quite well but only if the soil moisture is perfect, the tilth absolutely first class and there are no stones. If conditions are even a little dry or lumpy this technique results in the dry lumps falling back into the drill behind the hoe as it passes along, providing very poor physical conditions for the seed.

Making drills and sowing seeds takes up a relatively small proportion of the time spent on gardening. It is worth taking whatever time and care are necessary to create the best conditions as you can for the seeds. What I have always done is to use a sharp spade and push it in on the far side of the line, almost touching the string and throw the soil forward, making a 'V'-shaped drill. This can be done without lumps falling back into the drill or if they do, you can just repeat the process. If young children find a spade too heavy for making seed drills, a Dutch or push hoe can be used.

When making more than one drill, start with the outer one nearest the path and work in towards the middle of the bed. That way you avoid filling in the drill you have just made. Remember to position the garden line so that the bottom of the drill is just where you want it. In other words, the garden line will be nearer to you than where the actual row is to be. When the drills, made from one side of the bed, have been seeded, if the weather is dry and sunny, fill them in before going to the other side of the bed and working inwards again. If the drills are in no danger of drying out they can be left open so that when the inner drill is made from the other side you can avoid it being too close or far apart from the adjacent drill made from the first side. After drawing the soil back into the drills the ground should be level.

The depth of the drill should vary according to the size of the seed. Some books recommend covering with a depth of soil the same as the diameter of the seed. This is nowhere near deep enough; the soil will dry out to below that depth, leaving insufficient moisture for germination. Recommended sowing depths are given on seed packets and these are usually about right but the depth needs to be related to soil type. In a sandy soil seeds need to be sown deeper than in a heavy clay soil. The sandy soil will tend to dry to a lower depth than will the clay soil in the same weather conditions and over a given length of time. Also, a soil high in organic matter will hold moisture better than one low in organic matter. A silty soil is prone to 'capping'. This is where rain compacts the surface and forms a cap through which shoots from small seeds are sometimes unable to emerge.

If the soil is lumpy and lacking in organic matter, it is worth making the drills deeper and sprinkling some fine, well-rotted compost into them and sowing seeds on top of that. If it is the first year of the garden and there is no compost available, there is a little ploy that will help. The soil should be just moist, having been watered, if need be, then allowing time for the water to soak in (this could be some hours) before the final cultivation for the seed bed. After making the drill, turn a spade or fork upside down and use the horizontal handle (whether it is a 'T' or 'D') to pat down the soil in the drill. This might break up a few lumps but the main effect is to create a more continuous and level surface within the drill, so that the seeds will stay at that level. Without doing this, if the soil is lumpy in the drill, some seeds will fall between lumps and be too deep to grow to the surface, or will emerge much later than the rest, and some will land on top of a lump and be too shallow. If the thought of an upturned spade or fork, with children around, is too alarming, use a broom handle or buy a handle intended for a pitchfork, lay it in the drill and pat it down with a spade or fork. The drill will have to be straight to start with!

When sowing seeds, rather than shaking them straight out of the packet, which can result in over-crowding, pour a few into the palm of one hand and pick up a few between the finger and thumb of the other. Then, even with small seeds (lettuces and carrots are quite difficult, though) they can be sown individually the distance apart that you want.

The next decision to be made is whether to pat down the soil after backfilling the drills. To make the right decision you need to know what the weather is going to do between sowing and emergence of the seedling! Soil texture, structure, organic matter content and the current moisture status of the soil will also influence the decision. Then you have to decide how *hard* to pat down the soil. The seed needs to be able to absorb moisture to stimulate germination and thereafter to be able to draw in moisture to facilitate growth. If the soil is too loose, with pore space greater than the volume of solid material, it will tend to dry out unless there is frequent rain. The rain will have the effect of compacting the soil so that it will probably be able to maintain adequate moisture by drawing it up from below through capillary action. Creating conditions so that capillary action can occur is the reason for patting down the soil after sowing. Judgement and experience will tell you if and how much your soil needs to be patted down to achieve the right conditions. Conditions might be dry at the time of sowing, necessitating a fairly firm patting down but then there might be unexpectedly heavy rain before the seedlings emerge, capping the soil and preventing emergence. This happened in my garden one year and about 90% of brassicas and catch crops sown in between at the same time failed to come up.

When to sow seeds is a perennial problem. Many gardeners will be constrained by when they have time to garden. In schools, too, gardening will have to fit in with terms and timetables. For each crop and for each garden there will be a best time to sow. Soil moisture and temperature and forthcoming weather are all considerations. In the next chapter, guidance is given on sowing times for each type of vegetable.

In biodynamic agriculture there are certain days when sowing, planting, hoeing, harvesting and many other procedures are recommended, according to the positions of the planets. *The Biodynamic Sowing and Planting Calendar* is published annually by Floris Books. Over the years I sometimes wondered why a crop did badly for no reason I could think of. It is only recently that I have looked into the subject of biodynamic growing; I remain open minded but sceptical. There are so many factors that influence the growing of a crop. One reason I have not taken up working according to the biodynamic calendar is that there are so few days when a particular job can be done. Most people have to fit in gardening when they can, around life's other obligations. Beyond that, suitable weather conditions are usually the determining factor when jobs get done. It is not always suitable when the calendar recommends sowing, harvesting or whatever. It would be virtually impossible for a school to adhere strictly to the calendar. However, a trial could be done with, perhaps, one crop each year.

Vegetables One by One

ALLIUMS

In the rotation recommended, alliums are grown in the plot previously occupied by the tender crops – squash, sweetcorn, etc., which will have had compost dug in before they were planted out. After these crops are cleared in the autumn, the soil may be tested for its pH and if below 6.4, or 5.8 on a peat soil, garden lime or fine ground calcified seaweed should be applied and worked in with the cultivator or a rake.

GARLIC (*Allium sativum*)

It is advisable not to grow garlic from bulbs that have been bought for eating. They could be carrying virus or fungal infections or dormant cysts of nematodes. The variety might not be stated, nor whether it is a short or long dormancy type.

Both short and long dormancy types may be planted in autumn but short dormancy types *must* be. Short dormancy types have broader leaves and produce larger bulbs than long dormancy types. Short dormancy types mature and are harvested earlier than long dormancy types but will only keep until around Christmas time; whereas long dormancy types, if kept cool, dry and in the light, should still be good to use when the short dormancy types are ready for harvest.

The cost of 'seed' garlic might seem high but especially when starting a new garden it is advisable to buy in certificated stock. If you manage to grow good sized bulbs with good sized cloves, these can be used to plant for the next crop. Every few years you might want to buy in some fresh stock, perhaps to try a different variety or if your bulbs have become rather small.

Site and soil

An open site that gets maximum sunshine is preferable. The soil should be free draining, including throughout the winter. A heavy clay soil is not ideal for garlic. A silt or brickearth are considered to be best. If, as recommended in the rotation, alliums follow tender crops such as squash, there should be no need to dig in bulky organic matter as this will have been applied in the spring, before the tender crops were planted out. If your soil tends to be acidic, test for pH in the autumn and if below 6.4, apply lime.

When to plant

Garlic needs to have a period of at least a month in the ground in temperatures below 10°C. This stimulates the production of cloves. One year, as an experiment, I planted some garlic in early spring and later harvested bulbs that each consisted of just one, albeit slightly bigger, clove. It is advisable, therefore, to plant short and long dormancy types in the autumn. The timing is not very critical. I like to see the shoots up before the worst of the winter weather, so I can at least see where they are and that they are alive. They can then continue to photosynthesize throughout the winter whenever the temperature is high enough. In most of England, October planting is fine but September or even August would be advisable in colder areas. Timing might be more dictated by when beds are available after clearing the summer crops. After clearing crop debris, remove any weeds then a little work with the cultivator to about 10cm deep to loosen and level the soil is all the preparation needed. If lime is being applied, this should be done before cultivating.

Spacing and planting

Rows can be about 15cm apart and, if the cloves are large, plant at about 12cm apart along the row. Small cloves may be planted closer each way. Some books recommend planting up to 10cm deep in light soils. I recommend just covering the tops of the cloves. Do not push the cloves into the soil as this compacts the soil underneath the basal plate and then when the roots start to grow they will tend to push the clove out of the soil. Dig a hole with a trowel, put the clove in the right way up, backfill and very lightly pat down the soil. As an experiment, try planting some cloves on their sides and see what happens. This is one way of preventing cloves pushing themselves out.

Care

The freshly cleared and cultivated soil will attract cats. To prevent them defecating, as soon as the garlic is planted, cover the bed(s) with the crop debris that has just been removed. In the crop rotation recommended this will be the haulms of squash. If the garden is just being started and there is no previous crop debris, any twiggy, especially prickly, prunings will do, otherwise use wire netting. Squash haulms are good for this purpose as they rot down slowly but will not need to be removed. By the time the garlic shoots emerge there will be enough light getting through to the soil surface.

Apart from keeping the ground free of weeds, with garlic there is nothing to do until harvest. In practice, it might not be necessary to weed until the spring, as a short ground cover of weeds will protect the soil surface from compaction or erosion caused by winter rains. However, if there is annual meadow grass present, it should be pulled out before it flowers as it can run to seed all year round if the temperature is high enough for growth. Also, pull out any other weed that is seen to flower during winter. The minimum temperature for growth is only around 5°C.

Pests and diseases

In many years of growing garlic I have never had any pest problems with it. If you start by growing certificated 'seed' garlic it is unlikely that pests will be introduced into the garden. There are two fungal diseases which garlic is susceptible to. One is the soil-borne white rot and the other is rust.

White rot (Sclerotium cepivorum)

This does not produce spores but the fruiting bodies, or sclerotia, which are black and the size of a pin head or poppy seed, can remain in the ground for at least 20 years, although some sources say 7 and others say 15 years. The differences could depend on soil and climate but for the gardener, if there is white rot, it is very difficult to get rid of and normal rotations will not be effective. The first symptoms are a yellowing of the outer, or lower, leaves, although this might be less easy to identify in garlic than in onions. So, you might not notice the problem is there until you dig them up, by which time the diagnostic fluffy white stage might have developed into black, green and other colours. Affected plants, together with adhering soil and the immediately surrounding soil should be carefully put into a bucket and kept until you have a large bonfire.

If your soil is badly infected with white rot there are a few organically-accepted strategies to deal with it. It is claimed that application of plenty of compost in the soil has a beneficial effect. A mulch of eucalyptus leaves has also been found to have some effect (see the International Society for Horticultural Science website, www.ishs.org). Sclerotia are stimulated into development by exudates from the roots of alliums. Therefore, if a powdered extract of garlic is incorporated into the soil but no allium crop grown that year, the fungus will exhaust itself with no host to live on. This should be done at least a year after a crop of Alliums and when the soil temperature is between 15 and 20°C. This might have to be repeated a few times. It is a long-term strategy!

Once you know there is white rot in the soil, plant cloves 15cm apart each way and keep a look out for yellowing leaves. If unsure, carefully dig up affected bulbs to check if they have the disease.

Rust
This is easy to identify. The leaves and stems look as though they have been dusted with powdered rust. As with leeks, this disease appears in some years for no apparent reason but in most years you will not see any. If it does occur, pick off affected leaves at an early stage and burn them. However, even if left, it does not seem to affect the crop very much. High

nitrogen feeding, which promotes soft, disease-prone growth, together with damp conditions, will encourage the growth of rust but as garlic do not require high nitrogen feeding and their narrow foliage allows good air circulation, they are rarely affected.

Harvest

Harvesting at the right time is important. If left too long in the ground the outer skins covering the whole bulb can decay, exposing the cloves to fungal infection. They do not look so good either, with the outer layer of cloves exposed. The bulbs put on most of their growth during the last six weeks before they are ready to lift. The timing of harvest, therefore, is quite critical: too soon and yield will be below potential; too late and various rots could have set in. In most areas of England short dormancy types will be ready around the end of June. So, each week during that month, carefully scrape away the soil around a few bulbs to see how they are progressing. Long dormancy types might need another month to mature. Advice in books that bulbs are ready to harvest when the leaves turn yellow is not very helpful. The tips of the leaves can start dying off many weeks before the bulbs are ready. If you wait until all the leaves have gone yellow, it will probably be too late. The weather is also a consideration. If conditions are dry, a little extra time in the ground will do no harm, but if it is wet, then bulbs should be lifted as soon as you think they are fully grown.

In dry weather the plants may be left on the ground to dry off but if wet they should be brought under cover and spread out to dry. When the necks have dried so that they are no longer green but are still pliable, cut them off, leaving about 10cm if you wish to string them up for storage. If they get completely dry and crisp they will break when you bend them in the process of stringing up. For a neat appearance and to allow good air circulation in store, the roots should be trimmed off as shown in Figure 7.1. (See also Figure 7.2 on page 130 for how to string garlic and onions.)

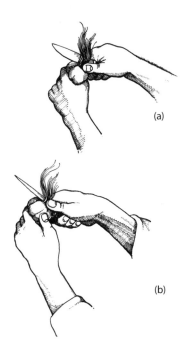

Fig. 7.1 Trimming garlic without cutting your thumb! (Drawn by Kevin Kimber.) (a) Correct method. (b) Risk of slicing top of left thumb.

Storage

Garlic should be stored in a cool place, in light, though not direct sunlight, with plenty of ventilation. They may be kept outside but protected from rain and brought inside only if a frost is likely.

Recommended varieties

My favourites are 'Germidour' for a short dormancy type and 'Cristo' for a long dormancy type. I prefer to eat garlic raw and 'Germidour' has good flavour but is not too hot; some varieties just burn the tongue. 'Germidour' can grow big, given good soil and weather – this probably depends on the temperature in June. The cloves have skins which peel off easily. 'Cristo' does not grow as large but it is a very handsome garlic. When the outer skins of the bulb have been taken off it is unblemished white. It keeps well into the spring.

ONIONS (*Allium cepa*)

Onions are a particularly good crop to grow in a school garden. Most people like eating them, they are easy to grow, easy to harvest, are likely to survive the journey from school to home without damage and, if need be, can be stored for months. They are also a convenient crop to use for trials looking at the effect of spacing on individual size, on yield per unit area and on the effects of different fertilizer applications. I would recommend using sets rather than seed with children up to the age of 12. Sets are miniature bulbs that have been grown from seed at high density, harvested early, stored in controlled conditions and sold early the following year to continue their growth. Because onions are biennial, stretching their growth over two years tended to result in some of them bolting. Now, however, sets are obtainable that have been heat treated, which kills the embryonic flower inside the bulb.

Site and soil

An open site with maximum sunshine and well-drained soil is preferable. The recommended pH is between 6.5 and 7.5 but I have grown excellent crops in soil with pH 6.4. If the soil does need liming, this should have been done in the autumn. If it has not been, liming in spring will have little effect on crops grown straight afterwards. Wait until the autumn and lime the plot where alliums will be grown next year. If your soil happens to be a silty loam or a brickearth, you have the best chance of growing excellent onions. If they are following crops that have had compost or manure dug in before they were grown, there is no need to apply more. However, if you think the soil is lacking in organic matter and you happen to have plenty of well-rotted compost or manure, then the crop will benefit from it. In a trial in 2005 looking at the effects of different application rates of urine on onion yield, I also applied an unmeasured amount of compost to half of each bed. The compost increased yield by an average of 6%. If compost is applied it should be done several weeks before planting to allow time for the soil to settle – onions grow better in a firm soil – and to avoid attracting the onion fly at the critical time of planting.

An application of urine a few days before planting the sets will provide nitrogen and potassium for the leaf growth of the onion. Leaves continue to grow until the day length is 16 hours. From then on leaf growth stops and the bulb starts to swell. The leaf area at that stage determines the potential for bulb growth. Apply no more than one litre of urine per square metre, (equivalent to approximately 60kg nitrogen per hectare), diluted with two litres of water and then wash in with a further two litres of water. If the soil is very dry to start with, apply a couple of litres of water per square metre before putting on the urine. If conditions are wet, allow a longer period between urine application and planting. Cultivate to a few centimetres to help the soil dry out to just a damp state suitable for planting.

When to plant
If you have not been able to buy heat-treated sets it is important not to plant them too early. If there is a cold period after planting, this simulates winter, which will stimulate the bulbs to bolt. Therefore, delay planting until it can reasonably be assumed that winter is really over. Of course, the later you plant, the less time there is for leaf growth, which largely determines eventual bulb size. So, if the spring weather is late and planting is delayed, the sets may be planted closer than

usual to maximize yield per square metre, as they are not going to get very big anyway. With heat-treated sets, they may be planted as soon as there is a period of good weather that will get growth started, provided that soil conditions are suitable, i.e. not waterlogged.

Spacing and planting

Aim for about 90 plants per square metre. If you have seven rows in a metre-wide bed or six in a 90cm bed, the sets need to be 7–8cm apart along the row. However, if you know there is white rot in the soil then allow 15cm each way between plants to reduce the likelihood of localized infection spreading to neighbouring plants. Before planting the sets, pull off any length of dead stem, taking care not to damage the shoot which might already have sprouted. If pieces of dead stem are left protruding from the soil, birds pull at them and pull the sets out. Perhaps they see the pieces of dead stem as potential nesting material. As with garlic, do not push the bulbs into the soil; make a hole with a trowel, put the bulbs in the right way up and just cover with soil, then gently firm the soil down around the onion.

Care

Hand weeding is all that needs doing until harvest. When the onion leaves are clearly visible it is just possible to hoe along the rows, if your hoe has been narrowed by sawing off each side, but it is very easy to catch the onions and damage them. Hoeing is not recommended for children. It is very satisfying, if the bed is covered in young weeds, to work steadily from one end to the other pulling out the weeds and revealing the neat rows of onions. Check at least twice a week for any signs of disease.

Pests and diseases

Hessayon (2006) states that of the many disorders that can afflict onions only four are common: onion fly, stem and bulb eelworm, neck rot and white rot. I have never seen onion fly, very rarely seen symptoms of stem and bulb eelworm, occasionally had neck rot; only white rot has been a serious problem but only in patches in part of the garden. So, if you are lucky and do not have white rot in your soil, onions should be problem free (see pests and diseases of garlic on page 122 for how to identify and deal with white rot). Following the cultural recommendations described in the Site and soil section on page 126 is the best way to avoid problems occurring. However, the weather is beyond our control and can cause a particular problem. If there is a long period of drought and then heavy rain before the bulbs are quite ready for harvest, this can cause 'saddleback', characterized by splitting at the base of the bulb. Again, I have rarely seen this. Affected bulbs should be used first, as they will not keep. Normally, the weather suits the onion crop, with good periods of dry weather, allowing ripening and harvest before any appreciable rain.

Harvest

Old gardening books recommend bending the tops over to hasten ripening. This is not now recommended as it damages leaves and can allow disease organisms to enter. Just leave the tops to bend over naturally. At this stage sprouting inhibitors produced in the leaves are transferred to the bulb. Therefore, the leaves should be left intact to allow this process to occur (Tucker, 1982). When all, or nearly all, of the tops have 'gone down' the bulbs may be lifted out of the ground. A small, close-pronged fork is ideal for this. If the soil is dry and the weather remains dry, the bulbs can be left on the ground for roots and tops to dry off but should be brought under cover if there is any chance of rain or even if there are heavy dews. The staging of a greenhouse or anywhere with good light and ventilation will do. The picture on the back cover illustrates the yield and density of crop obtainable from a bed.

Storage

If you intend to store onions by stringing them up, do not allow the stems to become completely dry and brittle or they might break in the process of stringing. Some plants might have developed thick necks, which do not dry properly, neither will the bulbs keep for very long. Hessayon (2006) suggests this is caused by too much nitrogen in the soil. Tucker (1982) suggests it is caused by a cool growing season. Thick necked onions should be used first.

In a school it might not be *necessary* to store onions at all but making strings is a useful skill and fun to do. So, all suitable bulbs could be strung up, hung in the classroom for a while before being pulled or cut from the string and handed out for children to take home (see Figure 7.2). If onions are to be stored, keep in a cool, dry place in the light but not direct sunlight and with good air circulation. That is the conventional

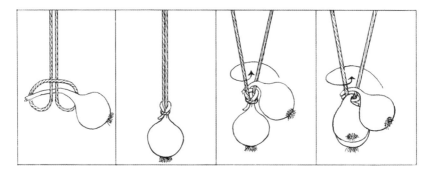

Fig. 7.2 How to string onions and garlic.

wisdom. However, a couple of friends keep their onions in strings, near the high ceiling of a farmhouse kitchen, which I assume is warm most of the time, and they keep remarkably well. So, perhaps temperature is not critical. They will survive a few degrees below freezing without damage, provided conditions are dry.

LEEKS (*Allium porrum*)

Leeks are one of the most 'generous' crops. From small seeds grow nutritious, tasty plants, part green, part onion-like and they obligingly stand all winter providing fresh produce whenever you want it. They respond well to any improvements you make in soil structure and fertility and are good crops to use for trials of different spacing or feeding. Their extensive fibrous roots help to improve soil structure. They are hardy, and some varieties particularly so. In January 1982 my leeks (var. 'Musselburgh') survived $-26°C$. Leeks will tolerate strong wind, being frozen in the ground and covered in snow.

Site and soil

Leeks do well in a deep, well-drained, fertile soil with a good level of organic matter and a pH of 6.5–7.5 but they will tolerate most soils. The range of pH within which leeks grow best is higher than other temperate vegetables. If the pH is suspected to be low, in the autumn before growing them, test the soil. Making controlled adjustments to pH is not an easy exercise, however. Outside of a laboratory, testing soil for pH might not be reliable, either. For 20 years I grew excellent crops of leeks in soil that always seemed to be pH 6.4, just outside the optimum, according to books. In a clay soil it can take up to two years for a lime application to have its full effect. The latest time it should be applied, therefore, is as soon as possible after the previous crop has been cleared in the autumn. Incorporate it well into the soil using the cultivator.

Dig in compost or manure in early spring, two or three weeks before sowing. If no compost or manure is available, apply urine to the bed(s) a few days before sowing, at a rate of about one litre per square metre, diluted. Application dilution can be 1:1 but then add two to five parts water, depending on soil moisture conditions. The moister the conditions are, the more days in advance this needs to be done, to allow the soil to dry to suitable conditions for sowing seeds.

When to sow

Leek seeds are fairly slow to germinate, generally taking 14–18 days, but they benefit from as long a growing period as you can give them. However, the soil temperature needs to be a minimum of 7°C. A late variety, to be harvested the following spring can be sown as late as June.

Spacing and sowing

Most books describe raising seedlings and then transplanting when they are pencil-thick. This provides a very neat result, with uniformly-spaced plants. However, it is time-consuming work and necessitates the use of much water to enable the plants to recover. Transplanting suits the commercial grower, where mechanization is used but in a garden, time and much effort can be saved with, I would suggest, no loss of yield. I have not done any trials to determine if there is a yield advantage in transplanting and would expect there might be a disadvantage due to the check in growth. To minimize the need for transplanting to even out the spacing along the rows, take particular care when sowing the seeds.

Depending on the width of bed, rows can be 25–30cm apart. In a 90cm bed, the rows could be 26cm apart at 6, 32, 58, and 84 cm from one edge of the bed. The final within-row spacing should be 10–15cm. It is useful to know how many seeds you have and what the total length of rows is. Then you can work out how far apart the seeds need to be sown.

Make the drills a few centimetres deep and as wide as possible. Cover the seeds with about 2cm of soil, depending on its condition: a good, moisture-retaining loam will need less covering than a poorer, lumpy soil that is prone to dry out. You should be left with shallow, 'V'-shaped valleys and ridges, with the seeds in the valleys. A catch crop of radish can be grown along the ridges. Gently tamp down the ridges with a spade or rake so that there is space to make a drill, or if only a small quantity of radish is being sown, individual seeds can be pushed in with a finger. If the soil is a little dry and no rain is forecast, the drills will need to be firmed. For the leeks, the handle of a spade or fork held upside down works quite well. If drills have been used for the radish, the same method can be used, or the back of the spade.

Alternatively, early carrots could be sown in between the leeks on the same day. The shallow 'V' shaped trench can still be used for the leeks but you will not be able to level out the ground before applying liquid feed (see 'Care' below) as the carrots will still be there. Applying the feed will be more difficult but the slope of the 'V' will help to direct the liquid towards the leeks. By the time all the carrots are harvested the leek leaves will probably be too large to allow the plants to be earthed up with a spade. As carrots are pulled, localized earthing up can be done with a trowel.

However carefully seeds are sown there will always be gaps and overcrowding. So, some transplanting will be necessary to even out the spacing along the rows but it is not necessary to be precise. If you were to end up transplanting half the crop just to achieve equidistance, it could cause more loss of yield, by interrupting growth, than tolerating uneven spacing. Aim for an *average* spacing of 10–15cm and as long as no more than three plants are growing right next to each other and there is no more than a 20cm gap anywhere, I would think that close to maximum yield will be achieved. Ease the plants to be moved out of the ground with a spade or small fork, or individually with a trowel, and plant straight away into a pre-dug hole. Fill in the hole before watering from a can with a rose. Always water gently; never swamp the soil so that the structure collapses into mud. This causes compaction, which will impede oxygen supply to the roots as well as water from rainfall. One watering should be sufficient because there has been minimum disturbance. If soil and weather are damp, it might not be necessary to water at all.

There seem to be three sizes of leek: thick, thin and very thin. I do not know if size is related to flavour but when transplanting I tend to use the largest plants first and discard the very thin ones. The size at this stage is an indication of future growth rates; large ones grow faster than the small ones.

If, at the time when transplanting is done the soil is too dry, do not transplant and rely on watering afterwards. Preferably on the evening before transplanting, water the plants that need moving and the ground where they will be planted. Before transplanting, check that the soil is moist throughout and that it is not dry below the watered surface layer.

Care

After any necessary transplanting, the soil between the rows can be loosened by using an upright fork as a cultivator. This will level out the surface and facilitate the liquid feeding. Leeks will benefit from feeding during their maximum growth period of summer. Soon after transplanting has been done is a good time to apply the feed. 1.5 to 2.0 litres of urine per square metre is appropriate, depending on how fertile you consider the soil is already. Apply at a dilution of 2:1 water to urine and then add at least another two units of water, depending on soil moisture beforehand. For this operation, remove the rose from the watering can and either use an attachable spout with a narrow outflow or cover three quarters of the can's own spout with masking tape in order to slow down the rate of flow, so that liquid can be applied in a more controlled way, directly on to the soil and avoiding getting it on the leaves. Apply along each side of each row of plants. When the soil has drained to a just moist condition it can be drawn up to the plants using a spade or push hoe, reversing the original ridge and valley arrangement. After that, the only care needed is hand weeding. A hoe is not appropriate as it is likely to damage the leaves.

A second catch crop

A second catch crop can be grown in between the rows of leeks. In most of England, hardy winter salads would be sown in August – late enough to prevent them flowering until the following year but early enough for them to grow to a reasonable size before cold weather inhibits growth. American land cress/early winter cress/Belle Isle cress/Normandy cress (*Barbarea verna*), Corn salad/lamb's lettuce (*Valerianella locusta*), winter purslane/miner's lettuce/claytonia/Cuban spinach (*Montia perfoliata*) are examples. Rocket (*Eruca versicaria*) would be sown in late August, or early September in warmer areas.

It could be said that if the spacing is right for the fertility of the soil, there will not be room for an inter-crop of salads or anything else – I have not tried it myself. However, intercropping could be practical, for the following reasons. If the salads are sown soon after the liquid feeding and earthing up of leeks, which will probably be in July, they should be able to establish themselves well enough before the outer leaves of leeks cover much of the ground. Some experiment might be needed to discover the best time to sow for your area. In warm/ southern areas a July sowing might be early enough for salads to start flowering the same year. Sow on two or three different dates over a period of a month. If the leeks are an early variety, they could be harvested carefully, with minimal soil disturbance, allowing the salads, which are not likely to have been killed by over-shadowing leeks, to take over the bed and continue growing throughout the winter whenever temperatures are high enough (see 'Harvest' section below for how to get leeks out without disturbing any in-between crops). If the leeks are a late variety, the salads could grow large enough to provide some pickings in early winter, before the leek foliage smothers them too much.

Pests and diseases

Leeks are subject to the same pests and diseases as onions and garlic. However, I have only ever seen two diseases on leeks – rust and white rot – and no pests. They are more prone to be affected by rust than onions but less prone or are less affected by white rot than are onions and garlic. Lack of space between plants and high nitrogen feeding are said to lead to rust problems. However, I have grown good sized leeks very close together and some years they got rust and other years they did not; there seems to be no correlation between spacing or feeding and the incidence of rust. Urine is not just a nitrogen fertilizer; it also contains phosphorous and potassium. The latter helps to harden tissue and improve resistance (Pollock, 2002). If leeks are badly affected by rust, pick off the leaves and burn or put into a hot compost heap. Only the outer leaves will be affected. When the weather turns cold the rust disappears.

Harvest

Some varieties are ready in late summer and may be used through the autumn. Others are intended for winter and spring harvesting. If they have grown well it should be near impossible to pull them up, as the roots will be long, numerous and thick. If you try to pull leeks up they can snap off just above root level. It is easier to dig them up with a small fork. Be careful not to let soil from the roots fall between the leaves of neighbouring plants. Much of the soil can be shaken off at ground level. The roots can be cut off *in situ* and left to rot. If you intend to leave the roots where they are, there is no need to take the plant completely out of the ground. Loosen them with a fork, pulling with one hand at the same time and cut off the roots as soon as you can see where to cut. Alternatively, if the leeks are not too deep, you can just push a knife into the ground and cut off enough roots to allow the plant to be pulled out. However, you might cut a worm doing this, as they can often be found amongst the roots. Otherwise, take the plants to the compost heap and trim them there. If you wish to keep leeks for a few days out of the ground before using, leave the roots on and put them in a bucket with enough water to cover the roots and store in a cool place.

Commercially, there is much waste involved in the harvesting of leeks. Most of the green part is cut off with one chop of a knife. The leaves are perfectly edible and more nutritious than the white part, containing more vitamin A than cabbage, although not as much as kale (Hills, 1971). The outer leaves can be a bit tough and coarse, though. So, after trimming the roots, pull off the outer two or three leaves right down to the base, leaving a clean white shank. Then hold the plant upside down and make two chops in the air with a sharp knife at angles so that the outer, coarser leaves are cut near to where they start being green but the inner, more tender leaves remain increasingly intact the nearer to the centre of the plant they are. In other words, the younger the leaves the more of each is left to eat. The very youngest, in the centre, will be left uncut.

Recommended varieties

There are many to choose from. Some mature in autumn, others are very hardy and go on growing throughout winter and can be used until early spring. Some have relatively long white shanks while others are shorter and thicker, with relatively more green leaf. Some have more flavour than others. 'Musselburgh' is very hardy and reliable with good flavour, so is the later maturing 'Siegfried'.

BRASSICAS

Brassicas – cabbage, broccoli, etc. – are the most difficult group of vegetables to grow well, as they are very likely to be infested with a number of pests and diseases that can leave you with no crop worth eating. However, there are ways of avoiding or dealing with these problems. Brassicas are mostly biennial. Resist the temptation to sow too early. A cold period of weather can simulate winter and result in plants bolting. This is

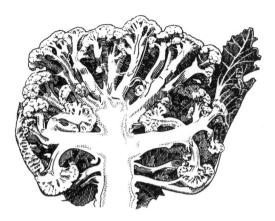

a particular problem with spring-sown cabbages but with any brassica a cold period with slow growth makes plants more vulnerable to pests and diseases. With purple sprouting broccoli and spring cauliflower there is plenty of time for them to catch up from a late sowing.

In the rotation recommended for a five plot rotation within a four plot design (see Figure 3.6 on page 53) brassicas share a plot with legumes. It does not matter which half is used for which, as their positions are reversed the next time these two crops are grown on the plot four years later, thus giving an eight year rotation for brassicas and legumes.

PURPLE SPROUTING BROCCOLI (*Brassica oleracea*), Italica group

Site and soil

Some books say that broccoli needs shelter or will need staking but I have had plants fall over during the winter that went on to produce a crop of sprouting as good as the plants that remained upright. So, stake if you wish to keep a neat appearance but from the point of view of yield it does not seem to be important. The soil needs to be well drained and not prone to becoming waterlogged in winter. If there is compost

available, dig some in over the whole bed a few weeks before
sowing, if possible, to allow the soil to settle. Brassicas grow
better in a firm soil. Unless you are in a high rainfall area and
have very free-draining soil, the pH should be suitable following
the allium crops, before which lime may have been applied.
However, if you know that there is clubroot infection in the
soil then it would be advisable to apply lime in the autumn
before sowing brassicas.

Brassicas are prone to more pests and diseases than most crops.
Therefore, anything that can be done to help them grow fast
and strong to 'grow out of trouble' is worth doing. A general
application of urine over the whole bed will be of considerable
benefit. Apply about 1 litre/m^2, diluted 2:1 with water and
washed in with one to two litres of water, depending on soil
moisture at the time. If conditions are wet, this needs to be
done long enough before sowing for the soil to dry out to a
suitably just-moist condition.

When to sow

Spring is the time to sow broccoli but in western Europe spring
can be an up and down affair, with periods of mild weather
alternating with cold, dry winds or cold, saturating rain. In
adverse conditions delicate young plants can succumb to pests
or diseases. Traditionally it is recommended that all seeds,
except beans and peas, are sown during the waxing moon. In
most of Europe, some time during the waxing moon in April
will be the right time. In areas that become dry by May, a
month earlier might be advisable. At the other extreme, where
little growth occurs before the end of April, waiting until May
would be better. Brassicas will do well if their growth is steady
and not much interrupted by very cold or very dry conditions.

Spacing

I recommend sowing all spring-sown brassicas in the positions where they are to remain. This saves having to transplant, which takes time and effort and causes a check in growth of the plants, which then need watering. The space they occupy for such a long period is not a problem, as catch crops of radish, lettuce and spring onions can be grown in between during the summer. Or, if you have enough seed, extra broccoli plants can be grown and eaten as young greens at a time of year when there is little else fresh and green.

In an adult's garden, where beds might be 120cm wide, there is just room for three rows, but in a metre or 90cm bed two rows should be grown. Position the rows 25cm from the edge of the bed. That leaves space for a row of lettuce in between, with a row of radish either side of it and a row of spring onions along the edge of the bed. If there are not enough broccoli seeds to allow continuous sowing along a drill, sow a few close together at positions 50cm apart along the row. Try to leave a centimetre between seeds at each place so that when you pull out the surplus plants the roots of the one you are leaving will not be disturbed. Thinning out should be done before the plants are 10cm high. The lettuce and spring onions can be sown at the same time as the broccoli but it might be better to wait until conditions are a little warmer before sowing radish, so that they grow quickly, without too many checks to their growth due to cold spells of weather.

Care

If catch crops are being grown it will be impractical to use a hoe. So, it is essential to begin hand weeding as soon as the vegetable seedlings are up and can be identified. When the broccoli plants are between 20 and 25cm high they will benefit from liquid feeding. Because you will not want to get urine on the catch crops it is necessary to reduce the flow from the watering can so that application is more controlled (see the section on care of leeks on page 135). About 1.5 litres per square metre is adequate, diluted 2:1 with water and washed in with another litre of water if the soil is moist or rain is imminent, or more water if the soil is dry. If extra plants are being grown for eating as greens, they can have more feed. Before I started using urine on young brassicas, any spare plants eaten were tough and bitter. Feeding them with urine makes them sweet and tender (delicious with walnut oil and salt). The following year, as soon as the plants show signs of new growth, apply another liquid feed. The same volume can be used. As there will be no catch crops in the way and as the roots will have spread over a much larger area by then, use a down-facing rose on the watering can and apply up to a 30cm radius from the stems.

Pests and diseases

Flea beetle (Phyllotreta nemorum)
This is otherwise known as turnip flea, and is likely to be the first pest to appear on brassica plants, even at the seedling stage. These creatures are about 3mm long and have the characteristic habit of jumping up in the air when disturbed. This habit can be exploited. Lawrence Hills (1971) describes how to make a 'flea beetle trolley'. I have to admit I have not tried this but suggest it is within the capabilities of upper junior children to construct and use. I wonder if the design might be improved by making the trip wire adjustable to suit plants at different stages of growth, as the flea beetle does feed on plants over a period, albeit a fairly short one while the plants are young. Also,

perhaps the board, with the greased paper attached, could protrude further forward to avoid the possibility of beetles jumping forward and sideways or simply landing on the ground ahead and not being further disturbed (see Figure 7.3).

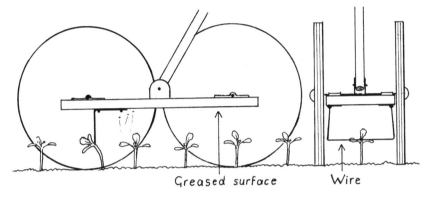

Greased surface   Wire

Fig. 7.3 Flea beetle trolley. (Adapted from Hills, 1971, p. 144.)

When I described this contraption to a Norwegian vegetable farmer, suggesting it could be scaled up to a field version, spanning a bed, he immediately suggested an improvement to the design. A field surface would not be perfectly even over the width of a bed and plants might also be different heights. A single bar might be low enough to damage some plants but too high to touch others. Instead of having a bar he suggested that the underside of the 'vehicle' could have numerous pieces of string hanging down. They would not damage the plants but should disturb the beetles enough to make them jump. Clearly, further research is needed.

Flea beetles make characteristic small round holes in the leaves from the earliest, seedling leaf stage. The problem is worst in dry weather and can result in the death of the plant. Keeping the soil surface moist will reduce the problem and also help the plants grow faster and recover. When watering delicate seedlings, turn the rose on the watering can to face upwards to create a more gentle 'rain.' I have seen small birds, for example house martins and sparrows, hopping over the brassica beds pecking at the ground. I always hope that they are eating flea beetles! In most years flea beetles are not a very serious problem and keeping the ground damp is fairly effective. They will also attack radish and turnip leaves and other brassicas.

Cabbage aphid (Brevicoryne brasssicae) and peach aphid (Myzus persicae)

These pests feed on the underside of leaves. Attacks can come when plants are still small or later when near fully grown. Both can carry virus diseases, e.g. cauliflower mosaic and cabbage ring spot or leaf spot, but I have never known either of these to be a serious problem. Small birds eat the aphids and usually numbers diminish quite quickly. However, a severe infestation, especially in dry weather when growth is slow, can cause considerable puckering and distortion of the leaves and, therefore, retard growth. Liquid feeding and water to promote good growth will help plants grow out of trouble and recover.

Swede midge

This pest causes the growing points of plants to stop, producing 'blind plants'. The bases of existing leaf stalks become swollen. Symptoms are noticed in the summer when plants are half mature. For several years this was a serious problem in my garden, in one year affecting 95% of savoys. Then, just as inexplicably, it disappeared, rarely to return. Hessayon states that it is uncommon except in northern Britain and the south west. This might indicate that wetter areas are more at risk. I know of no deterrent herb or preventive measure. Pull up affected plants and burn as soon as possible.

Cabbage root fly (Erioischia brassicae)

The small, white larvae of cabbage root fly can be a very serious pest. Of all the brassicas I have grown, purple sprouting broccoli seem to be the most resilient against it and spring cauliflower the most susceptible. All brassicas are susceptible to some extent, including radishes and turnips. The first symptoms are outer leaves turning yellow, with characteristic purple edges often showing first, generally a sign of starvation and stress. Growth is slowed and young plants might die. I once had a bed of large, good looking spring cauliflower plants which suddenly started falling over as so much of their roots had been eaten away by the small white grubs. There can be three infestations during the year. In England the second is said to occur in July although I have never noticed an infestation occur any earlier.

Special discs with a slit to the centre are sold to be placed around the young plants to prevent the fly laying its eggs in the soil. I have tried these. I have also tried larger squares of thick carpet underlay and squares of thick black polythene stapled around the plant stems. I found none of these to be effective in saving the plants. If I applied the collars early enough to prevent the fly laying eggs, the plants were still small enough to have their stems eaten through by tiny black slugs that were attracted to the moist, warm conditions under the collars. Try collars, but I cannot recommend them. Putting them on and then disposing of them at some stage is another little chore I would rather not have to do.

There is a biological method of deterring the fly and, at the same time, attracting and feeding bees: plant thyme amongst the brassicas. I have found this to be well over 90% effective. One plant, at least 20cm across, per square metre will be plenty. In a larger garden, half that density would be adequate. This need not be expensive. When planting the thyme out in the early spring, bend down one or two of the longer branches of each plant, cover part of the stem with a little soil and cover this point with a stone. By the next spring the layered branches will have rooted and you will have more plants to move on to the new brassica plot. Later in the season, look out for large leaves of brassicas shading out the thyme. Cut leaves off if necessary. Honey bees, in particular, as well as some butterflies, are attracted to thyme flowers.

Slugs

These can be a problem in some years on young plants. In my experience only the small light grey, small brown and small black slugs feed on living plants. The very large slugs seem to prefer green stuff that has already been uprooted or cut. In a private garden going out at first light with a sharp knife or after dark with a torch and a sharp knife is the surest and quickest way of dealing with them. Otherwise, pieces of slate, tile, flat stones or large leaves may be placed next to where slugs are a problem. Each morning these can be lifted and any slugs hiding underneath can be dealt with. Using salt on slugs and snails does work but it certainly is not a quick death and could be a painful one. Collecting slugs in a bucket and removing them to well away from the garden is an option but avoid touching them with bare hands. The slime is impossible to wash from skin. It can be removed by abrasion with soil or sand.

Snails

These can be a problem at all stages of maturity – of the plants and the snails. Throughout summer large numbers of young snails can cause serious damage to even large leaves. They are easy to lift off with the point of a trowel and squashed on the ground.

Caterpillars

There are three types that are common and almost guaranteed to infest brassicas:

Cabbage moth (*Mamestra brassicae*): The caterpillars are greenish or dull brown with darker markings and tend to feed at the heart of the plants. They are difficult to get at on cabbages and can ruin a hearting cabbage by riddling it with holes. With broccoli and spring cauliflower plants they are easier to find. Pick them off and squash underfoot.

Small white butterflies *(Artogeia rapae)*: The caterpillars are plain green and are usually found singly, not in large numbers and often lying motionless along the mid-rib of a leaf. When the butterflies are seen in the garden it is time to start regular inspections of the underside of leaves, at least twice a week, looking for tight clusters of tiny orange eggs. These can easily be squashed between finger and thumb or, if near the edge of the leaf, torn off.

Large White butterflies (*Pieris brassicae*): The caterpillars are larger than the small white and are distinctly coloured with a black and yellow pattern. They are easy to find and, especially in the early stages, tend to stay together in a large group. Sometimes it is worth breaking off a whole leaf to tread on the entire brood at once. Frequent inspection of brassicas is recommended. It is much easier to deal with pests if caught in the early stages. It is said that vast numbers of these caterpillars are destroyed by the parasitic larvae of *Apanteles glomeratus*, an ichneumon fly (Chinery, 1986) but I have never seen this.

Perhaps I never left caterpillars on the plants long enough to give the predators a chance but by then much damage would have been done.

For a number of years I grew outdoor tomatoes amongst the brassicas, approximately one per square metre. This was about 95% effective in deterring cabbage white butterflies. Then, one year, the tomatoes had very little effect. So, it is worth trying. It could be effective in most years.

Pigeons

My experience of pigeons in a rural garden was that they did not come into the garden except in the harshest winter, I think once in 20 years. A farmer told me that they like to have a clear flight path. There is usually something edible on a bigger scale, anyway, in the fields. Urban pigeons seem to behave differently and do come into small gardens, especially in areas where some people put out food for birds. In a school garden there should be no excuse for pigeon damage, with all those creative, imaginative children around. Scarecrows can be made, or various reflective, jingling or clacking things, windmills, streamers, etc. Or if you would rather be more subtle and not make the garden look cluttered, try putting in a few stakes and stretching black thread between them, criss-crossing the plants. Birds coming in to land will not see the thread but are deterred by the threat of entanglement when their feet make contact with it. I have only tried this on a small scale a long time ago but cannot say how effective it was as pigeons rarely came into my garden anyway. It is a rather tedious technique and not cheap. Using various waste materials and lots of imagination is probably the best strategy in a school. The necessity of scaring the birds can be taken as the starting point for some craft work that could add style to the garden rather than make it look cluttered with junk.

Club root

This is caused by a soil-borne slime mould, *Plasmodiophora brassicae*. Spores can live in the soil for 20 years or more (Pollock, 2002). If the soil is infected with this organism it thrives if the pH is low and if drainage is poor. Spores can move through soil moisture towards the brassica roots. This process is slowed if the soil can drain quickly to field capacity. A high pH is also inhibiting to the development of the disease.

Symptoms are slow growth, and leaves turning pale and eventually yellow. On lifting the plant the roots will show the characteristic swelling. They are not hollow and do not contain maggots. Burn the whole plant as soon as possible. Some weeds are natural hosts to club root, for example charlock (*Sinapis arvensis*), shepherd's purse (*Capsella bursa-pastoris*) and wild radish (*Raphanus raphanistrum,* subsp. *raphanistrum*).

Avoid buying in plants or accepting donations; grow from seed in the garden. If it is a serious problem in the soil of a school garden it is not very helpful to be advised to be careful to avoid transferring soil from one part of the garden to another, when there are many children walking about and sharing tools. So, this is one situation where I would advocate not growing one type of vegetable – this includes turnips and swedes.

Harvest

Books usually advise picking the large central shoot first as it encourages the growth of the other shoots but often some side shoots develop before the central one and it is tempting to let the central one get bigger before picking it. Wherever you pick, more shoots will develop but they will be progressively smaller.

SPRING CAULIFLOWER (*Brassica oleracea*, Botrytis group)

Some catalogues describe these as winter varieties. The earliest variety is 'Medaillon F1'. This will mature in late February to March, presumably only in favourable areas of England or southern Europe. 'Celebrity' and 'Wainfleet' mature from April to May and 'Maystar' in May to June. There is also an old variety 'Purple Cape' (1834) which matures in March.

Site and soil

Follow the advice as for broccoli except that they will benefit from a little more compost dug in to the soil before sowing. Try to do this a few weeks before. Cauliflowers are more sensitive to trace element deficiencies than other brassicas. Three or four handfuls of seaweed meal per square metre thoroughly mixed in with the soil at the time of incorporating the compost will provide a range of trace elements.

When to sow

Spring cauliflower may be sown at the same time as sprouting broccoli. However, the young plants do seem to be more delicate than broccoli and if they will be cropping later than broccoli it would do no harm to sow cauliflower a little later, even up to a month later. There will be plenty of time for them to catch up and they will benefit from growing in warmer conditions with fewer interruptions due to bad weather. If this means they will still be very young when prolonged dry weather sets in, this is one crop which might need watering, especially if flea beetles are a problem (see pests and diseases below).

Spacing

To produce large cauliflower heads grow no more than four per square metre. In a school garden it would be preferable to grow a larger number of smaller heads. Six, eight, nine or twelve plants per square metre are possibilities. I have always found that there are fewer seeds of cauliflower in a packet than other brassicas. You will probably have to sow no more than two or three at each position. If you are growing three rows in a bed there will not be room for a catch crop of lettuce but you should be able to squeeze in rows of radish and spring onions.

Care

Daily inspection of the plants is advisable! Cauliflowers seem to be the favourite for brassica pests. Give priority to cauliflowers when allocating thyme plants as root fly deterrents. Feed as for broccoli but allow a quarter litre of urine per plant. Be particularly thorough and prompt with weeding; these plants need all the help they can get.

Pest and diseases

Cauliflowers are subject to the same pests and diseases as broccoli but seem more susceptible to most of them. They are particularly sensitive to conditions caused by trace element deficiencies. A shortage of molybdenum causes **whiptail**. The symptoms are poor growth and narrow, strap-like leaves. Molybdenum might not actually be deficient in the soil; the condition can be brought on by the soil being too acid. Test the pH in the autumn before sowing and if it is below 6.5 add lime according to instructions on the packet to suit your soil. Use the cultivator to incorporate it well into the soil. **Boron deficiency** will cause young leaves to be distorted. Later, the heads will be small and brown patches can develop on them, by which time it is too late to remedy the situation. Making sure the pH is high enough and the use of seaweed meal incorporated well into the soil before sowing should enable both these problems to be avoided.

Harvest

It is a matter of judgement as to when the heads are ready. You want them to maximize their yield but they should be cut before they start to open out and become 'stalky'. Eventually they would turn into yellow flowers on long stems, typical of brassicas. The leaves immediately surrounding the cauliflower are also good to eat.

BRUSSELS SPROUTS (*Brassica oleracea,* Gemmifera group)

Site and soil

Brussels sprouts require essentially the same conditions as broccoli except that, if compost is to be incorporated before sowing, it is more important, with sprouts, that it is done as soon as it is practical in the year to give the soil time to settle and become firm. If your soil is light and friable (ideal for many other crops) it might be beneficial to allow children to walk (not stamp) on the soil before cultivating the surface to make a tilth just deep enough to sow the seeds.

When to sow

As for broccoli (see page 140).

Spacing

As for broccoli; aim for about four plants per square metre. Catch crops of lettuce, spring onions and radish may be grown in between during the summer.

Care

As for broccoli. Make sure not to exceed the recommendation of one litre per square metre (i.e. 0.25 l per plant) of urine when plants are 20 to 25cm high. Too much nitrogen can cause the sprouts to be open rather than the preferred tight buttons.

Pests and diseases

As for broccoli. When the lower leaves start to go yellow, break them off to allow good air flow around the plants. This will help to prevent fungal infections.

Harvest

Pick the lowest first and work upwards. Then you can eat the top, which is like a loose cabbage.

Recommended varieties

There are many to choose from but in a school garden you might as well grow an F1 hybrid. They can be more reliable than open pollinated types and it does not matter if all the plants mature at the same time.

CABBAGE (*Brassica oleracea,* Capitata group)

Cabbages require the same conditions as other leafy brassicas – high pH, good soil organic matter content, firm, moisture-retentive but well-draining soil and feeding with nitrogen when young. They are subject to the same pests and diseases as broccoli but watch out, in particular, for early signs of the cabbage moth caterpillar. These will bore into the middle of the developing heart where they are then difficult to get at. In the early stages the caterpillars can be found between outer leaves at the base of the plant.

LEGUMES

Legumes provide a wide choice of types to grow, from the easy and productive broad bean and the also productive climbing beans to the more time-consuming, less productive but sweet tasting fresh peas. All the legumes that can be grown in whatever climatic zone you are in are fairly straightforward to grow and present fewer pest and disease problems than brassicas. In temperate zones rhizobium bacteria will be present in the soil, enabling the plants to fix nitrogen from the atmosphere. The large seeds of legumes make them easy for children to sow and, of course, broad or runner beans are an old favourite for classroom germination to demonstrate seed development. Legumes occupy the third plot in a five plot rotation (see Figure 3.4 on page 47) or share the second (with brassicas) in a four plot plan (see Figure 3.6 on page 53).

BROAD BEANS (*Vicia faba*)

Broad beans are probably the easiest legume to grow and are likely to be affected by only one serious pest and no serious diseases. It is also likely that many children will never have eaten them. Picked at the right time, before the beans get too big and tough, they are delicious served with new potatoes, which should be ready at about the same time.

Site and soil

Broad beans grow better in a slightly heavier soil than other beans prefer but they are tolerant of a wide range of soils. For autumn-sown beans it is important that the soil will not become waterlogged. Some shelter from strong winds is also necessary. Autumn-sown beans can crop up to a month earlier than spring-sown ones and will normally produce a higher yield. However, it is only advisable to sow in autumn if winters are likely to be not too severe. Although the plants are hardy they will not survive very severe frost, prolonged periods of freezing wind or waterlogged soil. They will, however, survive quite well under a covering of snow, provided there was not a prolonged period of freezing and dehydrating wind before the snow.

If compost is available, dig some in before sowing, a couple of weeks before, if possible. If sowing is to be done in the spring, this is one crop for which, because of its early sowing date, incorporating compost in autumn could be recommended. Broad beans have a relatively high demand for potassium. Some wood or bonfire ash mixed in with the compost is a good source. Or, think ahead and incorporate extra ash in the compost that is to be used for beans. Potassium will help the plant resist chocolate spot infection. Do not use a urine liquid feed before sowing or at any stage during growth. A high nitrogen fertilizer will have no effect on yield.

When to sow

For autumn sowing you need to know your local climate; sow at such a time so that they grow no more than a few centimetres tall with two or three leaves and little length of stem showing before winter temperatures virtually cease further growth until the spring. If they are taller, depending on the climate, they are likely to suffer from cold winds or be flattened by snow. In lowland England or mild, maritime areas, early November is the usual time to meet these requirements. In colder areas an earlier sowing might be necessary.

The above recommendation is further complicated by folklore recommendations to sow beans and peas on or shortly after the full moon! I have not done sufficient trials to come to a conclusion one way or the other but there is one thing to be said in favour of folklore like this: if you follow it, the beans get planted, as opposed to not getting planted! If you need to sow later to avoid plants getting too big before the worst weather, can you afford to wait a whole month to the next full moon? One year I might have sown late, I cannot remember, but I do recall that the weather was very cold in December and early January and the beans did not come up until well into the new year but grew normally from then on. So, in autumn, it is probably better to err on the side of sowing late rather than too early.

Spring sowing really means late winter; in lowland England and mild, maritime areas, this will probably be in February. In colder areas it will be when snow has gone, the ground thawed and at the first signs of growth in nearby weeds

Spacing
Autumn-sown broad beans will 'tiller', which means that they will produce two, three or four stems. Therefore, they should be given more space than when sown in spring. Aim for a maximum of 16 plants/m^2. If the bed is a metre or 90cm wide, four rows are convenient, whether autumn or spring sowing. In autumn sow at 25 to 30cm along the row and in spring at 20cm

spacing along the row. Spring-sown beans are likely to produce only one stem. In the first year or two of a new garden there is likely to be a dense covering of annual weeds. If beans are sown in a grid pattern, i.e. in line across as well as along the bed, this will make it easier to hoe across as well as along the bed while the bean plants are small.

Care

Broad beans do not need feeding during their growth. Because of the wide and precise spacing of the plants it should be possible to hoe between them while the plants are only a few centimetres high. After that hand weeding is required.

Pests and diseases

Bean seed beetle (Acanthoscelides obtectus, and others)
Small, round holes in dried beans are the exit holes of the adult beetles. You should not find affected beans in bought seed. The grub eats part of the cotyledon rather than the embryo so the bean will probably grow but might produce a weak plant. So, it is better not to sow any affected seed. Eggs are laid in the pod as the beans are growing but the larvae are unnoticed if beans are eaten fresh. Small, pale, circular patches on the surface of the bean indicate the presence of the grub inside. If you store dried beans in paper bags, for the first two or three weeks adult beetles, which are about 4mm long, will be emerging from the beans and can be heard as they try to escape from the bags. Some will cut a hole in the bag to get out.

Black bean aphid (Aphis fabae)
Commonly known as blackfly, this pest normally begins to infest the growing tips when the plant has nearly reached its

final height and produced a few trusses of flowers, so that pinching the tops out below the lowest aphid completely stops the infestation at little cost to yield. However, in 1987 and at a different garden location in 1998, the infestation was very rapid, in far greater numbers than was usual and appeared not just at the growing tips of plants but on lower trusses of beans at the same time. Pinching out the tops would have been ineffective. In 1987 the infestation came earlier than usual too. In 2005 in another location the infestation was sporadic over a period of two or three weeks on only a few randomly distributed plants and on various parts of them. Pinching out affected parts was effective in stopping the pest, although some plants had to be 'pinched out' below the lowest truss of beans! The conclusion is that you need to be vigilant and inspect plants at least three times week in May and June, although in any one area, the danger period is not that long. Even if there is no black fly, when the plants have set four or five trusses of beans the tips can be pinched out anyway and used as a spinach-like vegetable. In most years the absence of the growing tip will prevent the fly from settling on plants.

Pea and bean weevil (Sitona lineatus)

This pest leaves characteristic U-shaped notches around the edges of leaves but this is not a serious problem unless it strikes early on very young plants, which I have never known it to do.

Chocolate spot (Botrytis fabae)

The name describes quite accurately the appearance of this fungal infection, the symptoms being brown circular patches on the upper surface of leaves. Plants are more susceptible to infection if they are short of potassium. Incorporating some wood or bonfire ash into the soil or using compost to which plenty of ash has been added, should help prevent infection. The development of the disease is also encouraged by damp conditions. Keep the ground free of weeds to allow good air flow between plants. If the plants seem to be crowded and have chocolate spot, try a wider spacing next time.

Harvest and storage

For eating fresh in summer, it is best to harvest before the part of the bean that is attached to the pod turns brown or black. Experience of the shape and feel of the pods will tell you when the beans are at the stage you prefer them.

To produce dried beans, for seed or winter stews, just leave the pods on the plants until they turn black and brittle. It is a good idea not to leave the lowest truss to dry but to eat them while green, as these pods can become damp and mouldy and attacked by slugs and snails in a wet season. To collect beans for next year's seed pick only healthy-looking pods from healthy-looking plants. I tend to choose the longest and straightest pods and no more than one pod from any one plant. Take the beans out of the pods, discarding any with exit holes of the bean seed beetle, and store in paper bags to allow for any further drying.

The dried pods can be composted. The stems can be pulled up, broken or folded into two or three and also put into a compost container. A pair of thick gloves is advisable for this task. It will be difficult to get much in the bin – you will need to stand inside it and tread down the contents. Use the bean stalks to start a new heap, so that you will not be compacting ordinary compost underneath. I once completely filled a container with bean stalks, compacted as much as possible. A few months later

I lifted the bin off, revealing what looked like a giant, high fibre pudding. They had not rotted but left exposed to wind and rain began to break down and were gradually fed into another compost heap. Alternatively, bean stalks can be fed into the compost a few at a time. Coarse material is useful to layer in with soft stuff, as it creates air spaces within the heap.

If the bean plants need to be cleared away before the beans are dry – to sow a late catch crop or winter salads – the whole plants may be pulled up and stuffed into a hedge or hung on a temporary 'washing line' to continue drying.

Recommended varieties

▶ For sowing in autumn or spring: Aquadulce Claudia, Super Aquadulce, Imperial Green Longpod, Witkiem Manita.

▶ Spring-only sowing: Green Windsor.

▶ Dwarf varieties: The Sutton (30cm), Bonny Lad (40cm). Dwarf varieties are multi-stemmed and need more space per plant. In a metre or 90cm wide bed three rows would be appropriate, with just nine plants per square metre.

FRENCH AND HARICOT BEANS (*Phaseolus vulgaris*)

There are dwarf, or bush, varieties as well as climbers. I have not done trials to compare yields but climbers will probably produce more than dwarfs, assuming optimum spacing for both. Some varieties of dwarf and climbing beans have been bred for drying. These tend to have larger seeds and are contained in pods which dry readily, maintaining their shape and which are easily snapped open to release the beans; whereas some other varieties shrink tightly around the beans, making it difficult to get them out. Beans grown for drying can be eaten whole, while the pods are still soft, or left a little longer until the beans in the pods are fully grown but before they begin to dry, when just the beans are eaten. At that stage they are known as flageolets.

French bean flowers are pollinated before they open, which means that it is very unlikely, though not impossible, for different varieties grown in the same garden to cross pollinate. Therefore, saved seed should come true to type.

Site and soil

An open, sunny but sheltered site is ideal for French beans. They respond to a somewhat richer soil than is required by broad beans. A few weeks before sowing, dig in some well-rotted compost over the whole bed. A pH range of 6–7 is suitable.

When to sow

Phaseolus beans are not hardy. When sowing directly in the ground, therefore, it is important to time this so that they will come up after the last likely spring frost. This is always difficult to predict, of course, but sowing just after a May full moon will probably be safe. If you are in an area where it would not be safe at that time, then perhaps the area is not suitable for this crop. However, I have obtained reasonable yields from a late June sowing in a year when there was a plague of slugs that, despite my best endeavours, devoured two previous sowings! A trial carried out by the Henry Doubleday Research Association (HDRA) obtained good yields from the variety 'Safari' sown on the 4th of July in south east England (HDRA, 2001). It is very important to do any cultivating and bed preparation at least ten days before sowing, to avoid the depredation of the bean seed fly (see 'Pests and diseases' below).

Spacing and sowing

In a metre or 90cm wide bed four rows can be fitted in. Aim
for about 30 plants per square metre, which means a spacing
along the row of around 12cm. However, if you are growing a
variety for dried haricot beans I would recommend a spacing of
15–20cm within the row. This is a good crop to experiment
with using different spacings and comparing yields. Because of
the wide spacing it is practical to sow individually, making a
hole for each bean with a trowel. Using this method causes less
soil disturbance than would occur if drills were made, thus
minimizing the risk of attracting the bean seed fly (see 'Pests
and diseases'). Patting the soil down gently with the trowel
after sowing each bean leaves a slight depression, so that you
can see where each has been planted. This enables you to
position them in whichever pattern you want, whether opposite
each other or staggered. Sow at 4–8cm depth, depending on
soil texture and moisture: the heavier or more moist the soil,
the shallower the beans should be sown.

Care

The roots of dwarf beans are not very substantial and in strong
winds plants will work loose. If such conditions occur and
there is insufficient shelter, draw soil up around the plants and
firm it down. Apart from that, weeding is all that needs doing.
Once the leaves have covered the area of the bed there will be
no more germination of weeds. There will always be a few
weeds that manage to emerge just before the bean leaf canopy
closes but they will probably remain very thin and retarded and
not flower, unless they manage to grow above the bean foliage.
Only perennial weeds with good root resources are likely to do
this.

Pests and diseases

French beans can be affected by many pests and diseases but I have rarely encountered serious problems with any of them. In some years there can be unusually high populations of slugs, snails, bean seed flies or aphids. In some years none of these will be a problem. I have never seen a serious infestation of any disease. Maintaining good soil structure and drainage, building up organic matter and maintaining good fertility with compost, urine and trace elements, will provide favourable conditions for plants to resist infection. However, there is one pest that is probably the most common cause of crop failure – the bean seed fly – but the problem is easily avoided (see below).

Slugs

These can be a serious problem in some years and in some gardens. Most common are the small pale grey field slugs (*Derocerus reticulatus*) but small brown and small black ones might also be found. They come out of the soil at night to feed but there is a time lag in their movements. So, you will have to wait until it is dark before finding them in the evening, but in the morning they can be caught out just after dawn. For the non-squeamish a sharp knife is quick and effective. Do not cut them in half, as the front portion remains alive and possibly in pain. Cut nearer the front. If you prefer non-lethal methods of control they can be picked off and taken elsewhere. Wear gloves as the slime cannot be washed off the skin but can be abraded off using sand or soil. Slugs can be attracted to particular spots using large leaves, pieces of slate or flat stones left on the soil surface. Each morning lift them up and remove any slugs. Rhubarb or brassica leaves are good for this purpose.

Snails

As with slugs, these can be a problem in some years or in some gardens. Their habits are much the same as those of slugs. Snails seem to have a particular affinity for plastic. I find many under thick black plastic, used to cover the final stage of composting. Snails are easier to handle. So, removal is my preferred method of control. In summer large numbers of very small ones might be found turning foliage into 'lace'. These can be lifted off with the point of a trowel and crushed on the ground. If there are any thrushes in the area put adult snails where they are likely to be found and eaten. If there is no 'anvil' nearby, provide a stone or brick for the convenience of the birds. However, in many areas the presence of free-ranging cats means that thrushes are rare or absent.

Black bean aphid (Aphis fabae)

I have never known this to be a serious problem on French beans. If I do find them on the underside of leaves I just ignore them. Healthy plants should not be unduly affected by the low populations usually found. The aphid overwinters on *Euonymus* (spindle) bushes.

Bean seed fly (Delia platura)

This can be a serious pest, destroying 90% of seedlings. The adult flies are inconspicuous, like small house flies. They may be seen flying very close to the ground when you are digging or cultivating the soil. They are attracted to freshly disturbed soil, compost and manure. The larvae feed on organic matter as well as on seed and seedlings of peas, beans and onions. To avoid problems, do any cultivating and incorporation of compost at least ten days before sowing. This is known as sowing into a 'stale bed'. Sow with a trowel, with minimal soil disturbance, rather than make drills. By the time the beans start to germinate, which is the stage when they are most vulnerable, if there are any fly larvae present, from eggs laid when cultivation was done, they will have developed beyond the stage when they would attack the seed or seedlings (Wheatley, 1979). If beans fail to come up, it is always worth digging around with a trowel to try to find out why. Typical symptoms are beans partially eaten inside (before or after germination) or tunnelling in the stems.

Birds and mice

In my experience, these are not a problem with French beans. Whereas broad beans and early-sown peas can be eaten by these larger pests, by the time the non-hardy French beans are sown, birds and mice are, presumably, well supplied by other foods. Birds – jackdaws and pheasants, for example – will be interested in higher protein foods, such as insects, to feed their young.

Root aphid (Smynthurodes betae)

The symptoms are poor growth in plants, which wilt in warm weather, even when the soil is moist. I have never knowingly had root aphids on a crop. Crop rotation helps to avoid the problem. It is difficult to control organically if it does occur.

Anthracnose

This fungal infection and **halo blight**, caused by a bacterium, are both carried on the seed. Do not soak seeds before sowing, as that can spread the pathogens to all if one is infected. Both are rare, in my experience. The symptoms of anthracnose are brown, sunken patches on the pods. Halo blight is so-called because brown patches on the leaves are surrounded by a yellow margin or 'halo'. Pull up infected plants and burn.

Foot and root rot

Various fungal infections can cause the base of the stem to darken, soften and gradually die off. Leaves also dry up and die. Pull up and burn infected plants.

Harvest and storage

Where a crop of green beans is required, start picking as soon as some are large enough. Continue picking as often as necessary to prevent any pods getting too mature and tough. This will encourage continued flowering. It is important to stress to children to hold the stem of the bean with one hand while pulling at the pod, so as not to loosen or uproot the plant, which is easily done. One-handed picking is possible; with a strong thumbnail the pod can be snapped at the very top.

Beans grown for drying, known as haricots, require a little more care and attention if they are dwarf varieties. In northern and western Europe it is unlikely that all the pods will fully dry before autumn rain and general dampness causes mould to develop. The pods will also become soiled by rain splash. Plants should be left in the ground for as long as the weather is reasonably dry. If there is space under cover – a greenhouse or well-ventilated room – at the first sign of sustained wet weather, the whole plants may be brought in and spread out and then the pods picked off later. If space is unavailable inside, the first frost needs to be anticipated by a couple of weeks, which is not an easy task in our climate. A frost will spoil any beans that are not dry. The plants are easily pulled up and can then be tied in bunches of five or six and hung from the branch of a tree or along a south-facing fence until all the pods and contents are dry.

Climbing beans grown for drying are easier as they can simply be left on the plants until dry. If a frost is forecast any pods not yet dried can be picked and spread out indoors. French beans are not attacked by bean seed beetle. So, when the dried beans are taken out of the pods you will not find any with an exit hole.

Recommended varieties

There are many varieties of dwarf and climbing French beans for eating when young. Choose one that you think will suit your conditions and taste. For a given area of ground, climbing beans will produce a higher yield than dwarf beans.

- ▶ 'Blue Lake' is a climber and a good, reliable variety. If, accidentally or deliberately, allowed to ripen, the white dried beans are easily shelled out and are good for winter use. Soak for twenty four hours before cooking.

- ▶ 'Brown Dutch' is a dwarf variety grown for drying. They have an attractive amber colour that makes them look like baked beans. The flavour is excellent – they need nothing added to flavour them. They were regarded as a little difficult to ripen in the British climate and, perhaps one year in three they would be but with global warming they should be easier over a larger part of Europe. 'Horsehead' is supposed to be better adapted to a cooler climate but perhaps the flavour is not quite as good as Brown Dutch.

- ▶ 'Pea Bean' is a climbing variety. The best thing about this variety is its attractive seeds – each bean is half deep red and half white, but the yield is poor and the pods might contain only two or three beans. Even when pressure cooked they are not as tender as other varieties.

▶ 'Barlotta Lingua di Fuoco' (tongues of fire) lives up to its
spectacular name. In the course of ripening the pods go
through a stage of having bright red streaks which later turn
maroon. It is quite productive and the pods can have six or
seven attractive speckled beans in them. When fully dry the
pods are easy to snap open and, after soaking, the beans are
tender enough just boiled and do not need to be pressure
cooked.

There are many varieties of climbing bean grown for drying
from many countries – the US, Canada, eastern Europe – and
with some strange and interesting names that speak of their
history. Try different ones each year. *Phaseolus vulgaris* are
self-fertile and do not cross pollinate. So, it is possible to grow
more than one variety in the same year and save the seed.
However, not all types are suitable for drying, except to collect
a few seeds. With some varieties, as the pods dry they shrink
tight around the beans, which are then difficult to get out.

RUNNER BEAN (*Phaseolus coccineus*)

Runner beans are really perennials but in areas where frosts are
frequent in winter they are grown as annuals.

Site and soil
Runner beans will crop best in a sheltered position in deep,
fertile soil containing plenty of organic matter. They originate
from Mexico and thrive at altitudes of 1,800–2,500m (5,500–
7,600ft) where frequent heavy rain in July, August and
September follows a hot, dry growing period. In Europe this
means that watering might be necessary from the start of
flowering in order to get the best results. In a site with a high
water table and good soil, good yields can be produced without

watering. Some shelter from high winds is advised, partly so that pollinating bees will not be deterred and also to avoid plants and their supports being blown over.

If the topsoil is already more than 30cm deep and high in organic matter, characterized by a dark brown colour and dark staining on the fingers when soil is rubbed between them, then normal cultivation, if necessary, and seedbed preparation is all that will be needed. Traditionally, a 30 × 30cm trench is dug and filled with kitchen scraps during winter, then filled in and allowed to settle for a few weeks before sowing. Some sources also advocate putting thick cardboard and newspaper in the trench and watering them before backfilling. The theory is that these materials will hold moisture that will then be available to the plant roots. The volume of this material is not great compared to the volume of soil the roots will occupy, and the volume of water the materials can hold will be low compared to even the daily requirement of the bean plants. Cardboard and newspaper have a high carbon to nitrogen ratio. If the material were soaked in urine it would be better but I would imagine it would still leave a compacted layer of not entirely natural material that will constitute a temporary barrier to root penetration. I wonder if anyone who advocates this practice has ever reopened different parts of a trench at monthly intervals throughout summer and autumn to observe the conditions. Digging in or putting into a 20cm deep trench some well-rotted compost would, I suggest, be better than unrotted kitchen scraps or paper and cardboard.

In a bed, if trenches are to be dug, there need to be two, occupying each half of the width of the bed, to allow a good spread for the roots to grow into. As well as spreading the compost horizontally it is a good idea to try to ensure that it is spread vertically, after all, roots naturally occupy a range of soil depth. So, dig each trench 15–20cm deep and nearly half the width of the bed, put in some compost and, with a fork, mix it in with the soil below or turn it in with a spade. Backfill most of the soil and incorporate some more compost before backfilling the rest of the soil. This should be done at least two weeks before sowing beans, to avoid the problem of the bean seed fly (see 'Pests and diseases' below). If the compost is not well rotted, application should be several weeks before sowing.

When to sow

Runner beans are not at all frost hardy. So, there is no point raising plants early and then having to go to great lengths to protect them or having to keep plants under cover getting pot-bound. In a school garden you might decide that it is preferable they only start cropping when the autumn term begins. In England, with terms beginning in early September, a June sowing would be appropriate. Otherwise, a May sowing would be recommended. In very mild areas an April sowing might be safe. A few days after the full moon is as good a time as any or perhaps better (see Kollerstrom's annual publication).

Spacing and planting

The ideal way of growing runner beans is to provide hazel sticks, 2–3cm in diameter. Old coppices in woods provide the best rods, as the taller trees draw up the hazel growth straighter than if grown in the open. Ash is good too. Bamboo canes will be the only option for many urban gardeners and they are fine, if rather smooth and slippery when new. Hazel sticks will last for no more than two years. After that they are too brittle and weak, although a thick one might be strong enough for three years. Do not leave any sort of sticks in the ground any longer than necessary. They should be stored under cover when not in use.

For a primary school garden the sticks need to be about two metres tall after being pushed into the ground as far as they will go, and at least 2.5m for older children and adults. Ideally there would be one stick per plant, but two plants per stick will result in little loss of yield. In a metre-wide, and wider, bed put in two rows of sticks, about 25cm in from each side of the bed. The sticks should be 40cm apart along the row. In a 3m long bed, for example, there would be 14 sticks, with 30cm to spare at each end of the bed. I normally put the sticks in after the plants have emerged but, to reduce the risk of damaging the plants, with children I would recommend putting the sticks in before sowing.

To prepare the sticks you will need a short log of hard wood, to use as a chopping block, and a sharp hand-axe. Ten year olds should be quite capable of doing this job, once they have been given clear instructions on technique and safety. Eye protection can be worn, although it really is not necessary. It is always good practice to blink for half a second when chopping anything but in 30 years of pointing bean poles I cannot recall ever having a problem of anything flying up into my face. What is important is to keep the hand that is holding the stick well away from the end that is being cut. Make a point at the top end as well, to deter birds from perching and messing over the plants. Think ahead to a cold, windy, autumn day when the sticks have to be taken out and the bean haulms taken off. The stems can be cut near the ground – no need to pull the roots out – the sticks pulled up and the haulms pushed off at the thin/

top end. It can be annoying if they keep snagging on the stumps of twigs. So, chop these off to make the poles smooth. This can be done with the pole resting on the chopping block, turning it upside down to trim the top half. Do the trimming before making the points, otherwise they will get blunted.

Traditionally, bean sticks are put in at an angle so that the two rows cross and are tied there to a horizontal pole. This causes much crowding of the plants as they meet where the sticks cross. I have always put the sticks in vertically, treating each row separately. I have not done trials to compare yields using the two methods but it seems to make sense to give the plants as much air space as possible above the bed. When erecting the poles they can be pushed in further if hands are damp, giving a better grip. A few soft leaves or some grass rubbed between hands is one way to dampen them. A horizontal pole is tied (lashed) to each upright one along each row (see Appendix III). This pulls the row of poles into a straight line and gives it stability. Avoid using plastic covered wire to tie the sticks. This is fiddly to take off when dismantling in autumn. Natural fibre twine is strong enough and can quickly be cut and loosened.

A row of tied-in bean poles can be used to demonstrate wave motion, although it might be difficult to see this in the short rows of a school garden. Hold one end of the horizontal and give it a single and rapid sideways movement and watch the sideways wave travel down the row of sticks.

An alternative arrangement, if few sticks are available, is to tie two strings between wider-spaced sticks, one string close to the ground and the other connecting the tops, then to tie in vertical strings between the two. There can then be one plant per stick or string. However, this involves much work and string. Also, the plants that are on strings can be blown about in strong wind and might crash into the plants on the poles. Two plants per pole is a reasonable compromise.

With two rows of poles 40cm apart along the row and two plants per pole a density of 9.33 plants per m^2 is achieved. This is close to the optimum of 10.7 per m^2 recommended from trials at Wellesbourne (Bleasdale, 1979) although, really, in calculating the plant density, the area of one adjacent path should be added to that of the bed. Assuming a path width of 50cm, that would add on half the area of the bed, bringing the density down to just over 6 plants per m^2. In theory, therefore, the number of plants could be increased to 14 per m^2 of bed, which would mean having three per pole, or preferably, two and one in between on string. Three per pole would make them too crowded and probably not give a proportional increase in yield. The more even the planting pattern is, the higher the yield. The same, presumably, applies to above-ground spacing as well, to allow maximum light-gathering in the leaves.

Direct sowing usually results in an acceptable germination rate, provided there is a gap of at least ten days between any cultivation or compost application and sowing. The statutory minimum germination rate for runner beans is 80%. If there is enough seed, sow some spare beans between the rows to transplant to any gaps later. Sow by making a 5cm deep hole with a trowel, minimizing soil disturbance so as not to attract the bean seed fly.

Which way up the bean is planted probably makes no difference to growth but children might like to think they are helping it by planting the right way up. To find out which is the 'right way up', soak a few beans for 24 hours and then carefully prize apart the two cotyledons. Before doing that, notice at which end of the central scar (where the bean was attached to the pod) are two tiny bumps. When the bean is split into the two halves, on one will be seen a tiny root pointing 'down' and above it a nascent pair of leaves, also pointing down, but which will straighten up when they emerge from the soil.

Care
When the beans have come up, hand weeding can begin. The bean foliage will soon cover most of the bed, suppressing any further weed growth, except along the edges of the bed.

The plants might need some encouragement to start climbing the right pole or string. Some plants seem determined to go for one half a metre away, or more. Sometimes it is better to let it have its way but try to find another nearby plant to take its place, to maintain the same number of plants per pole. If the site is exposed to strong winds it might be necessary to help young plants to start climbing by tying them to the poles until they are firmly attached. Use wool or soft string. Tie the wool/string tightly to the pole first and then tie in the bean stem so that it is just touching the pole but not bound tight.

When the plants begin to flower, unless you are confident the soil contains plenty of moisture, watering will be necessary to ensure good 'setting' of the flowers. There is an old idea that poor pod-setting is due to dry air around the flowers and that spraying the flowers with water twice a day will help. This is not the case and spraying with water can actually reduce pod-setting (Pollock, 2002; Salter, 1979). Lack of moisture in the soil is usually the cause of flowers failing to develop pods. Sometimes birds can be responsible for removing runner bean flowers. If this is happening, it provides scope for children to make all manner of bird-scaring devices – windmills and shiny or flappy things.

In 2009 I spent a few minutes on most days during the flowering period observing bees on the runner beans. All the honey bees and large bumble bees that I saw did not enter the front of the flower but, instead, pierced the side of the flower at the base to extract the nectar. This does not pollinate the flower. One small type of bumble bee did enter the front of the flower. I am no expert in bee identification but it could have been *Bombus pascuorum.* Once or twice I also saw what might have been *B. sylvarum.* I did not record the numbers of flowers that grew into beans but guessed that the 'setting' rate was only about 10%. Half the row was watered on two or three occasions but this made no noticeable difference. Perhaps the volume and frequency were insufficient.

When the leading shoots reach the top of the poles, pinch them out. There is no point having stems waving about in the wind, unless you want to take it over to the next pole because the plants there have not grown well.

Pests and diseases
As for French and haricot beans (see page 163). The black bean aphid (*Aphis fabae*) is common on runner beans but I have never known them to be a serious pest. Whether runner beans have a better chemical defence mechanism than broad beans or whether there are more predators about at the time of year, I do not know. I have never done anything to try to control this pest. It does not seem unduly to affect the plants.

Harvest and storage

Start picking as soon as any pods are big enough. If beans are allowed to develop in the pods this decreases further flower production. If you find a large pod that has previously been missed, it should be picked. The beans can be taken out and cooked along with younger pods. Although modern varieties have been bred to be stringless, runner beans are more tender and have a nicer flavour if eaten young. Frequent picking, every day if necessary, will ensure a continuing crop of tasty beans.

If you wish to save your own seed, wait until half way through the cropping season before selecting a few pods to allow to mature. This will have some effect on green bean production but waiting any later will not give the beans time to develop fully. They are unlikely to ripen and dry on the plant. At the first threat of a frost they must be brought inside and left in a well-ventilated place. As long as the pods are not going mouldy the beans may be left in them. Runner beans in the pods take much longer to dry out than broad beans, peas and haricot beans. Taken out of the pods and spread on trays they dry in a matter of days. If soaked for 24 hours before cooking, runner beans are tender and tasty.

PEAS (*Pisum sativum*)

Peas eaten from the pod at just the right time of maximum sweetness are relished by children. They are not the highest yielding crop in terms of the space they occupy or the effort required to grow them but are a 'must' in a child's garden. A mangetout 'sugar snap' variety will provide more food per square metre and are just as tasty, raw or cooked.

Site and soil

An open, sunny position in a well-drained soil with good structure and containing plenty of organic matter is ideal. Peas will tolerate quite a wide range of pH but near to neutral (for soil this is 6.5) is ideal. Dig in well-rotted compost in early spring, or at least two weeks before sowing and, using the back of a fork, leave the surface loose and level. The compost only needs to be applied along the middle third of the bed, although if there is plenty, it can go in over the whole bed and benefit the catch crops that can be grown alongside the peas. Carrots will do well alongside peas and are likely to escape the attention of carrot root fly. However, if they are to be grown the compost must be well rotted and dug in as early as possible before sowing, to avoid the carrots growing in a forked or multiple-rooted way.

When to sow

In most of Britain, by sowing early, late February, or late, in May, an infestation of pea moth will probably be avoided. The moth is most active in July. Round-seeded varieties of pea are hardy but wrinkled-seeded ones are sweeter. Wrinkled-seeded varieties are prone to rot in cold soil. So, if you want sweet, tasty peas and to avoid pea moth, a May sowing is recommended. In Britain this means that they will crop during the school summer holidays – an extra incentive for holiday weeders to come in and reap their reward. Look at the maturing times in seed catalogues or on packets and work out when to sow for when you want to reap.

Spacing and sowing

Many books describe and illustrate how to take out a wide, shallow trench and then space out the peas within this. This method can be a little difficult and also causes considerable soil disturbance which will, if they are around, attract the bean seed fly. Two other methods can be recommended. One is to make four or five drills, 8–10cm apart and 4–6cm deep. The peas are then dropped into the drills about 6cm apart. The other method, suitable for schools given there are plenty of willing hands, would be for the peas to be placed on the surface at the above-mentioned spacing and then pushed into the soil to the depth of a child's forefinger. This will only work if the soil is loose, friable and moist.

Along each edge of the bed a row of carrots or spring onions may be sown and then, about 10cm inside of those, a row of radishes. An early maturing carrot is recommended for this use: 'Amsterdam forcing', 'Nantes 2', 'Napoli F1' or 'Sugarsnax' are all suitable.

Care
When the seedlings have emerged, it is time to put in the supports. Dwarf varieties can be grown without support but it is advisable to have some sticks in case of unusually heavy rain or strong winds which can leave the plants flattened to the ground and the pea pods splashed with soil and liable to get eaten by slugs. The ends of hazel branches are the best natural material for pea supports but plastic pea netting or wire netting can be used. Plastic netting needs to be well supported by posts and tight strings, otherwise it will sag and blow about and damage the plants. Hazel sticks are sufficiently bushy and rigid. For dwarf peas there only needs to be 20–30cm sticking out of the ground. Put a row of sticks in alongside the multi row of peas and also some between the rows, being careful not to get too close to the plants. For taller varieties do exactly the same

and then put in taller sticks along each side and some in the middle as well. The seed packet should state how tall the variety will grow. Make sure the sticks are a little taller, as you might be surprised how well the crop grows.

The large sticks will need to be sharpened to make them easier to push in deep enough to be firm. The quickest method is to use a sharp axe on a chopping block. Make sure the hand holding the stick is well away from the trajectory of the axe; obvious advice but I once chopped the back of my left hand while pointing pea sticks.

Weeding must be scrupulous, for when the peas are fully grown it is very difficult to find and pull out weeds from amongst them but pea foliage is not dense enough to prevent weeds from flowering and seeding.

Watering
If the soil is dry when peas are in flower they can fail to develop pods. In very dry weather, water the crop throughout the flowering period. Apply 8–10 litres per metre of the multi row twice a week. This might seem a lot but in hot, dry conditions it is essential for the water to reach the level of the roots and not evaporate before doing this. As always, some judgement is required to assess how much water is needed. Although it might disturb a patch of any catch crops being grown alongside the peas, it would be interesting to dig a hole close to (a few centimetres from) the peas to look at the soil profile and see how moist it is at different depths. Then, the day after watering, dig another hole in a different place to see how far down the water penetrated.

Pests and diseases

Seed beetle

Small round holes in the seed indicate it has been host to a grub of the seed beetle. It is unlikely that affected peas will be found in seed bought from a good supplier but do not sow any that do have holes, as they will either fail to grow or produce weak plants.

Mice

In some gardens mice might dig down and eat peas even before the shoots emerge from the soil, although this is only likely to be a problem with early-sown peas. If the peas are sown in late spring, as recommended above, then the mice are likely to be able to find other sources of food. They can clear a whole bed of peas overnight but, short of that, at the first sign of damage, traps will need to be laid. Whether fatal or humane box traps are used they should be checked twice a day. A soaked pea is appropriate bait. It might need to be tied with cotton to a fatal trap to prevent it being taken without the trap being sprung.

Bean seed fly

Sow into a stale bed to prevent infestation by this pest. (See the section on stale beds on p.112, and p.163 for pests and diseases of French and haricot beans.)

Pea and bean weevils (Sitona lineatus)

These pests make characteristic U-shaped notches around the edges of leaves. They are only a serious pest if they attack very young plants, which I have never known happen.

Foot and root rot

The bases of the stems turn black or brown and start to rot;

leaves turn yellow and shrivel. Various fungal species can be the cause. Pull up and burn any affected plants. The problem tends to occur where the soil is cold and wet. So, May-sown peas are unlikely to be affected.

Pea thrips (Kakothrips pisivorus)
Adults may be around at any time from May to September, depending on local climate. They are small, black insects, 2mm long. The nymphs (not larvae, there is no pupal stage) are a similar shape and size but wingless and yellow. The symptoms of an infestation are distorted pods and leaves with silvery patches which later turn brown. Pea thrips thrive in hot, dry weather.

Pyrethrum insecticides may be used. Although its toxicity is low to mammals, the pea pods should not be consumed if they have been treated. Pyrethrum insecticides are highly toxic to aquatic life. I have never found pea thrips to be a serious problem. The fact that they thrive in hot, dry weather could indicate that spraying plants with water at such times might reduce the problem, although I have not tried this myself. While I do not recommend annual digging, having a *totally* undisturbed soil surface, especially if covered with mulch, provides ideal conditions for thrips to hibernate over winter, ready to infest crops the following year. I recommend, as standard practice after a crop is finished with, removing the remains for composting, hoeing any weeds, then cultivating with the cultivator or a rake the top few centimetres of soil. If there has been an infestation of any over-wintering insects, leave the soil for a few days before sowing another crop. This gives birds a chance to find them.

Another possible strategy, if thrips are a serious annual problem, might be to try companion planting. *Chrysanthemum cinerariaefolium, C. coccineum* and *C. marschalli* are sources of pyrethrum. Growing these flowers next to peas can have some deterrent effect but, again, I have not tried this.

Pea moth (Cydia nigicana)

This moth produces the well known 'maggots' (caterpillars) found eating the peas inside the pods. Peas sown late, in May to early June, may escape infestation. After feeding on peas the caterpillars drop to the ground and hibernate in white cocoons over winter. If an infestation has occurred, as soon as the peas are harvested pull up the plants and cultivate the soil to a depth of 10cm each day for a few days to give the birds a chance to feed on the cocoons.

Powdery mildew

This can be caused by infestation by any of a number of fungal species. White powdery patches appear first on the upper surface of leaves and can then spread to the underside and other parts of the plant. The problem is worst in dry seasons and in sheltered gardens where the air around the plants might be moist. Pull off and burn any affected leaves as soon as the problem is noticed. If plants are being adequately watered during flowering and pod set, the problem is unlikely to occur, provided the water is applied to the ground and not over the plant. After harvest, pull up and burn any affected plants.

Harvest

It is important to explain to children that both hands should be used when picking peas: one to hold the stem near the top of the pod and the other to pull the pod, otherwise the plant can be pulled away from the sticks or even uprooted. Experience will soon tell you at what stage peas are at their best. Frequent picking encourages further flower formation.

POTATOES (*Solanum tuberosum*)

Potatoes are divided into three categories according to the time they take to mature: earlies (often referred to as new potatoes), second earlies and maincrop. If the garden is not big enough to grow all three types, earlies allow more flexibility. They may be planted late, after spring bassicas are finished, every second year, in the Figure 3.6 type rotation and, if planted early there is time to grow a catch crop after they have been harvested.

Site and soil

An open, sunny site with good air flow and a deep, friable soil containing plenty of organic matter will give the best results. A pH between 5 and 6.4 is suitable but if your soil is naturally more alkaline it is not a big problem. Common scab tends to develop in alkaline soil but it only affects the skin; eating quality is not affected.

When to plant

Potatoes are half hardy. The slightest frost will kill any exposed foliage but the plant will shoot up again. 'Seed' potatoes are, of course, not seeds but ordinary tubers grown by specialist growers in areas and in conditions where pests and diseases are minimal. Seed potatoes should be bought as early in the year as possible to ensure the varieties you want are still in stock and also so that the shoots on the tubers will still be small and tight and, therefore, undamaged. As soon as possible they should be spread out to 'chit', which means allowed to sprout. For this they need to be indoors but where there is good natural light, some ventilation and where there is no risk of their being frozen. Shallow boxes used to transport fruit and vegetables, obtainable from a greengrocer, are ideal for chitting potatoes in, or, if there is room, egg boxes or trays. Place them with the 'eyes' or shoots upwards. Most of the eyes are at the opposite end to the little stump where the tuber was attached to the plant. In conditions of good light the shoots will grow very short and strong, with a few small, tight leaves. If the lighting is poor the shoots will grow long and thin, looking for light, and liable to be damaged in the planting process.

Potatoes need to be planted much deeper than seeds. So, there is no point planting them when the soil will still be too cold for growth at the planting depth, about 15cm depending on how deep the top soil is. The soil temperature should be at least 10°C and rising. It can take three or four weeks for the shoots to emerge from the soil, depending on temperature and planting depth. If you know when the last spring frost is likely to be (impossible to predict, of course!) you can work back from that when to plant. However, there is no need to be quite so cautious; it is always worth taking a chance to get the crop off to an early start, provided the soil temperature is high enough. It is not difficult to protect a bed of young shoots if a frost is forecast. Horticultural fleece or a couple of layers of newspaper kept in place with sticks or stones will be enough to protect them. Spring frosts occur on calm nights, so these sorts of coverings are not likely to be blown away.

In England, Good Friday is the traditional time to plant potatoes, but that is probably because it was the only day off that agricultural workers got at the time of year that was about right for planting them. In cooler regions, where spring is later, planting in May will still leave plenty of time for the crop to grow, especially in more northern latitudes because of the long summer days. If cloches are available to go over the rows, the plants will grow very well under them until the risk of frost is over. There is no need to plant early varieties days or weeks before maincrop. Earlies, second earlies and maincrop can all be planted around the same time. Indeed, some people say, 'plant your earlies late and your lates early!'

Spacing and planting

Ideally, to produce the maximum yield, potatoes would be grown in equidistant rows over the plot at the optimum spacing for each variety. This would necessitate digging up the paths between beds – hard work and time-consuming. Growing two rows per bed is a compromise worth making. To compensate for the loss of growing area on the paths, tubers can be planted a little closer along the rows than normally recommended. Although unlikely to occur with early varieties, the leaf growth on adjacent beds should touch across the path, so that as far as utilizing available light energy is concerned, the whole of the plot area will be used. Three rows of earlies can be grown in adult-sized beds of 1.2m width.

In a new garden where the soil has just been dug and cultivated and if there is no compost yet made, there is no point digging a trench to plant potatoes. Tubers can be planted by digging a hole with a trowel for each one. Thereafter, digging a trench is recommended.

Even with the bed system, where the beds are never trodden on, the soil can become more compacted than is ideal for potatoes. Digging a trench serves three purposes:

1   It enables compost to be incorporated in what will become the root zone.

2   It allows the tubers to be planted at the right depth.

3   Digging and backfilling, effectively, cultivates and loosens the soil.

Method for digging potato trenches

The soil needs to be at or just a little below field capacity. If it is dry, apply sufficient water one or two days before, using a can with a rose. Put a garden line lengthwise down the middle of the bed and another along the edge where you are standing. With the concave, upper face of a sharp spade facing you, make a cut 5–10cm on your side of the string in the middle. Try to make the cut at an angle, with the spade handle leaning away from you. This has to be done by thrusting at arms' length, as the feet cannot reach to push the spade in as with digging. The cut will form the far side of a V-shaped trench (Figure 7.4 (I)). The string in the middle of the trench can then

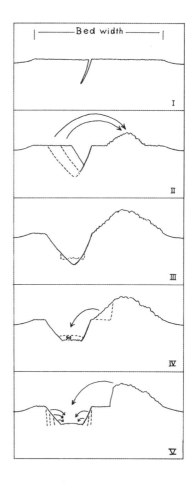

Fig. 7.4. How to dig a potato trench.

be taken out. With the spade held in the normal way, cut the other side of the 'V', lift the soil out and throw it forward (Figure 7.4 (II)). This process should be done in two or three stages, according to the state of the soil and your strength. So, the first cut might be only 10–15cm from the initial cut of the far side of the trench. Work back to about 10cm from the string at the edge of the bed. The purpose of the first cut to define the far side of the trench becomes apparent when digging out the soil, making it easier. Without the cut, if the soil is compacted an unnecessarily large volume of soil will be pushed up by the spade and if the soil is loose it will keep slipping back into the trench until an 'at rest' angle is reached. With the pre-cut far side of the trench one lifts out only as much soil as is necessary, and the far side of the trench does not keep slipping down. If the top soil is very shallow, stop digging any deeper as soon as the soil colour starts to change, otherwise a spade depth (25cm) will be about right.

For the next stage a long-handled, thin-pronged muck fork is ideal but an ordinary digging fork will do. Move the prongs each way along the base of the trench, taking in some of the soil from the sides so that you end up with a base of loose, level soil 10–15cm wide (Figure 7.4 (III)). Well-rotted compost can then be spread in the trench and worked in with the fork by moving it each way along the trench, as before. The potatoes are then planted on to the bed of loose soil mixed with compost (Figure 7.4 (IV)).

Spacing
The effect of spacing on crop yield is maximized by plants being equidistant at the optimum density. This is easily achieved with onion sets and large seeded crops such as beans. Potato tubers

naturally produce several shoots, each growing into what amounts to an individual plant. Ideally, allowing just one shoot per tuber and planting at the optimum spacing would produce the maximum yield per square metre. Since most potatoes produce several shoots it would be rather wasteful and expensive only to allow one shoot per tuber. However, early potatoes need to have a higher ratio of tuber volume to shoot number than maincrop because they need good reserves of nutrients to promote early growth and to be able to re-grow if the first shoots to emerge are killed by frost.

It is difficult to give precise spacing for tubers because the optimum depends on three factors: how many shoots will grow, how fertile the soil is and how large and spreading the top growth will be. The size of top growth varies according to the variety. King Edward, a maincrop, has long haulms and needs more space per plant than Desirée, also a maincrop but with much smaller tops. Early varieties tend not to have very large top growth but are mostly more bushy than Desirée. With a small early tuber (16–20 per kg) planting at a within-row spacing of 15–20cm and assuming there are two shoots per tuber, and two rows per bed, would result in 20–26 shoots or 'plants' per m. Larger tubers should be given a little more space, assuming they only have two shoots each. Maincrop varieties need between 20 and 40cm within-row space, depending on the eventual size of the top growth and the size of the tuber.

Filling in the trench
If the soil is rather hard and lumpy, to reduce the risk of damaging the shoots when backfilling, use your hands to break up some lumps over the tubers until the shoots are covered with fine, loose soil. Otherwise use a spade to take just enough

of the dug-out soil to cover the shoots (Figure 7.4 (iv)). Then, using the spade with the concave side facing you, slice off the soil from the far side of the trench. With the spade still facing you, slice soil off the near side of the trench. If the soil is loose and friable, more can be sliced off with each action than if it is more compacted. The soil falls into the trench, further covering the tuber. This process, effectively, cultivates the soil as it is sliced up. Work back until the sides of the trench are vertical (Figure 7.4 (v)). Then go to the other side of the bed and spade in the dug-out soil. An easier way is to use a draw hoe to pull the soil in from the side where you have been working. Finally,

Fig. 7.5(a) Filling in a potato trench using a draw hoe.

Fig. 7.5(b) Filling in a potato trench: converting V to a square-sectioned trench.

the cultivator can be used to even out the surface, taking care not to go too deep and catch the potatoes. There should be a slight valley in the soil surface where the trench was. The result of this backfilling technique is as if a flat-bottomed, square-sectioned trench had been dug out but only half the volume of soil has actually been lifted. The plants have plenty of loose soil around them for roots and tubers to grow into. However, if there is an abundance of compost or farmyard manure available, then dig out a spade-width, flat-bottomed trench and put plenty in, mix it in with some soil and then plant the potatoes.

Care

As soon as potatoes are planted urine can be applied. If the weather is warm and sunny it is better to apply it before the trench is completely filled in, so that a little more soil can be spread in order to prevent the volatilization of ammonia, which causes an unpleasant smell and is a waste of nitrogen. If conditions are generally dry, with no rain forecast and especially if, when the trench was dug the soil was found to be dry under the surface, it would be better to apply some urine, diluted 1:4 urine to water, on top of the compost or manure in the bottom of the trench before planting. One litre of urine per three metre length of trench is enough. Then apply the same amount again, also diluted, when the trench is about two thirds filled in. The reason for this is that if all the urine, even diluted, is applied on the surface when the weather is dry and warm with no prospect of rain, evaporation will draw the moisture, along with the valuable urine, to the surface, where nitrogen will be volatilized and lost. If rain is forecast within the next week, apply another two litres per three metre length of row, diluted 1:4, just before the rain, if possible. If no rain is forecast for at least a week, the extra two litres of urine can be applied straight after planting or within a few days. This surface application can be applied more concentrated – 1:2, followed by two litres of water per metre of row to wash it in. The urine and water should go on over the full width of the trench. By now the soil over the trench will have sunk down a little. This is useful not only because it prevents urine and water running off on to the path but if there is a frost after the potato shoots are up, they can be covered with newspaper and sticks with less chance of damaging them if there is a gap under the paper.

A day or two after the surface application of urine a catch crop of radish can be sown – a row or two down the middle of the bed and one along each side. The radish will have been eaten before the potatoes need earthing up. Until then there is nothing to do except hand weeding and there should be very little of this to do. Any small annual weed seedlings will be destroyed in the earthing up process.

When the potato shoots are about 20cm tall they should be earthed up or 'moulded'. To do this, soil will be drawn from the centre of the bed and also from along the two outer edges. These are areas that will not have been loosened by the trench digging process. Therefore, the soil might need to be loosened with a fork before being drawn up towards the plants. A long-handled, thin-pronged muck fork is ideal, but a digging fork will do. It may be used as a harrow if the soil is not too compacted. Otherwise you might need to stick the prongs in and lever the fork back and forth before using it as a harrow. Then use a draw hoe to pull some soil from the middle towards the nearest row and from the far side of the bed towards the other row. Then repeat the process from the path on the other side of the bed. When the tops have grown another 15cm or so, they can be earthed up again. Be careful, when earthing up, not to bury any leaves or damage them. The second earthing up might need to be done with a spade if the shaft of the hoe gets in the way of the leaves too much.

Do not neglect the hand weeding. Weeds might be hidden by the potato foliage but they can still flower and produce seed.

Pests and diseases

Hessayon (2006) describes six pests, eleven diseases and eight environmentally-caused problems in potatoes. You will be very unlucky if you ever see half of these. Buying good quality 'seed', chitting them in good light, planting at the right time in deep, fertile soil and feeding with urine will result in healthy, vigorous plants able to withstand many pests and diseases. Potatoes are known as 'hungry feeders'. The nitrogen in the urine will promote good growth and the potassium helps plants withstand adverse conditions. One year I did a trial whereby most of the crop was fed with urine but about a third had none. The summer was dry. The plants which had not had an application of urine turned yellow and started to die off nearly three weeks before those that had been fed. The latter stayed green, continuing to photosynthesize and feed the tubers. The yield of the fed rows was twice that of the others though not, presumably, just because of the extra three weeks' growth but also from the fertilizer effect.

Potato black leg

This is caused by a bacterium *Erwinia carotovora* var. *atroseptica*. The symptoms are premature yellowing of the leaves and a characteristic blackening of the stem just above as well as below ground level. As soon as symptoms are noticed, carefully dig up the whole plant, including, if possible, the seed tuber, and put into a compost bin that will get hot. Any new potatoes may safely be eaten.

Potato late blight
This is caused by the fungus *Phytophthora infestans*. The first symptoms are rounded brown patches at the tips or along the edges of leaves. Eventually, a fine, white mould develops on the underside of these patches. It often starts on the lower leaves, hidden by those above. So, careful and frequent inspection, at least twice a week, is advised. Blight used not to occur until August, although in recent years it has been starting earlier, even late June. Early varieties are rarely affected and the fungus only begins to develop when weather conditions suit it. Two consecutive 24 hour periods with temperatures no lower than 10°C, and a relative humidity of 89% or more for 11 hours in each of the 24 hour periods are the conditions required for the fungus to become active. Two days of damp, drizzly weather are almost guaranteed to trigger the development of blight. The damp atmosphere favoured by blight is the reason it often starts on the lower leaves, where ventilation is poor. If you can manage to pick off all infected leaves and if the weather suddenly turns dry and sunny, it is possible that the blight will develop no further. If you wish to spray with a fungicide, the time to do so is as soon as the above-described weather conditions have occurred, i.e. before any symptoms have developed. Follow carefully the instructions if using a copper-based fungicide such as Bordeaux mixture, as copper is highly toxic to soil organisms, including earthworms and nitrogen-fixing blue-green algae, and tends to accumulate in the soil. Although commercial growers spray against blight every ten days as a preventive measure (on maincrop, at least) in my

experience, a single spraying, or at most two, is sufficient. With earlies, which might be harvested in July, it is unlikely to be necessary to spray at all.

If you do not wish to spray and have been unable to control the spread of the disease by picking off affected leaves, the tops must be cut off close to the ground to prevent mature zoospores from being shed on to the soil and washed down to infect the tubers. It is safe to compost blight-infected foliage provided the heap will get sufficiently hot, at least 60°C. Potato tops have a high water content and if put into a compost heap altogether will become soggy and airless. So, mix the potato tops with coarser, drier material.

If the potatoes are going to be stored, it is important to wait at least two weeks after cutting off the tops before digging them up. This allows time for the spores to die off on and in the soil, avoiding their coming into contact with the tubers as they are dug. This is another reason why earthing up is important, to give a good protective covering of soil. With earlies that are going to be eaten soon they may be dug any time after the tops are removed.

The blight spores only survive the winter on tubers. So, it is important to dig up the whole crop – something I have never been able to achieve, and neither do farmers! When the tubers you have missed grow in the following spring, dig them out as soon as possible, chop them up and burn them or put them into a hot compost heap.

Although blight is not usually a problem with early varieties there are a few that are recognized as having some resistance, Orla and Premiere, for example.

Potato cyst nematodes/eelworms (Globodera pallida and
G. rostochiensis)
These are tiny transparent parasitic worms less than 1mm long
which feed on the roots of potato plants. The symptoms are
stunted growth with lower leaves withering away and upper
leaves pale green and wilting during the daytime.

Eelworm life cycle: The female develops a spherical cyst which
contains between 200 and 600 eggs, each containing a fully-
formed juvenile. The mother dies, leaving the cysts in a
dormant state. Hatching is stimulated by exudates from the
roots of the specific host plant. In the absence of the host plant
there is a spontaneous hatching of about 30% each year for
G. rostochiensis and 20% for *G. pallida* depending on soil type
and temperature. So, the longer the gap between potato crops
on a given area of soil the better for controlling the population
of nematodes. However, hatchings can continue for 25–30
years and in exceptional situations, eggs inside cysts can remain
viable for over 40 years. Populations can attain enormous
numbers; heavily infested land can contain 300 eggs per gram
of soil. At 10 eggs per gram there is a noticeable effect on crop
yield. For this reason it is important to buy certified seed
potatoes. During the years 1998–2000, 97.6% of 20,000
samples taken from Scottish seed potato-growing land were free
of viable potato cyst nematode (Pickup, 2002).

The spherical cysts adhering to the roots are about 0.5mm in
diameter and may be visible through a strong magnifying glass.
If nematodes are sufficiently numerous in your soil to cause a
serious depression of yield there is nothing that can be done in
the short term, organically. As soon as it is clear that crop

growth is being seriously depressed by nematodes, dig up and burn affected plants. A crop rotation of at least five years will reduce populations and maintain them at tolerable levels. Farm-scale trials are going on involving a sacrificial crop of *Solanum sisymbriifolium* which stimulates eggs to hatch but which is fully resistant to the nematodes.

Wireworm

These are the larvae of various species of click beetle, including *Agriotes lineatus, A. obscurus, A. sputator* and *Athous haemorrhoidalis*. Wireworm are numerous in grassland and can, therefore, be a serious pest in soil recently converted from grass. Populations decline with continued cultivation but still remain in lower numbers, as they will feed on many different plants and vegetables. They have distinctive orange, shiny bodies with three pairs of legs at the front and grow to about 2.5cm in length. They tend to cause damage to potatoes in late summer. So, earlies are unlikely to be affected. If the garden is kept weed-free the adult beetles are less likely to lay eggs.

Potato common scab

This is caused by *Streptomyces scabies*, an actinomycetes, which are filamentous bacteria. The symptoms are raised, corky patches, a few millimetres across, on the skin. The problem usually only affects the skin and the inside of the tuber is unaffected. It is quite safe to eat affected potatoes cooked in their skins. In fact, some people claim it improves the flavour. Common scab is likely to occur in the first year in a garden converted from grassland. Thereafter, it is common in dry conditions in sandy soils lacking organic matter and also in alkaline soils.

Aphid (Myzus persicae)

The 'greenfly' that affects potatoes also attacks peach leaves. It is pale green or yellow, sometimes pink. Although aphids can carry viruses I cannot recall seeing symptoms in potato plants of either of the two most common, leaf roll virus and mosaic virus. Nor have I ever noticed aphids in such numbers as to cause direct harm to the plants. Well nourished, vigorous plants are less likely to succumb to any pest than plants under stress or plants which have been over-fed with nitrogen. Although urine contains nitrogen it is roughly balanced with potassium and phosphorous.

Magnesium deficiency

The symptoms are yellowing of the leaves in between the veins, leaving a thin band of green next to the veins. The yellow area can eventually turn brown and brittle. The problem is likely to occur on very acid soils or on sandy soils after heavy rain. The lower, older leaves are affected first, as any shortage within the plant results in the transfer of the element to the new, growing leaves. So, it is not uncommon to see symptoms late in the season. Early potatoes are unlikely to be affected except in extreme soil conditions described above. The use of compost to build up organic matter in the soil and the inclusion of some seaweed products will provide adequate sources of magnesium.

Harvest and storage

Dry conditions are preferred for digging potatoes. Any of four types of tool can be used. I used to use a spade, reasoning that even the small tubers would not be missed and also because if the spade hit a potato it was a clean cut. Some were always missed, of course, including embarrassingly large ones, found in the following spring when they grew. However, a spade is quite hard work as all the soil the plant has grown in has to be lifted several times. A standard digging fork allows soil to pass between the prongs so that you are not actually lifting it, but small potatoes can be missed. A five-pronged fork will catch a few more small ones but the overall width of the fork is greater, which makes it harder work as more soil is being moved with each dig. I now prefer a small, four-pronged fork. The prongs are closer than the standard fork and less soil is being moved with each dig.

Varieties vary in the extent to which the tubers are spread out under the ground, but earlies tend to be fairly compact. Nevertheless, to begin, insert the fork near the path, well away from the middle of the ridge and work inwards until the first clump of tubers is found.

Maincrop potatoes have rougher skins and will take longer to dry than earlies if the soil is damp enough to stick to them. The first row tubers will have to be put on the ground to dry where they were growing but those from subsequent rows can be spread where the previous row was lifted, having first flattened the surface with a spade so that they do not sink into the soil when you drop them. If the soil is damp, after an hour or so the tubers might need to be turned over to dry the undersides. If potatoes have to be lifted in wet conditions they can be spread out in a greenhouse, cold frame or brought indoors and spread out on newspaper to dry.

Potatoes can be stored in shallow boxes that may be stacked but allow regular inspection to check for any rots. I have always used paper sacks as this method takes up less space, but tipping them out to check for rot is more of a problem. If this is done a month or so after harvest most potential rots will have started to develop by then so that one more check is probably sufficient, provided that storage conditions are near ideal.

Potatoes need to be kept in darkness. Light causes changes that turn them green and poisonous. A reasonably dry atmosphere is required with ventilation. Ideally, the temperature should not fall below 4°C for lengthy periods. One year, as an experiment, I left half of my potato crop in the ground. The winter turned out to be particularly cold and other gardeners' potatoes stored in outbuildings were ruined by frost. (I brought my sacks indoors for the worst period of weather.) When I came to dig up those that had been left in the ground I found they were perfectly sound. In the autumn, after clearing away the haulms, I had earthed them up again to make sure the tubers were well covered. Then, fortunately, there was a good covering of snow before the coldest weather set in. The snow and the soil provided sufficient insulation, but it is difficult to believe that the temperature of the soil surrounding the tubers remained above 4°C throughout the winter.

Recommended varieties

One of the great things about potatoes is that there are so many varieties available that you could try several each year for many years before repeating any. There are also various cooking criteria and pest and disease resistance characteristics to help make choices. Edwin Tucker's garden seed catalogue for 2009 listed 111 varieties. It also lists varieties under various pest and disease characteristics. The RHS recommends four early varieties: Accent, Foremost, Red Duke of York and Winston. Of those, I have only grown Red Duke of York, which is a very attractive potato with a bright red skin. Home Guard is a reliable early. Orla has good blight and black leg resistance.

Second earlies recommended by the RHS are Charlotte, Kondor, Picasso and Roseval. I can recommend Linzer Delikatess and Balmoral (see back cover for a picture of a crop of Balmoral).

Maincrop potatoes recommended by the RHS are Desirée, Maxine, Navan and Nicola. I can recommend King Edward for its flavour and creamy texture when mashed. However, it has two drawbacks. It is very susceptible to late blight; it has long haulms which can sprawl on the ground and get damp and also, along with some good sized tubers, will produce many small ones. In 2009 I grew Sarpo Mira, one of three blight resistant Sarpo varieties developed in Hungary. It was not a particularly bad year for blight but Desirée was affected whereas Sarpo Mira had no blight at all, and continued growing into October, when an early frost killed them off. Sarpo Mira is susceptible to early blight but recovers from it by producing new growth. It produced a good yield of large, smooth-skinned tubers. Sarpo varieties are the ones to choose if you wish to avoid having to spray against late blight. However, I think Desirée has slightly more flavour than Sarpo Mira (I have not tried the other two Sarpo varieties). Desirée has upright haulms, some blight resistance, good yields of what can be very large tubers in fertile soil, with few small ones. It grows fast and is known as an early maincrop. Although Tucker's catalogue does not include it in the slug resistant list, I have found it much less troubled by slugs than many other varieties. It is good for boiling, mashing, baking, roasting and chipping. Tucker does not include it in the salad list but in 1999 I met a canny grower on the Isle of Skye who separated his small Desirée and sold them as salad potatoes in little punnets for a pound. Marketing is a wonderful thing!

CUCURBITS: COURGETTE, MARROW, PUMPKIN AND SQUASH

This is a very diverse genus and includes many colourful and tasty crops, but the common names can be confusing and do not always reveal their true botanical relationships. There are 27 species originating in North and South America (Phillips and Rix, 1995). Three species account for most varieties grown outside the tropics and subtropics: *Cucurbita maxima, C. moschata* and *C. pepo*.

Cucurbita maxima includes pumpkins, autumn and winter squashes, and gourds. *C. maxima* originated in South America. They are vigorous and trailing. Goldman (2004) gives eight groups, within each of which are several varieties:

1	Australian Blue.	5	Mammoth.
2	Banana.	6	Turban.
3	Buttercup.	7	Zappallito.
4	Hubbard.	8	Miscellaneous, unclassified.

C. moschata includes winter squashes, butternut types, cheese squashes and trombones. Goldman gives four groups:

1 Neck (or Cushaws) includes curved/crooknecked and straight, e.g. 'Canada Crookneck', 'Ponca Butternut'.

2 Cheese Pumpkin.

3 Tropical Pumpkin, e.g. 'St. Petersburg' the sweetest moschata and high in beta carotene.

4 Japonica, e.g. 'Chirimen' and 'Futtsu'.

C. pepo includes marrows, pumpkins, courgettes, summer and winter squashes. Goldman gives eight groups:

1   Pumpkin, subspecies *pepo*, e.g. 'Connecticut Field' (sold for Hallowe'en lanterns) and 'Winter Luxury Pie'. 'Styrian Hulless' ('Gleisdorfer Olkurbis') and 'Lady Godiva' are grown for their seeds rather than the flesh.

2   Acorn, subspecies *texana*, e.g. 'Delicata' (sweet potato squash), 'Gill's Golden Pippin', 'Table Queen' and 'Thelma Sanders'. Acorn squashes do not keep long.

3   Scallop, subspecies *texana*, includes various 'pattypans'.

4
5 } Crookneck and Straightneck, subspecies *texana*.

6   Vegetable Marrow, subspecies *pepo*, includes 'Long Green Trailing', the common marrow grown in Britain – speckled dark green with yellow ribs – and 'Vegetable Spaghetti'.

7   Zucchini, known as courgettes in Britain, includes 'Golden Zucchini' and 'Nano Verde di Milano' – green courgette.

8   Cocozelle, grown in Italy and Turkey, e.g. 'Cortata Romanesco' and 'Cocozelle' which is like a mini vegetable marrow.

The classification into summer and winter squashes refers to whether the fruit is normally used in late summer or kept until fully mature and stored for winter use. Winter squashes can be used in summer, although they have little flavour then, but summer squashes will not keep for very long into winter. The *Cucurbita pepo* species contains both summer and winter varieties of squash.

There are several other species grown in North and South America but the three named above are the more common ones grown in Europe. Within each species the different varieties can cross-pollinate. So, if you wish to harvest your own seeds to grow, only one variety from each species can be grown in the same garden but bear in mind that bees can fly for miles. Hand-pollination can be done to get round this problem but involves taping up the female flowers to prevent them opening, then opening them at the optimum time and pollinating with a male flower.

All the above cucurbits require similar growing conditions. So, the following may be used as a guide for any of them.

Site and soil

These crops are very responsive to soil fertility. I have grown Golden Hubbard squash (*C. maxima*) for many years and in the ordinary beds most plants produce one good sized fruit, some will have a smaller one as well and a few will have two large fruits. However, occasionally I have grown a spare plant or two on a compost heap where each plant can produce three large fruits.

An open site that gets maximum sunshine but which is also sheltered from strong winds is preferable. A deep, well-drained soil with plenty of organic matter is also important for good results. In the spring, preferably a few weeks before planting out, dig in well-rotted compost centred on where each plant will go. Each patch of compost can be 50–60cm in diameter. A few days later some urine may be applied to the same areas as the compost, at a rate of one litre per plant area, diluted 1:2 and then washed in with another couple of litres of water. If the soil is already wetter than field capacity, dilute the urine with less water. If heavy rain is forecast, there is no need to wash in the urine with water.

When to sow and plant

All of the cucurbita species are not frost hardy. So, in temperate areas with a relatively short growing season it is best to sow in pots indoors or in a greenhouse, cold frame or under cloches. Nine centimetre pots are big enough, or large yoghurt pots will do, provided a few holes have been punched in the base.

Using peat is like burning fossil fuel. Peat formation is a long-term carbon capture process. Once it is extracted and used in a garden it begins to break down or oxidize, releasing carbon dioxide. Any other peat substitute, bought potting composts will have necessitated fossil fuel use to process, package and transport. I have always just used riddled garden soil. That is fine if the soil is friable with plenty of organic matter in it but if it is not like that then for the first few years you might need to use a bought-in potting compost. Leaf mould is an alternative material for potting soil but with that and also with soil from recently dug grassland, there could be a problem with nematodes attacking the seeds. Rotted turf is a traditional material to use for potting soil. If the garden has been made from grassland there will, at least, be a supply of this in the second year.

One year I used soil from a heap accumulated the previous summer from hoeing and raking up weeds between the beds. The soil in this heap was from compacted paths and had never had any compost or fertilizer applied. During the winter I had poured many litres of urine on to the heap. In the spring, when it had dried to an appropriately damp condition, I riddled this and used it for half of the pots to grow the squash plants in. The rest of the seeds were sown in ordinary garden soil, also riddled. About three weeks later when the plants were ready to plant out, those grown in the urine-enriched soil were twice the size of the others.

If sowing in pots under glass it will be two or three weeks before the plants will be ready to plant out. Count back from the date of the last likely frost to work out when to sow. If later than usual frosts are forecast and planting is delayed, being kept in pots for another week or two does not seem adversely to affect the plants' future growth and fruiting. Once the seeds have germinated, open the ventilation on hot sunny days.

Spacing and planting

Seed catalogues and packets should provide the information as to whether the particular variety has a trailing or bush type of growth. If a bush type, an equidistant spacing is desirable but if the plant is going to grow a few metres of stem, equidistance is less important. What is important is that the over all plant density is optimum, which will vary according to the fertility of the soil and the particular variety. For bush varieties, courgettes for example, in a bed up to a metre wide, one row along the middle is appropriate, allowing 90cm between plants. There will be time and space for a catch crop of radishes along each edge of the bed, or, if they can be sown earlier, lettuce and spring onion. Trailing varieties require a little more space over all. Allow about one square metre of bed per plant. This can be achieved by having two rows and an along-the-row spacing of 1.5–2.0 metres, or, in a metre-wide bed, one row, with plants a metre apart along the row. The trailing stems will put down roots from nodes along their length, so that they will be taking water and nutrients from many points in the bed, not just from where the plants were planted. If more than one bed of trailing plants is grown, it is advisable to have all the beds next to each other so that the plants can roam freely across the paths without interfering with other crops (see the following section).

Care

Trailing stems grow fast and sometimes several seem intent on aiming for the same place, resulting in over-crowding. Before they put down new roots they can be lifted up and turned to encourage them to go in a different direction. Sticks can be put in to keep wayward stems in place. In particular, sticks might be necessary to prevent shoots trailing over neighbouring beds and plots.

Weeding is necessary but once the entire area of soil is covered by the foliage of trailing plants, there will be very little subsequent weed growth. So, it does not matter if the paths between adjacent beds of squash disappear under a mass of foliage, as you will not need to go on them to do anything. Having paths covered by leaves effectively increases the size of the garden, as far as the area for photosynthesis is concerned.

Apart from weeding and trying, with trailing varieties, to prevent overcrowding and spreading into neighbouring beds of different crops, there is nothing to do until harvest.

Pests and diseases

Hessayon (2006) describes quite a number of diseases but they are mostly problems affecting cucumbers and particularly when grown in a greenhouse. I have grown squash for many years and courgettes in a number of years as well and cannot recall having any major pest problems and only minor problems with disease. Squash can even be grown where there are rabbits, as can potatoes and garlic, although the latter two will suffer some nibbled foliage.

Slugs and snails

These can attack seedlings. Inspect the plants in the evenings and early mornings and remove or kill any offending creatures. Providing a flat stone or large leaf – rhubarb or cabbage – nearby will attract slugs to hide underneath, from where they can be removed each morning.

Cucumber mosaic virus

This is a serous disease that affects cucumbers and marrows. Although courgettes and marrows are both *Cucurbita pepo*, marrows are a subspecies, *pepo*. Cucumber mosaic virus can overwinter in chickweed, which acts as a bridge from one season to the next (Burchill, 1979). Viruses are spread by aphids.

Powdery mildew

This can be caused by various fungal genera. Leaves and stems are covered in white powdery patches. This usually only occurs in late summer after prolonged dry weather when the soil is dry but the air is becoming moist. The problem can be avoided by keeping the soil adequately watered but without wetting the leaves. This is difficult to do with trailing plants when beds and paths are covered with foliage and it is difficult to walk anywhere without treading on the stems. I have never known powdery mildew to strike early enough for it to be a problem. In late summer it merely speeds up defoliation, allowing the sun to ripen the fruits a little earlier. However, if it does occur earlier in the year, remove any affected leaves as soon as possible and try watering the soil.

Grey mould (Botrytis cinerea)

This can occur on young fruit in wet or humid conditions with insufficient airflow. I have only encountered this on late, secondary fruits, which would probably not grow to be fully ripe anyway. If the site is particularly sheltered and liable to be damp, the spacing might need to be more generous to allow adequate airflow. Also, keep the beds free of weeds.

Pests

Squash seeds are the best bait for mousetraps! If seeds are sown directly into the ground, watch out for tell-tale holes and missing seeds. In theory, mice could also steal from pots under glass but I cannot recall this ever being a problem. There will usually be a few black aphids on the underside of leaves and although they can carry virus infections, I have never known aphids cause a problem directly. Squash plants are not attacked by rabbits. Whether other cucurbits are also rabbit resistant, I do not know.

Harvest and storage

Courgettes and marrows should be cut as required and at the size preferred. Continual cutting will encourage flowering and more fruits. Summer squash, too, can be cut as and when needed. Winter squashes should be left as long as possible, to ripen in the sun. When the leaves are obviously dying off and no longer photosynthesizing much – they will probably also be covered in powdery mildew – it is a good time to remove the haulms and just leave the fruits to continue ripening. If any trials have been done, involving different treatment to plants, you will need to know which fruits belong to which planting positions. In a school garden one child could go to each plant and give the stem a tug and see which fruit moves! It could be several metres away. Another child can then cut the fruit free and carry it to the plant site. The whole plant can be pulled up and removed before the fruit is placed in position.

When cutting the fruit, cut the actual stem close to but either side of the thick corky stalk of the fruit. The piece of stem will eventually dry to a crisp but if the stalk is cut it can let in fungal rots. If you wish, place the fruits upside down to ripen the part that has been resting on the soil. If there is a frost forecast, bring the squashes indoors. One year all of mine got frosted – about a hundred fruits. There was a patch of ice, like a cap, on top of each one but, contrary to dire predictions in books, they kept as well as usual. The frosted patch remained a slightly darker colour of orange. It is advised that the storage temperature should not fall below 4°C, but during the cold winters of the early 1980s the unheated room where mine were kept must have been below that for many days and nights. For longest-term storage the optimum conditions are 10°C at 60% relative humidity (Sumption et al., 2005).

In a school where there will not be enough fruits for anyone to take home more than one, long term storage will not be a requirement. However, the flavour of winter squash does improve if they are kept a few weeks. They will keep well at room temperature, or in an unheated room, where they can be appreciated for their decorative value. They need to be in a dry room with ventilation. Christmas is a good time to eat them.

One of the many good characteristics of winter squashes is that if they do begin to rot they do so from the outside and slowly. So, if you do wish to keep a number for use throughout the winter, inspect them twice a week. Symptoms of rots can be pale grey soft mould next to the stalk or at the other end, or dark sunken spots anywhere else. If caught soon enough, affected parts can simply be cut out and the rest will probably be unaffected and good to eat. In fact I have sometimes thought they taste even better when the first signs of rot have appeared!

Recommended varieties

There are many to choose from and seed companies seem to increase their range every year. It is interesting to study the catalogues, look at the pictures, read the descriptions and also to ask fellow gardeners what they would recommend. In a school you probably will not want to grow large specimens but rather, a larger number of smaller fruits, so that more children can take one home. According to Goldman (2004) squashes should be grown at their optimum spacing; you will not get more, smaller fruits per square metre of a large-fruiting variety by planting them close together. Instead, they will be less likely to fruit at all. So, if a large number of small fruits are required, grow a small-fruiting variety at its optimum spacing. If you wish to keep your own seed, only one variety from any one species can be grown.

▶ *Cucurbita maxima* varieties tend to be large but 'Buttercup' produces fruits of 1–2kg.

▶ *C. moschata* contains a number of 'Butternut' varieties. The name is a clue to the flavour!

▶ *C. pepo* includes the courgettes. The problem with them is that they need frequent picking at the time British schools are on holiday. Left unpicked they will grow to marrow-sized fruits. The squash 'Delicata' is also known as the sweet potato squash – again, a clue to its quality.

BEETROOT (*Beta vulgaris* subsp. *Vulgaris*)

Beetroot are easy to grow and can give good yields per square
metre. Some children might be unfamiliar with them but if you
can harvest some when small, young and sweet, cook and serve
them hot, many children could be 'won over' to liking this
nutritious vegetable. It is also worth leaving some to grow large
and using them for soup (see harvest and storage below).

Site and soil

Beetroot will grow best in an open position with full light and
in a reasonably well cultivated and fertile soil. Deep cultivation
is not necessary but a compacted soil might cause problems. In
a school garden, where space could be very limited, they might
not warrant a whole bed to themselves from the spring. So,
they can be regarded more as a catch crop, growing between or
after other crops. They will do better in a light soil rather than
one with a high clay content. The preferred pH is around 6.5.
The yield of beetroot will benefit from an application of urine.
Apply up to 1.5 litres per square metre a few days before
sowing. If the soil is already moist, dilute 1:1 with water and
then apply another 1.5 l per m^2 of water. If the soil is very dry,
apply 2 litres of water per m^2 then 1:1 urine, then another 2
litres of water. If the soil is not particularly fertile to begin
with, this quantity of urine will have a dramatic effect on yield.
Try a control area where only water is applied at the same rate
as the total liquid for the urine application.

When to sow

Beetroot seed germinates well at relatively high soil
temperatures but not at temperatures below 7°C. So, do not be
in a hurry to sow in the spring. A good crop can be obtained by
sowing after the first early potatoes are harvested. In that

situation they will benefit from whatever compost has been applied for the potatoes and also from the cultivation done while digging these out. Beetroot could also be grown in single rows between winter and spring brassicas but sown later, after the latter have emerged and the soil has warmed up a little.

Spacing and sowing

Spacing depends on whether you want to grow small roots in a short time or large ones over a longer period. The number of rows per bed can be the same but the within-row spacing can be varied. The conditions and fertility of the soil will also affect what should be the optimum spacing for maximum yield. The better the soil the greater the potential for growth so the more space each plant requires. In a bed 90cm wide there is room for five rows, 20cm apart and allowing 5cm between the outer rows and the path. In a one metre bed, six rows may be fitted in, 18cm apart and also allowing 5cm each side. Drills should be at least 2cm deep or 3 or 4cm in a light or lumpy soil prone to dry out. As the seeds are large it is easy to place them fairly precisely where required. Large seeds may be sown singly but small seeds should be sown in pairs, in case one produces no plants or plants lacking vigour. If small roots are required, allow 6 to 10cm between each sowing position. For large roots, 12 to 15cm is appropriate. Each seed is really a cluster and will usually produce between two and four seedlings.

When the first two leaves have appeared, pull out the surplus plants, leaving the biggest or healthiest-looking one at each position. This should be done very carefully, causing as little root disturbance as possible to the plants being left to grow. When the soil is just moist provides the best condition for doing this. Alternatively, to avoid the risk of damage, all the seedlings may be left in and allowed to grow as clusters of roots but they will be small.

Care

The only maintenance needed is weeding. Beetroot seedlings will come up relatively quickly so they may be left until well established and rooted before any weeding need be done.

Pests and diseases

Black bean aphid

This is described as a pest in some books but I have never noticed this or any aphids on beetroot even in years when broad beans are heavily infested.

Mangold fly (leaf miner)

This can be a problem in some areas. Small white grubs burrow inside the leaves, causing them to blister. The blisters turn brown. Pick off infested leaves as soon as symptoms are noticed.

Forked roots

These can occur in stony soil or in soil with a high clay content that has not been sufficiently cultivated. Heavy soils will benefit from applications of organic matter for the previous crop, e.g. early potatoes, or in the autumn before.

Manganese deficiency

This results in yellow patches between the leaf veins. If the problem is severe, the whole leaf will turn yellow and the edges curl inwards. If the pH is too high, this has the effect of 'locking up' manganese, making it unavailable to plants. If the pH is not too high but there is a deficiency of manganese anyway, adding dried seaweed to the compost heap or raking it into the soil a few months before sowing should provide enough of this trace element to avoid crop deficiency. For a quick remedy if symptoms have appeared, try spraying with a seaweed solution.

Boron deficiency
This causes leaves to wilt in the summer and blackened voids to develop within the root. Too high a pH can 'lock up' boron and make it unavailable to plants. If it is known that the soil is deficient, an application of borax may be made but it is important to follow the recommended application rates and avoid overdosing. Including dried seaweed when making compost or applying it to the soil a few months before sowing should help to avoid the problem. For a quick remedy if symptoms have appeared, try spraying with seaweed solution.

Sparrows
The first year I grew beetroot the seedlings were eaten by sparrows. For several years I covered the seedbed with netting until the plants were well established. Then, one year I did not bother and the sparrows did not touch them. I have had no problem with bird damage since!

Harvest and storage
In school gardening, beetroot are best eaten young and straight from the garden. Whatever their age, beetroot may be pulled out of the ground or eased out with the help of a small fork, being careful not to damage the skin anywhere on the root. The tops may be twisted off or cut, leaving 3 or 4cm of leaf stem so that, when being cooked there will be little juice from the root

'bleeding' into the water. Unless you intend to blend the beetroot with the cooking water to make soup, the roots should not be peeled before cooking, otherwise much of the juice and flavour will leach into the water. Boiled or pressure cooked and then peeled, young beetroot are delicious served hot, especially with new potatoes. If making soup, cut into small pieces to reduce cooking time but only use as much cooking water as you wish to incorporate in the soup. The chunks do not need to be covered with water; they will cook in the steam.

Beetroot are not so sweet late in the year and although they will survive one or two light frosts, the flavour is not so good afterwards. So, for storage, harvest well before any frost. For long term storage of large roots, make a clamp. Dig out a shallow hole, place a layer of beetroot in it and cover with a little soil before stacking another layer of beetroot, and so on. Make sure all the roots are covered by enough soil to protect them from frost. The thickness of soil required will depend on the climate in your area. In most of Britain, 5 or 6cm will be adequate. One year when I came to collect roots from the clamp I found several of them entirely eaten away by small rodents, leaving just a thin layer including the skin. Old books will tell you to use straw to cover the roots before covering with soil. I have not tried that but would imagine it would make the clamp even more attractive to rodents – bed as well as breakfast!

Recommended varieties

I like the cylindrical ones. They tend to have smoother skins and because they are 'high rise' I imagine they yield more per square metre, although I have not done a trial to establish if that is so. 'Cylindra' and 'Forono' are commonly available.

'Boltardy' is the most commonly available round rooted variety and is reliable.

CARROTS (*Daucus carota*, var. *sativus*)

Carrots are a must for children's gardens. They are relatively easy to grow, although not without challenge, but the smell and flavour of a freshly pulled carrot makes any effort worthwhile, plus, of course, they are so nutritious and good for young teeth to chew on. They are one of the best crops to grow from the point of view of the amount of food produced per square metre, provided they are grown well and you get the spacing right, i.e. optimum for the soil conditions.

Site and soil

Carrots grow well in a deep, well drained light loam. Heavy clay soils will be more difficult to grow good carrots in. Stony soils will tend to produce forked roots. If the soil is very stony and you wish to grow a whole bed of carrots, this is one occasion where it might be worthwhile changing the texture of the soil, at least on the surface. Prepare the bed using the cultivator and then leave for a few days. If there is some rain during that time, that will help, by washing soil off the stones on the surface. Then use a rake to rake off stones on to the path on each side of the bed. They can then be shovelled up and dumped somewhere. Do not leave them on the paths, they will make hoeing very difficult.

In a heavy clay soil it is not worthwhile trying to grow long varieties. They will grow distorted and branched roots. Choose a short-rooted variety. If there is some well-rotted compost available it is worth making the drills deeper and filling them with finely sieved compost, lightly firming it down and then sowing on top of that. Incorporation of organic matter will gradually improve a clay soil over a period of years.

Carrots do not have a high requirement for nitrogen. In the first year of a garden, if the soil is heavy or otherwise deficient in organic matter, if there is some well-rotted compost available, incorporating it thoroughly, as long as possible before sowing, will be beneficial. In subsequent years, soil that has had plenty of organic matter incorporated in the previous year is ideal. The cultivation done during the process of digging up potatoes will be a good preparation for carrots the following year, provided the soil is covered with a cover crop of some kind to prevent too much compaction over the winter. An early variety of carrot may be sown after lifting early potatoes, in late June or early July. If an early maturing maincrop, such as Desirée, is harvested in August, a sowing of lamb's lettuce or corn salad (*Valerianella locusta*) can be established and provide good ground cover, as well as nutritious winter salad. In the following spring this can be hoed off, the top few centimetres of soil cultivated to create a seedbed and carrots sown. If maincrop carrots are to be sown, this can be done in June (see below) which means that the corn salad can be left to seed. The seed is easily collected but the other great benefit is the effect the corn salad plants have on the soil. Each plant has a large volume of very fine roots, which improves soil structure.

With carrots it is worth taking especial care with soil preparation.

When to sow
The worst problem with carrots is carrot root fly. By sowing an early and a late crop the problem can largely be avoided. Early

carrots grow well under glass cloches but if glass is deemed too dangerous for children, various designs of rigid plastic or polythene on wire frame cloches are available. Horticultural fleece can also be used to cover a bed of early carrots but slugs can be a problem in the comfortable microclimate created. If cloches are not available and if fleece is too much trouble or environmentally unacceptable, any sufficiently large sheets of used plastic can simply be weighted down on the bed a few weeks before sowing in order to warm the soil. Do the bed preparation first so that the prepared surface gets warmed and remains at the surface for the seed to be sown into. The plastic can be put back on the bed after sowing to hasten germination and seedling growth. After about ten days check under the plastic each day and remove it as soon as the first seedlings are showing. It could take more than two weeks for the first shoots to appear. A late sowing of carrots can be defined as being immediately after early potatoes are harvested – late June or early July. In favourable areas, with at least three months' growing season left, a maincrop variety can be sown. Otherwise, sow an early variety, which will mature in a shorter time.

Spacing and sowing

For every soil and other conditions there must be an optimum plant density for carrots but within a relatively wide range the crop yield is little affected. So, you can choose to have large carrots or a larger number of small ones, with a similar total yield. Also, with carrots, it is not necessary to try to achieve equidistant spacing. The foliage bends gracefully over to meet that from the next row, so that all of the area is used for photosynthesis. For early or maincrop carrots, a row spacing of 15cm is recommended (Bleasdale, 1979). Spacing within the row depends on how fast you need the crop to grow. Bleasdale explains that for fast growth but not maximum yield, a relatively low plant density is required (54–75 per square metre) which means that the within-row spacing needs to be about 9cm. For seed sown in early May for autumn harvest he recommends 160–215 plants per square metre, which would require a within-row spacing of 3–4cm. From my experience, the 9cm seems over generous and the 3–4cm seems a little too close. Also, I would not recommend sowing in early May and expect a long growing season, unless you have some very good carrot fly protection. Therefore, for early varieties, whether grown early or as a fast maturing late crop and also for maincrop varieties, which will have a little longer to grow, I would recommend a within-row spacing of about 5cm. It is important to sow individual seed at that spacing, to avoid the necessity of thinning out. Pinching out young carrot plants damages plant tissue, releasing the scent that attracts the root fly.

It is difficult to allow individual seeds to fall from a pinch of seeds between finger and thumb. Children will tend to sow much too thickly. So, they must be encouraged to take great care when sowing and not to be in a hurry. The actual sowing of seeds takes such a small proportion of the total time spent gardening, it is worth taking whatever time and care are necessary to achieve the best possible conditions for the seeds, including the spacing you want. Make the drills 1–2cm deep.

Care

Careful hand weeding is very important. If a 'stale bed' has been used this will reduce the population of weeds somewhat (see p.112 for information on stale beds). Care must be taken not to bruise the carrot plant tissue, as this will release the strong scent that attracts the carrot root fly. If the seed has been sown too thickly and the seedlings need to be thinned out, this should be done as late in the day as possible – at dusk, when root flies have 'gone to bed'.

Pests and diseases

Carrot fly (Psila rosae)

The larvae of this pest tunnel into the roots, initially just under the surface, leaving the characteristic brown lines of collapsed tunnels. The first symptoms are a reddening of the outer leaves, which later turn yellow. Affected carrots should be used as soon as possible or, if they have already become unpalatable (the flavour quickly becomes unpleasant) consigned to a bonfire. In some areas carrot fly is rarely a problem, whereas in others it might be impossible to grow clean roots. It probably depends on the proximity and population density of the wild carrot, the natural host plant, and also other gardens where carrots are being grown.

Some books recommend growing carrots between deterrent crops or planting certain herbs next to them. Carrots and onions may be grown in alternate rows but when the onions are harvested the carrots are left defenceless. Leeks, therefore, are said to be a better deterrent crop. Tansy is supposed to keep the fly away. I have tried these three ploys but none appeared to have any effect. I suspect the fly is not so easily fooled. Even though, to us, the smell of carrots might be masked by a stronger smell, if there is the scent of carrot in the air, perhaps the fly can detect this and find the crop.

I have not done controlled trials but some experience indicates that, contrary to Hessayon's advice, growing carrots in single rows, to spread the risk, in between taller crops seems to have some protective effect. So, you could have a row either side of peas, which occupy only the middle third of a bed. Winter and (the following) spring brassicas are relatively small in the summer, so carrots could be grown in between the rows. If it is practical to sow early enough, a 'catch' crop can be grown where cucurbits, sweetcorn and tomatoes will be planted later. Carrots will continue to grow in between these summer crops for some time, especially under sweetcorn, where there is plenty of space between the stems. After harvesting early potatoes, in late June or early July, is also a good time to sow carrots. The cultivation done in the process of digging out the tubers will benefit the carrot growth.

Carrot flies stay close to the ground when flying. So, some sort of barrier around where carrots are grown is a fairly reliable way to keep them off. Some stakes and fine mesh material, or clear plastic, are required. The barrier needs to be a minimum of 60cm high. However, in a school garden constructing and looking after this might be too much to cope with. Sowing only early and late, and growing single rows in different places, are easier ploys and might be enough to produce a reasonable crop. On the other hand, if the beds are small enough and all the same size it could be worth making one or two permanent structures that can easily be removed and stored. Then you can grow full beds of carrots and get a good yield. The barrier will have the added benefit of protection from wind and creating a slightly modified microclimate that encourages growth. However, the lack of air movement around the foliage could allow the development of downy mildew, especially in a damp summer.

It is important to sow carrots at the optimum density to avoid the necessity of thinning out (see 'Spacing and sowing', below).

Pinching the seedlings to pull them out releases the scent that attracts the fly. In a private garden thinning out can be done at dusk, as carrot flies are not active at this time. It is better to leave the crop a little overcrowded than risk attracting the fly – better to have lots of little carrots than none at all!

Carrot willow aphid

This can be a problem in a warm, dry summer. The leaves become distorted, discoloured and stunted. The aphid can transmit the *motley dwarf virus* which causes yellow mottling on the leaves and a red tinge on the tips of leaves. Over all growth is restricted by both these problems. However, I have rarely seen the symptoms of either. As with many pests and diseases, it seems that creating a fertile soil with a good friable structure makes plants less susceptible. So, if carrots are not a success in the first year of a garden, do not give up. Each year of soil improvement will be of benefit to this crop, particularly.

Split roots

These are not caused by a pest or disease but can occur when there is heavy rain following a long dry period.

More than one root per plant

This can occur in heavy clay soil, stony soil or soil where manure or compost has been added too recently. Grow carrots in soil where compost or manure has been applied before the previous crop.

Harvest

Damaging the green, top part of the carrot plant releases the scent that attracts the root fly. In a private garden, where a few carrots are needed each day, this is not a problem as they can safely be pulled at dusk, when the fly is not around. In a school garden the entire crop can be harvested within a few days. If you are growing an early and a main crop this could be a problem, as the main crop could be at a vulnerable stage at the time the earlies are harvested. If carrot fly proves to be a problem in your area you could, a) grow either an early crop or a main crop, not both; or b) grow both but if the main crop are already up and growing when the early crop is harvested, construct a barrier to protect the main crop.

Carrots are not always easy to pull up by their tops without snapping off above ground or part way down the root. The size of the roots, how tapered they are, whether they are so close as to be touching, and the friability of the soil will all influence how easy they are to harvest. It might be necessary to use a fork or spade to loosen the soil along one or both sides of the row.

Recommended varieties

If the soil is shallow, stony or has a high proportion of clay, choose a short-rooted variety such as Chantenay. A good early variety is Amsterdam Forcing and a heavy cropping maincrop is Autumn King. There are a few varieties that have been bred to resist root fly, Fly Away F1 and Resistafly F1 for example. There are many other varieties, of different size, shape and colour, to choose from.

LETTUCE (*Lactuca sativa*)

This is a very popular crop and fairly easy to grow. It can be sown early where tender crops are to be grown later, or in between slow growing crops, or as a late crop where crops have been harvested early.

Site and soil

An open, sunny position is best but some shade is tolerable when temperatures are likely to be at their highest and the conditions dry. A fertile, moisture-retentive soil is important for good quality lettuce. To achieve these conditions dig in some well-rotted compost or manure, preferably a few weeks before sowing. Lettuce will benefit from some extra nitrogen. Apply diluted urine at least a week before sowing. About one litre of urine per square metre should be enough. A fairly neutral pH is preferred. So anything between 6.4 and 7.0 is acceptable.

When and where to sow: inter-cropping and catch-cropping

Tender crops, such as cucurbits, sweetcorn and tomatoes, cannot be planted out until the danger of frost is over. If the ground where they are to grow can be prepared a few weeks in advance, lettuce may be sown in between where the main crops are to be planted. There will not be time for the lettuce to mature before the tender crops are planted but that does not matter. There can be an overlap period where lettuces occupy the in-between spaces and are cropped as the tender crops grow and eventually fill all the space in the beds. Lettuces grown in between tender crops can be sown over a period of a few weeks to give a continuity of supply, avoiding shortages or gluts. Because squash and courgette grow quite fast after planting out and soon cover the ground, make the first sowings of inter-cropping lettuce in the beds where cucurbit crops are to be planted. The last inter-crop lettuces may be sown where sweetcorn is to be grown. Even when the corn plants are fully grown there is enough space and light at ground level for lettuces to remain in good condition until needed. Indeed, the partial shade will help to prevent the lettuces bolting if the weather happens to be particularly hot and dry.

Winter and spring brassicas and also leeks are relatively slow growing and have enough space between the rows for lettuce to be grown during the summer. The lettuce can be sown at about the same time as the brassicas and leeks. Between leeks grow the smaller varieties of lettuce, e.g. 'Tom Thumb' and 'Little Gem'.

After harvesting early potatoes, garlic and early (autumn-sown) broad beans, there is time to grow a late crop of lettuce.

Spacing and sowing

In a whole bed of lettuce the row spacing needs to be 15–20cm for small varieties and 25–30cm for large types. If grown between other crops, sow single rows. It is easy to sow lettuce too thickly. Germination is generally good. So, try to drop the seeds individually, a few centimetres apart, into the drills and later take out surplus young plants, leaving those to grow on at 15–20cm intervals for small varieties and 25–30cm for large types. Do not let plants grow too much and become crowded before thinning out, as this could encourage bolting. Aim at a drill depth of about 1cm, a little more in light soils prone to drying out.

Care

All that is needed is to weed carefully by hand. For watering, see under 'Tip burn' below.

Pests and diseases

Lettuces are subject to quite a long list of pests and diseases. However, given good soil conditions and reasonable weather – warm but not too hot and sufficient rain without any long dry spells – a good crop, with few problems, can be expected.

Aphids

These can ruin a crop and can carry mosaic virus but I cannot recall ever seeing them on lettuce. The problem is most likely to occur in spring in dry weather. Inspect daily and at the first sign of infestation, pick off affected leaves and water the plants. Try to water the ground around the plants, avoiding getting water between the leaves, which will encourage slugs, not that they need any encouragement. Slugs can often be found between the outer leaves, without doing much damage.

Root aphids (Pemphigus bursarius)

The symptoms are slow growth even in moist soil in good weather. Leaves can turn yellow and wilt. The problem is most likely to occur in late summer. If the plant is pulled up, small lumps of what look like white powder will be seen on the roots and in the surrounding soil. These consist of a waxy material that protects individual aphids. Crop rotation will reduce the likelihood of infestation. There are some resistant varieties: 'Avoncrisp', 'Avondefiance', 'Debby', 'Lakeland', 'Salad Bowl' and 'Sigmaball'.

Cutworms

These are the larvae of several moths, including Garden Dart (*Euxoa nigricans*), Turnip Moth (*Agrotis segelum*), Heart and Dart (*A. exclamationis*), Large Yellow Underwing (*Noctua pronuba*) and Lesser Yellow Underwing (*N. comes*). The symptoms are wilting and dying of the plant. If lifted, the root may be seen to have been eaten right through just below the surface. Cutworms can work their way along a row. Keeping beds free of weeds can help interrupt this progression. Digging around the site of an affected plant with a hand fork or trowel might reveal the culprit.

Root knot eelworms

These are microscopic and quite a rare problem in Britain. Above-ground symptoms are stunted growth and pale leaves. The roots will have gall-like swellings on them. Affected plants should be burnt, together, if possible, with the soil immediately surrounding the roots. Lettuces should not be grown on the same site for at least six years.

Wireworm

These can be a problem on ground recently converted from grassland. Wireworms are the larvae from various species of click beetle, including *Agriotes lineatus, A. obscurus, A. sputator* and *Althous haemorrhoidalis.* They can be up to 25mm long, are generally orangey in colour with segmented bodies and three pairs of legs at the head end. They can eat through the stems of plants just below the soil surface. With each year of cultivation their numbers diminish.

Leatherjackets

These are the larvae of crane flies or 'daddy-long-legs'. The most common species are *Tipula paludosa, T. oleracea* and *Nephrotoma maculata.* They can be up to 4.5cm long and are greyish brown. There can be large numbers in grassland and, therefore a problem in the first year of a garden if it were grass previously. They feed on the roots of various crops. The symptoms are yellowing leaves, wilting and, possibly, death of the plant. Eggs are laid in late summer and hatch in two weeks. The larvae feed on grass roots in autumn, are inactive in a cold winter and continue feeding in spring and throughout the summer. They can be encouraged to come to the surface by laying black plastic on the grass after rain, or watering if conditions are dry. The next day as the plastic is peeled back, the grubs can be collected, or left for blackbirds, thrushes and starlings to eat if there are plenty of these birds around. However, the grubs will soon go back into the ground. So, if this natural method of control is used, it might need to be done several times. All this is probably unnecessary if the turf is to be taken off, as most of the larvae will go with it. Then when the ground is dug, any deeper individuals will be seen and can be removed to a bird table.

Slugs and snails

These can be a problem with seedling and young plants especially. Snails can easily be picked up and taken away but if slugs are picked up with bare hands they leave slime which does not wash off; it has to be abraded off with sand, or soil containing sand. Placing a piece of slate, large leaf or anything flat and opaque, such as a piece of weighted-down black plastic, will attract slugs underneath over night. Each morning they can be removed. Keep surrounding soil surface free of any other plant debris, as this will also attract slugs under it. In my experience it is the small pale grey and black slugs that eat live plants. The large black or brown ones seem to prefer dead vegetation.

Botrytis (Botrytis cinerea)

This fungus looks like pale grey or brownish velvet. On lettuce stems a reddish-brown rot develops. The fungal spores enter the plant through diseased or damaged tissue. Take great care in handling if transplanting. This disease is most likely to occur in cool conditions with high humidity.

Downy mildew (most likely Bremia lactucae)

The first symptoms are yellowing between the veins on the

upper surface of older leaves, with pale grey mould underneath.
It is most likely to occur in damp conditions and on young
plants. Avoid watering and pick off infected leaves as soon as
possible. The whole plant can die if the problem is left to
spread.

Tip burn
This is a physiological disorder caused by a lack of available
calcium. The symptoms are a 'scorched' brown appearance on
the leaf margins. Very dry conditions can make calcium
unavailable to the plant, or the soil pH might be too low. Soil pH
cannot be changed quickly. Apply lime in autumn for crops that
need a raised pH the following year. Only if the soil is *very* dry
to a depth beyond most of the root, and also to prevent bolting,
plants should be thoroughly watered. To avoid triggering an
infestation of downy mildew, avoid getting water on the leaves.
Also, to avoid rapid run-off, it might be necessary to loosen the
soil around the plants with a fork or trowel. Use a reduced flow
attachment to the watering can, or simply tape over three
quarters of the holes in the rose. A reduced flow of water will
make it easier to avoid run-off or getting water between the
leaves.

Harvest
Any type of lettuce can be cut with a sharp knife at ground
level and taken away whole. Or, a few outer leaves may be
picked off and the plant left to continue growing. This is
particularly appropriate with the loose leaved varieties, for
example, Salad Bowl and Oakleaf.

PARSNIPS (*Pastinaca sativa*)

Site and soil

Parsnips will grow best in a deep sandy or silty loam, although good crops can be grown in heavier soil. If the top soil is less than 20cm deep a short rooted variety should be grown. An open, sunny position is also preferable.

When to sow

A mid to late spring sowing will be more successful than an earlier one. A late sown crop seems to be less susceptible to canker. Germination is slow.

Spacing and sowing

Parsnip leaves are larger and more spreading than beetroot but, as with other crops, a wider spacing will result in larger roots than a closer spacing. A row spacing of around 25cm is appropriate, giving four rows in a 90 or 100cm wide bed. Sow at stations 10–25cm apart along the row, depending on whether small or larger roots are required. Small roots seem to be less susceptible to canker. Sow in drills about 2cm deep. As it takes a long time for parsnip seedlings to emerge, in order to know where to expect them to appear, a few radish seeds may be sown in the drills in between the parsnip seeds. There is also space and time for a row of radish between each row of parsnips.

There are UK statutory minimum rates of germination for vegetable seeds but parsnip is exempted because the germination rate can be very low. One year I sowed 12 seeds at each station but there were still a few gaps in the rows! So, sow at least four at each position where you want a plant to be. Alternatively, sow individually along the drill with seeds almost touching each other, if you have enough. Surplus seedlings can be pulled out later, as necessary.

Care

Pulling weeds out is all that should need to be done. Damage to the roots can allow entry of fungal infections. So, hand weeding is recommended rather than hoeing.

Pests and diseases

Carrot root fly

This can also affect parsnips (see under carrots for more detail). However, parsnips do seem to be less susceptible than carrots.

Parsnip canker

This is caused by fungal infection and is the most likely problem to affect the crop. The top of the root turns black and rot spreads from there. A late sowing at close spacing, producing small roots, are two ways of reducing the likelihood of infection. Also, some varieties are resistant.

Celery leaf miner (larvae of fly *Euleia heraclei*)

Leaves develop dry, brown patches where the interior tissue has been eaten by the maggots. Pick off affected parts of the leaves and squash them to kill the larvae within.

Harvest

Loosen the soil carefully around the root with a spade or fork, being careful to avoid damage. For children, avoid varieties that are recommended for showing. Choose shorter ones.

Recommended varieties

Avonresister is one of the shortest varieties and also resistant to canker. Sow at 10cm intervals in rows 20cm apart.

SWEETCORN (*Zea mays*, VARIETY *rugosa*)

Sweetcorn was developed from a natural mutation of maize.
Whereas maize produces starch in the kernels, sweetcorn
produces sugar. Sweetcorn might not be the most productive
crop in terms of food per square metre but they are statuesque
plants providing a sweet and tasty seasonal treat. They also
produce a large volume of coarse biomass for composting.

Site and soil

An open site with full light and plenty of sun is important but
shelter from strong winds is also desirable. The soil needs to be
free draining, with a good organic matter content but sweetcorn
is fairly tolerant of a range of soil textures, although it does not
grow well in clay. A slightly acid soil, pH 6–6.5, is ideal.

When and where to sow

In warm, lowland areas of Britain sweetcorn may be direct-
sown. As a grass, it is not closely related to any other garden
crop. So, it could go anywhere in the rotation, but as a tender
plant requiring indoor germination in most areas and, as it
prefers a relatively low pH, it should be included with the other
tender crops – squashes and tomatoes, etc. Indoors, sow about
a month before the last spring frost is expected, after which it
will be safe to plant out. Germination is usually good. So, to
avoid wasting seed, sow singly in 9cm pots but discard any very
small or discoloured seeds. Some books recommend peat pots,
to avoid root disturbance when planting but I have never had a
problem of plants failing to thrive after planting (see Appendix
II). The plants should be in the pots long enough for the roots
to fill the space, so that they will hold the soil together, but

without being pot-bound. As sweetcorn will be the tallest of the crops in the 'tender' plot, plant them in the northernmost bed to minimize shading of other crops.

Spacing and planting

The male flowers are at the top of the plant and are descriptively called tassels, whilst the female flowers, usually only one or two per plant and looking like small, thin cobs encased in green leaves, branch out from the stem. From the end of the nascent cob protrudes a cluster of fine, yellow 'silks' which are the stigmas that receive the pollen. A grain of pollen from another plant (sweetcorn are not self-fertile) has to fall on each thread of silk for each kernel to develop and leave no gaps on the cob. The bed system is, therefore, particularly advantageous for sweetcorn. Good pollination in a single row would be less likely.

Opinions vary as to spacing. I tend to err on the side of close spacing. In a 1.2m bed four rows may be planted. In a metre or 90cm-wide bed I would plant three rows. In each case plant rows 30cm apart. Spacing along the row is also 30cm. However, if this seems too crowded (cultivars vary in size), spacing along the rows can be increased. In this case you could introduce a refinement, if planting rather than direct sowing, so that the leaves are aligned along the rows to fill the extra space! It should be noted that this close spacing is appropriate only if one bed is being grown. If two or more adjacent beds are grown, a wider spacing is recommended – perhaps just three rows in a 1.2m bed, and 40cm apart along the rows.

If plants have been grown in a greenhouse or conservatory where temperatures have been high, a transitional period of a week for the plants to 'harden off' is advisable. Transfer the pots to cloches or a cold frame. Both can be opened up in the daytime. Or, if the weather is really warm, pots can just be left outside and only brought inside again if the night temperature is forecast to be low. (See Appendix II for information on transplanting.)

Care

Catch crops of radish, rocket, spring onions or lettuce can be grown in between sweetcorn. Ideally, spring onion and lettuce would be sown about a month before planting out the sweetcorn. To be really intensive, any of these catch crops can be sown in drills going both ways, leaving squares for the sweetcorn to go into later. Precise measuring is called for! As the sweetcorn grows, lettuces will do well in the partial shade at the time of year when the sun is strongest. They will be less likely to bolt. If the site is unavoidably exposed to strong winds you might have to forgo the catch crops so that the stems of sweetcorn can be earthed up to support them. Alternatively, knock in stakes and support with strings. Keep the bed weed free. When the male flowers, or 'tassels', are fully out at the top of the plants, if there is no wind, tap the stems with a thin stick to see if pollen is being produced. It looks like fine yellow powder. If you do see it and the weather stays calm, tap the plants each day until no more pollen comes out. This will ensure good pollination and a minimum of gaps on the cobs.

Pests and diseases

Pests

Mice can be a problem with seeds sown directly in the garden. Put traps down. Birds, squirrels and badgers could be a problem in some areas when the cobs are fully grown.

Sweetcorn smut
This is caused by the fungus *Ustilago maydis*. Individual kernels swell up and eventually burst, releasing spores which can remain in the soil for up to five years. Remove and burn any cobs with noticeable swellings and cut out and burn any swellings (galls) on leaves or stems. The problem is only likely to occur in hot, dry weather.

Frit flies (Oscinella frit)
The first symptoms are longitudinal yellow stripes on the leaves of young plants. Eventually the leaves develop a shredded appearance. White larvae, 5mm long, may be found feeding at the base of leaves or in the stems. Growth is stunted and the crop will be poor. The growing point of the plant can be killed. The fly's eggs are laid near the base of the stem in early summer and hatch three weeks later. Healthy, fast growing plants are less likely to be attacked. If only a few plants are affected, pull them up and burn. If the problem is widespread there is little that can be done that season. Sowing seeds in larger pots and allowing plants to grow larger before planting out should avoid the problem, a) because the first egg laying period is likely to have passed and b) larger plants are less susceptible.

Aphids
These may be seen on the cobs in some years but they seem to cause little problem.

Harvest
When you notice the first cob with 'silks' starting to turn brown, it is probably ready to eat. You could test by peeling back the green leaves or husks and pressing a finger nail into one of the kernels, though not the very end ones, which will be

less mature. If what comes out looks like milk, it is ready. Hold the plant stem with one hand and snap the pod downwards. Peel off all the leaves, pull off the silks and cook as soon as possible, in a little boiling water for no more than a few minutes. As soon as sweetcorn is picked, the sugar in the kernels starts to change to starch. It might take a couple of days for a complete change but why lose any sweetness? The sugar in sweetcorn also turns to starch as the cobs mature. This is why it is important to harvest at the optimum time.

Recommended varieties

There are early, mid-season and late cultivars available. In southern, lowland Britain, late ones can be grown but in northern or upland areas it is advisable to grow only early cultivars. Sugar-enhanced varieties have the same amount of sugar as their antecedents but it takes longer for the sugar to turn to starch. Supersweet varieties have more sugar. Some suggestions are:

▶ 'First of All', normal sweetness, early and suitable for cooler areas.

▶ 'Sundance', normal sweetness, early, vigorous and suitable for cooler areas.

▶ 'Dickson', early, supersweet.

▶ 'Honey Bantam', early, supersweet, yellow and white kernels.

▶ 'Ovation', mid season, supersweet.

▶ 'Dynasty', late, supersweet.

TOMATOES (*Lycopersicon esculentum*)

Tomatoes are well worth growing in a garden, as the fruit can be left to ripen properly before picking, when they will then have more flavour than commercially grown fruit, which has to be picked before fully ripe in order to survive transport and not be over-ripe in the shop. However, growing tomatoes outside is unreliable; expect a crop one year in four, as they are susceptible to potato blight, although this can be avoided if you choose to spray with a fungicide. Blight usually strikes just as the fruit on the first truss are about to turn red. Outdoor tomatoes are, however, susceptible to fewer pests and diseases than those grown under cover.

There are two main types of tomato, in terms of the way they grow: vine and bush. A few varieties are intermediate. Vines would continue to grow until stopped by frost and can reach several metres in a glasshouse. Each type requires different methods of care.

Site and soil

An open, sunny site is best, or against a south-facing wall or fence. They will not do well in a shady position. Tomatoes like a well drained, fertile soil that contains plenty of organic matter.

When and where to sow

Sow in seed trays or small pots no more than eight weeks before the last frost is expected, if they are to be grown outside. Sow about 2cm deep. In a fine, moisture retentive soil sowing need not be quite so deep. As soon as seeds have germinated the plants need to be given as much light as possible. Any restriction on light will result in tall, weak plants and the fruit yield will also be reduced. I have only ever used glass cloches for raising tender plants but if a frost is likely I cover them with paper sacks over night. The same would apply to cold frames. A heated greenhouse or conservatory is fine. A south facing window will do, although light is restricted there. Ideally, the young plants would be grown in temperatures of 21–27°C.

When grown in trays, plants should be pricked out into pots when the first two proper leaves have grown. Hold the seedlings by one leaf and avoid touching the delicate stem. Lift out of the soil using the blade of a knife. If sowing direct into pots and you want to maximize the number of plants, sow one seed per pot and accept there will be some that do not emerge. If you have plenty of seed and only need a few plants, sow two or three per pot and pinch out the weaker plants.

As tomatoes are members of the Solanaceae family, logically, they could be grown in the same plot as potatoes but there will probably not be room. They are best grown with other tender crops in the plot where potatoes were grown the previous year. The ground will have been well cultivated and had compost or manure incorporated. They may also be grown spaced out amongst the brassicas as tomato plants do have some effect in deterring cabbage white butterflies.

Spacing and planting
If the tomatoes are to be grown all together in a bed, plant two rows per bed, about 25cm from each side, depending on the width of the bed. Along the row vine types can be planted about 40cm apart. The spacing for bush types will vary depending on variety – anything from 30 to 70cm. If grown amongst brassicas they can be between one and two metres apart.

Care

Vine tomatoes may be supported by canes or pointed sticks, or under cover, by strings. Use natural fibre garden twine or thick wool to tie plants to the sticks. Tie the string/wool tightly to the stick first then pass it round the stem once or twice before tying the ends together. The string should be loose round the stem, to allow for growth and so that it does not rub against the stick.

Bush plants do not need tying up but some of the fruit will hang down to the ground and be vulnerable to slugs and snails and also become splashed with soil. Straw can be spread around underneath the plants to reduce these problems. Pieces of wood could be used instead of straw. Intermediate plants will need some tying up but they do not have a single stem like the vine types. With vine types I have sometimes pinched out the lowest truss on each plant as soon as it appears, mainly to avoid the problem of slug damage on fruit but also to avoid soil-borne fungal infections that can be splashed up from the ground.

If there is a threat of frost after planting out and you do not have any cloches, an upturned cardboard box will do. Open out the flaps and weigh them down with stones.

On vine types it is advisable to remove the side shoots. These emerge from the base of the plant and also in the angle where leaf stems meet the main stem. Side shoots can be snapped off using finger and thumb, and can then be grown as cuttings. If they have grown several leaves, break off the larger ones, to reduce transpiration, leaving two or three young leaves at the tip and plant firmly in a small pot.

When the first truss has formed on vine plants, break or cut off any leaves growing at a lower level. Blight thrives in damp conditions, and the lower leaves can be where the blight starts. Removing them will improve air flow and allow watering without getting any leaves wet. At one garden I worked in I had planted a whole outdoor bed of tomatoes. They were doing well until, over one weekend, someone positioned a reciprocating sprinkler to irrigate the middle half of the bed. Within days that part of the crop went down with blight. Always water the soil around tomato plants not the foliage.

In general I resist watering vegetables but in a prolonged dry spell if tomato plants begin to show signs of drought, water every day if need be. Avoid just wetting the surface, leaving dry soil underneath. This will encourage roots to remain near the surface, making them more vulnerable to drought if, for any reason, watering is stopped. If you are unsure how much water is enough, wait a couple of hours after watering then dig a little hole near the plant and see how far down the soil is moist. Repetition of applying too much water and then leaving the soil to become dried out can cause blossom end rot or the fruits to split. So, with tomatoes, the rule of thumb is, quite a lot, quite often.

Keep the ground free of weeds. Weeds compete for moisture and impede air flow around the plants.

Pests and diseases

Tomatoes are susceptible to many pests and diseases, more so when grown under cover. However, I have only ever encountered one problem – potato blight – on outdoor plants. It is fairly easy to avoid blight on indoor plants. If grown in a well drained, fertile soil containing plenty of organic matter few problems are likely to be encountered, apart from blight, which

can affect any plant, given the right conditions, however
healthy it is.

Caterpillars

These are the larvae of the tomato moth. They are green or
brown. When young they feed on the leaves but later tunnel
into the fruit and stems. A daily inspection will enable you to
catch them while still on the leaves. If they are difficult to find,
try going out at night with a torch, as many caterpillars are
more active then. Pick off and squash them or feed to the birds
if you are confident they will be eaten before they can return to
the tomatoes!

Potato cyst eelworm/nematodes

If large numbers are present in the soil and infest the roots the
effects are stunted growth and wilting foliage, which might be
purplish on the underside (see under potatoes for further
information). If large swellings are found on the roots the cause
is root knot eelworm. Whichever eelworm is involved, carefully
dig up plants and burn them.

Red spider mite

The outdoor red spider mite (*Panonychus ulmi*) is not generally
a problem, as they are controlled by natural predators. The
glasshouse red spider mite (*Tetranychus urticae*) can build up to
large numbers in hot dry conditions. The symptoms might first
be noticed on the upper leaf surface, which begins to lose its
green colour, developing a fine mottling of paler green. On the
underside of the leaf will be numerous yellow-green mites 1mm
long together with spherical eggs. Using a magnifying glass you
might see two dark spots on the backs of the mites near the
head end. With heavy infestations a silky white webbing can

cover leaves and stems. The indoor mite turns orange or red in the autumn or winter.

Keeping the air humid can help to suppress numbers but avoid spraying the foliage with water as this might encourage blight. Keeping the soil moist, for plant growth, and dampening the floor will ensure a humid atmosphere. There is a predatory mite available called *Phytoseiulus persimilis* but it needs to be introduced before the pest mites have built up to large numbers.

Whitefly

Trialeurodes vaporariorum is the glasshouse whitefly, which has the appearance of a tiny white moth, about 2mm long, with a wing span of 3mm. They feed on the underside of leaves and fly up in clouds when disturbed. Eggs are laid under the leaves and hatch into flat, oval, scale-like nymphs. Adults and nymphs secrete 'honeydew' which drops on to leaves below. Sooty moulds then grow on the honeydew. Outdoors whitefly are not a problem as there are plenty of predators but in the glass house or polytunnel they can be a serious pest, sucking sap from the plant. Hanging yellow, flycatcher cards above the plants will help. There is a tiny parasitic wasp called *Encarsia formosa* that can be bought from suppliers of biological controls. *Encarsia* needs to be released before the whitefly population has built up to become a serious problem, as the wasp needs time to breed and increase its population. If the predators are introduced, the flycatcher cards should be removed as they will attract beneficial insects as well as pests. African marigolds (*Tagetes erecta*) may be grown alongside tomato plants and are said to deter whitefly.

Blossom drop

With this condition flowers wither and break off; pollination has not occurred. Dry conditions in soil and air are usually the cause. It is not usually a problem with outdoor plants. Water indoor plants with sufficient quantity and frequency to maintain soil moisture. In the mornings (to allow time to dry to avoid blight) flowers may be sprayed with a fine mist of water and the plants tapped or shaken to promote the shedding of pollen.

Blossom end rot

The symptom is a dark, sunken area at the end of the fruit. The cause is calcium deficiency, usually caused by the soil being too dry.

Blotchy ripening

Parts of the fruit remain green or orange when the rest of the fruit has ripened. The cause might be too high a temperature or potassium deficiency. Potassium deficiency is easily avoided by using compost to which urine and/or wood ash has been added during the composting process.

Buckeye rot

A grey spot is surrounded by concentric brown rings on unripe fruit. The infecting spores are splashed up from the soil surface. To avoid this the lowest truss on each plant can be tied up clear of the ground. Alternatively, pinch out the lowest truss (on vine types) as soon as they appear, which will also avoid slug problems.

Curled up leaves

An inward/upward curl of young leaves, provided they are a normal green colour, does not indicate a problem. Curling of older leaves could be caused by excess deleafing or too much difference between day and night temperatures. No action need be taken.

Dry set
The fruit develops to the size of a match head and then stops. This is rarely a problem on outdoor crops. The cause is the air being too hot and dry at the time of pollination. Mist the plants with water in the mornings.

Foot rot
A brown, shrunken area at the base of the stem. If this happens, the roots will also be rotting. It is caused by a fungal infection, and can be a problem with seedlings though it rarely occurs on mature plants. Avoid over watering. Remove affected plants, together with the soil around the roots, and burn.

Ghost spot
Small pale green or yellow rings appear on the fruit skin, caused by spores of the botrytis mould. It is not a serious problem and the fruit may still be eaten.

Greenback
The upper area of the fruit, around the stalk, remains green and firm when the rest has ripened. The cause is too high a temperature or a lack of potassium and, possibly, phosphorous.

Grey mould (botrytis)
Grey mould usually starts on a damaged stem and can spread to other parts of the plant. If caught in time, affected areas can be cut out. Improve the ventilation of indoor plants. Remove any decaying leaves or fruit plus a few more lower leaves to

improve air circulation. Perhaps plant further apart next year.

Leaf mould

Lower leaves are affected first. Yellowish patches appear on the upper surface while underneath patches of purplish brown mould are seen. Remove affected leaves and improve ventilation, especially at night. Avoid watering late in the day.

Magnesium deficiency

Lower leaves are affected first. The areas between the leaf veins turn yellow, leaving a narrow band of green next to the vein. Later, the yellow areas may turn red, purple or brown. Magnesium is leached from soil by heavy rain or over watering, especially in light, sandy soils. Deficiency is most common in acid soils. Excessive use of high potassium fertilizer can result in magnesium being unavailable to plant roots. A foliar feed of seaweed extract might help. If your soil is acid, sandy and in a high rainfall area and you suspect it is deficient in magnesium, use ground magnesium limestone for future applications of lime.

Potato blight

This is caused by the fungus *Phytophthora infestans* and is the most likely and serious disease to affect outdoor tomatoes. It can be avoided on indoor plants by watering the soil not the leaves and only watering in the mornings, so that any wetted foliage will dry off quickly. The first symptoms are brown patches on the edges of the leaves. A white mould develops on the underside of these areas. Affected areas spread until the whole leaf dies. Black patches appear on the stems. (For more information see p.193, 'Pests and diseases of potatoes'.)

Split fruit

This occurs after heavy rain or watering after the soil has become dry. The sudden spurt in growth causes the skin to split. Mould then develops on the exposed flesh. This can be cut off before eating but frequent inspection will enable affected fruit to be picked before mould sets in. Water indoor plants sufficiently frequently to prevent soil drying out, which might not be every day if the weather is cool and overcast. I try to resist watering outdoor plants. In most gardens, in most seasons the roots will be able to find sufficient water.

Stem rot

This is a disease of mature plants. The lower leaves turn yellow and the base of the stem becomes brown and shrunken. Black dots develop on the affected stem. Badly affected plants should be dug up and burned. The roots will be seen not to have decayed.

Sun scald

Fruits develop a sunken area with a pale, papery skin on the side facing the glass. Papery patches also develop on leaves. The cause is exposure to too much bright sun. Some shading is needed. Dampen the atmosphere by spraying water on the floor in the morning when watering the plants.

Verticillium wilt

This is caused by a soil-borne fungus *Verticillium albo-atrum*. The first symptoms can be yellow blotches on the lower leaves and brown veins. The yellow patches develop into brown dead spots. These symptoms progress up the plant but the top stays green. Leaves can wilt in hot weather but then recover in the cooler evenings, but sometimes no actual wilting occurs. If the stem is cut through, a brown ring will be seen. If cut longitudinally, two brown streaks will be seen a little way in from the skin, from ground level to as much as 30cm up the stem. If the problem occurs on indoor plants, change the soil before growing tomatoes there again, or choose a resistant variety. With outdoor crops, a four or five year rotation should be adequate to avoid infestation. The fungus needs longer than a 24-hour period of saturated soil to become active. Water indoor crops only when necessary; every second day might suffice. Avoid over watering at any time.

Viruses

There are several viruses that can infect tomatoes, producing a variety of symptoms. Leaves might be mottled and curled, thin and distorted, stems might have dark vertical streaks and growth might be stunted. Fruit can be mottled and bronzed. Destroy affected plants.

Weedkiller damage

Tomato plants are very sensitive to hormone weedkillers. Spray drift from a neighbour or residues on straw can severely affect plants. Leaves become distorted, thin and twisted. Leaf stalks and stems are also twisted. Fruit becomes plum-shaped and hollow.

Recommended varieties

There are many to choose from. One supplier I use listed 111 in their 2009 catalogue, while another had 46. Most varieties need to be grown under glass/plastic in Britain and northern Europe but that still leaves plenty to choose from for outside growing.

ASPARAGUS (*Asparagus officinales*)

Site and soil

A well-draining soil is essential. If there is a danger of water logging, or if the soil has a high clay content, consider creating a raised bed, with or without retaining boards. If possible, avoid a frost pocket but some shelter from strong winds is desirable. Asparagus does not like an acid soil but is tolerant of a wide pH range – 6.3–7.5. It is very important to clear the ground of perennial weeds before planting. Depending on how much space is available or how many plants (which are called crowns) you wish to grow, two rows can be grown in a 70cm wide bed or three rows in a metre wide bed. When clearing the bed of perennial weeds, make sure that the surrounding ground is also cleared, so that there is no possibility of roots creeping back in. Dig in plenty of compost or well rotted manure.

When and where to plant

Asparagus can be grown from seed but it will be three years before the first crop can be taken. It is more usual to buy one-year-old crowns and start cutting two years after planting. Plant in spring when the soil conditions seem suitable, not too cold or wet. Asparagus is a perennial crop which can remain productive for up to 20 years and, therefore, should be grown in a separate area from the rotational plots.

Spacing and planting

Two rows may be grown in a 70cm wide bed or three rows in a metre wide bed. For each row dig a trench 30cm wide and 20cm deep. Put in some compost and turn it in with a spade, not deeply but so that it is incorporated with the soil. Use the cultivator or a fork to mix it more thoroughly. If there is no compost available or if plenty was added during bed preparation, the trench does not need to be quite so deep. Loosen the soil along the base of the trench and form it into a curved ridge along its length about 8cm high. Or, as a refinement, use a trowel to create a dome of soil at each planting position (30cm apart, crown centre to centre) along the row. Spread the roots of the crowns over the ridge or dome. To allow a little more space for the roots the plants can be staggered – each plant opposite a space in the next row. Put back some of the soil and level it, with the centre of the crowns covered by about 5cm. When putting back the soil, use your fingers to work it in between the roots so that there is good root-soil contact and no large air pockets left. If necessary, crumble up any large lumps of soil used to cover the crowns. Add the rest of the soil as the shoots grow. It is important not to let the roots dry out before planting. Keep the crowns damp.

Care

Keep the bed free of weeds. Allow all the shoots to grow into 'ferns' for the first two years. If the ferns are exposed to strong winds, the rocking of the stems can cause damage to the crowns. Provide some support with strings along each side of the bed. Each year when the ferns have turned yellow cut them down, leaving stumps of a few centimetres.

Pests and diseases

Slugs and snails

These can eat the young shoots as they come up. Evening and early morning patrols with a sharp knife is one answer for slugs. Pieces of slate or large leaves left on the soil surface will attract slugs and sometimes snails to hide underneath, so that you need not get up quite so early in the morning. Snails can be removed to a safe distance or where a thrush might find them, or crushed under foot. I have never tried beer traps for slugs but many people find them effective.

Asparagus beetle (Crioceris asparagi)

This is 6–8mm long, has a red thorax and black wing cases with six square yellow markings. The larvae are up to 1cm long, grey and described as hump-backed. They eat young shoots as they start growing in late spring and two to four generations continue until early autumn. Adults and larvae also strip the outer skin from stems and eat leaves. Beetles and larvae may be picked off by hand throughout the season. If this is impractical, spray with pyrethrum at dusk so as not to harm beneficial insects. If the infestation has been particularly bad into the summer, cut the ferns off a little earlier than usual, just as they *begin* to turn yellow. Burn these or put into compost heap if you are confident it will get hot. This will destroy any adults, larvae and eggs that might be on the foliage.

Foot and root rots

Symptoms appear at the stem base, a darkening and softening of the tissue. The foliage wilts, changes colour and begins to die. Roots might also begin to rot. Various fungi could be responsible. Remove and burn affected plants as soon as possible. Also remove the soil immediately surrounding the roots. If you are going to have a large bonfire, keep the soil to add to it.

Rust

Various fungi cause symptoms of rust-coloured spots on the foliage. Cut out and burn or compost affected parts as soon as possible.

Violet root rot
This is caused by the fungus *Helicobasidion brebissonii*, (synonym *purpureum*.) The foliage turns yellow and growth is stunted. The roots are covered in dark purple strands and a large quantity of soil will stick to the roots when lifted. Black fruiting bodies (sclerotia) might also be seen. These drop to the ground and can persist for many years. The problem is most likely to occur in wet, acid soils in warm conditions. Remove and destroy affected plants as soon as possible, preferably before the fruiting bodies have developed.

Thin spears
There are three likely causes: cutting began too soon after planting, cutting continued for too long the previous year, or the soil is not sufficiently fertile.

Harvest
Two years after planting one-year-old crowns the first harvest can be taken. When the spears are about 15cm tall cut them at least 5cm below the surface, using a sharp knife or an asparagus knife, taking care not to damage any other shoots not yet visible. Only cut for five weeks in this first year. In subsequent years cutting can continue for eight weeks. Stop cutting in mid June even if the start of cutting was less than eight weeks before. Leave all subsequent spears to develop into 'ferns'. This allows the plant to build up reserves for next year's crop.

Recommended varieties
All male hybrids (AMH) are more vigorous than open-pollinated varieties and tend to have higher yields. They do not waste resources producing seeds. Some suggestions are:

▶ 'Backlim', all male hybrid (AMH).

▶ 'Cito', early AMH, high yielding long spears.

▶ 'Connover's Colossal', available as seed or crowns, early, thick spears.

▶ 'Guelph Millennium', AMH from Canada, suitable for cooler areas.

▶ 'Pacific 2000', AMH, highly rated for flavour, low fibre content (stringless).

▶ 'Purple Pacific', AMH, stringless, sweet and high yielding.

JERUSALEM ARTICHOKES (*Helianthus tuberosus*)

Jerusalem artichokes have nothing to do with Jerusalem nor are they artichokes. They are a tuberous relation of the sunflower and native to North America. The name is thought to be a corruption of the Italian *girasole articiocco* which means sunflower artichoke. When samples were first sent to Europe in the 17th century they were described as tasting like globe artichokes.

Site and soil

Jerusalem artichokes will grow best in full light but will tolerate partial shade. They are tolerant of a wide range of soil textures but will not thrive in very acid soils or where the ground becomes waterlogged in winter. A deep, fertile loam or sandy loam will give the best results. Dig in some compost or well-rotted manure before planting.

When and where to plant

Propagation is by tuber, as with potatoes. Best results will be obtained if they are included in the rotation, rather than being grown in the same place each year. If you have orientated the beds as near to east-west as possible, plant them in the northernmost bed, so that they will not shade other crops. As they are not closely related to any other crop, grow them in whichever plot you can spare the space. Planting may be done any time from when you begin to harvest, through to late winter or early spring, provided you do not damage any shoots.

Spacing and planting

In a 120cm wide bed you could squeeze in three rows, 50cm apart along the rows. In a metre wide bed, plant two rows, 40cm apart along the rows. Aim for no more than six plants per square metre. Select, for planting, undamaged tubers at least the size of a hen's egg. Depending on the stage of development, shoots will begin to curve upwards, indicating which way up to plant the tuber. Dig a hole with a trowel and plant at least 15cm deep. Firm the soil after filling in the hole.

Care

Keep weed-free, by hand or hoe. Unless you have a dwarf variety, artichokes can grow to 3m tall. In exposed positions they can blow over, exposing the tubers. To avoid this, or if you just want shorter plants, when they are about 1.5m tall (the height is not critical) cut the stems at just above a side shoot, or pair of leaves, at about a metre from the ground. They will produce new shoots, which can be cut again if they get too tall. The variety 'Dwarf Sunray' produces many flowers, which are decorative but if you are more interested in the crop of tubers, the flowers should be cut off. Tall varieties rarely flower in Britain. In autumn, plants can be left to die off completely, or, when the lower leaves have gone yellow, the stems can be cut off about 30cm from the ground and chopped up and composted. An old-fashioned heavy sickle is useful for this, holding the stem in one hand and chopping off convenient lengths with the sickle. The coarse stems are useful for providing aeration in the compost heap.

Pests and diseases

Slugs and snails sometimes eat the shoots as they emerge from the ground. Slugs also burrow into tubers during the winter, although this is not usually a serious problem. If there are mice in your area, they can do more serious damage to the tubers. Tell-tale holes in the soil next to the plants will indicate a rodent problem. If you only have a few plants they can be dug up and stored in a bucket of damp soil in a cool, rodent-proof place or in plastic bags in the fridge or a cool place. Unlike potatoes, artichokes will dry out in a couple of days unless kept cool and moist. If there are too many to store, consider putting traps down for the mice.

In over thirty years of growing Jerusalem artichokes mine have never had any diseases. They can, however, be infected by the fungus Sclerotinia (*Sclerotinia sclerotiorum*) which usually occurs at the base of the stem but can spread to any part of the plant. Its appearance is like fluffy cotton wool. Lift and burn affected plants as soon as possible.

Harvest

Harvest can be any time from when the leaves start to die off and throughout the winter, if the ground is not frozen. Push a fork in at least 30cm from the stem and, pulling on the remains of the stem with one hand, lever the stump out of the ground with the fork, together with whatever tubers remain attached. If the ground is hard you might need to loosen the soil all round the plant first. Invariably, there will be one or two tubers further out that will get speared by the fork. Try to get every tuber out, as they will come up the following year, in early May in England, which might be after you have sown another crop. Tubers are best eaten straight away but can be kept a few days or even weeks if suitable conditions can be provided. (See above under pests and diseases.)

Recommended varieties

I was given a few tubers from an old garden in Shropshire when I first started serious gardening. Most people probably acquire them in a similar way but there are named varieties: 'Fuseau' has long, smooth-skinned tubers; 'Dwarf Sunray' produces many small flowers.

Weeds

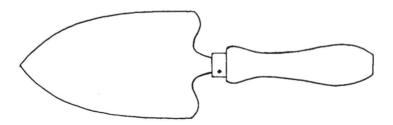

INTRODUCTION

Weeds are sometimes defined as plants where you do not want them to be. Grasses are weeds in a strawberry bed but strawberries would be weeds in a lawn and potatoes are weeds where they were grown, and missed being dug up, the previous year. More commonly, what we think of as weeds are, mostly, wild native plants that have adapted, over millennia, to the habitat where they are growing. Centuries of people trying to get rid of them in fields and gardens could have had an effect on their evolution: a constant process of selection for the most vigorous and best adapted to the conditions that farming and gardening provide.

The progeny of an individual weed that manages to grow and seed under the shade of a crop and unseen by the gardener will have a selective advantage. For a given species, the individuals that produce seed in the shortest time after germinating will also have an advantage. If the fast-maturing trait is inherited, successive generations will require more frequent weeding to control weeds with that trait. Weeding, therefore, could be likened to taking a course of antibiotics, where, if the patient fails to complete the course, a small population of only the most resistant (to the antibiotic) bacteria will remain in the body. When weeding, if you are intending/attempting to get every weed out but fail to, and if those left go on to set seed, repetition of this process could be selecting for increasingly problematic populations of weeds with particular strengths, such as:

1   fast maturing; growing and seeding in between sessions of weeding;

2   ability to grow and seed in the shade of crops;

3   perennial weeds that have roots more fanged and difficult to dig out, or roots which more easily break, leaving pieces to re-grow;

4   individual weeds that more closely resemble the crop they are growing amongst and which get missed out in the weeding process. (This last point might be a subjective impression and not actually true!)

WEEDING: SOME GENERAL POINTS

The saying about the shadow of the gardener being the best fertilizer is analogous to the problem of weeds. Walking round every part of the garden, more frequently in summer than winter, enables you to deal with weeds at the easiest stage, before they overtake the growth of seedling crops and certainly well before they set seed. It would be a good idea to regard weeding as the most important job in gardening, because if it is neglected, everything else becomes much more difficult, plus there will be many more weeds next year. Another saying is, 'one year's seeding, seven years weeding'. Each weed plant can produce thousands of seeds. Once seeds are within the soil they can remain dormant but viable for many years. There is a range of dormancy in seeds from each plant so that, even if they are near enough to the surface to germinate, only a percentage of them will do so.

How to deal with weeds in a new garden is dealt with in Chapter 2 and perennial weeds are covered in Chapter 4, but once a garden is established, weeding settles down to a year-round activity, with a peak in summer. For the first few years in a garden, having as your aim the elimination of all weeds is probably a good strategy. It provides the impetus to be assiduous and thorough. However, it is very difficult to get every weed out when there is a dense canopy of crops, and very few people live long enough working in the same garden to allow them to exhaust the seed bank in the soil. Then there are the wind-blown seeds that arrive each year from beyond the garden. So, elimination is never achieved. However, after only a few years a manageable equilibrium can be achieved.

I suppose opinions differ, perhaps according to one's character, but I found that at this stage I began to enjoy weeding. I think it is wise to regard it as a priority because if neglected there will be many more weeds thereafter, yields will be depressed, all garden operations are hampered by the sheer volume of biomass, and some weeds are hosts to crop pests and carriers of crop diseases. Think of the time spent pulling or hoeing each weed as avoiding having to spend a thousand times as long pulling or hoeing the descendents of that weed if it were left to go to seed. Weeding is a very good investment! I find it helpful and effective to adopt a methodical approach. On entering the garden at any time of year a hierarchy of priorities will be apparent.

PRIORITIES IN WEEDING

Flowering and seeding weeds

First of all, if there are any weeds going to seed, the seed heads should be pulled off and put in a bucket or bag to await burning, deep burial, immersion in water for two months or, if you are confident of achieving a hot compost heap, placed in the middle of an active one and covered with non-seedy material. The same treatment should be applied to weeds that are only at the flowering stage. If flowering weeds are pulled up and left lying around or put on the compost heap, unless the weather is very hot and dry, they can continue developing and produce seed. This is particularly noticeable with dandelion, sow thistle and groundsel. Once the flower and seed heads have been removed the rest of the plant can be put on the compost heap.

The technique of immersing seedy weeds in water for two months will kill the seeds but also produce some smelly liquid. This may be used as a fertilizer or just added to the compost heap, along with the fibrous remains of the weeds.

It is very important, having pulled off the flowers or seed heads of growing weeds, that the rest of the plant is pulled or dug up and put on the compost heap soon afterwards – preferably straight away, otherwise you might forget. The reason for this is that, having lost the main flowering stem, the plant is stimulated into producing side shoots to grow replacement flowers. These new shoots seem to develop more rapidly than the original flowering stem; they will be growing nearer to the horizontal and, depending on where the main stem was broken off, they will be nearer to the ground and, therefore, more difficult to see if surrounded by crops. This reaction can be clearly seen with sow thistle. They will, typically, produce five new shoots if the main cluster of flowers is broken off. So, you could end up with five times as many seeds than if the first cluster of flowers were left. This reaction could be an evolutionary adaptation to grazing.

If there is an area of ground awaiting cultivation it is a risky strategy repeatedly to cut off flowering weeds. Each time they are cut, new side shoots will grow, maturing to seed in a shorter time than the original growth would have done. This branched growth is closer to the ground and therefore becomes increasingly difficult to cut. Not all species are so problematic, however (see below). A better approach, depending on which weeds are present, might be to let weeds grow to the flower bud stage, then selectively pull them out, concentrating on those that would be the most troublesome if allowed to shed their seed. In my view these are weeds that produce wind-borne seeds or vast numbers of seeds, e.g. rose bay willowherb, thistles, groundsel, nettles, docks and fat hen. With a leather glove, most can be pulled out or helped with a fork. If docks are too big and there is not time to dig out the roots, if the stems are cut with secateurs or loppers at ground level it will be weeks before replacement stems can mature. Replacement dock shoots grow upwards and will become visible. Willowherb and nettles will break off just below ground but they will also take a long time to re-grow and will produce upright stems, making them clearly visible. With this strategy you are dealing with each weed once instead of repeatedly having to cut them off.

Clearing the paths

If there are perennial weeds coming up in the paths between beds or surrounding the garden, I would dig those out before weeding the beds rather than compact the soil further by walking on it. Annual weeds on the paths may be left until later, provided they are not in an advanced stage of flowering. In loose soils, a little compaction will make it easier to hoe the paths. However, there is an argument for doing first those jobs that might seem less important, to make sure they get done. If you always do the most urgent and important jobs first, it is possible that other jobs do not get done until they have become serious problems and are much more difficult to deal with. Clearing the paths, by digging out perennials and then hoeing annuals, is good for morale. It improves the appearance of the garden by clearly delineating the beds and allows clear access, but see 'hoeing' below. Rescuing smothered young crops might seem more urgent but because it is urgent, that job will get done anyway. By clearing the paths first, problems there are 'nipped in the bud' before they can spread to the beds, whether by perennial roots or seed from annuals.

Rescuing smothered young vegetables

After dealing with seeding weeds and also, perhaps, clearing the paths, the next priority could be to pull out a dense growth of weeds that is smothering a bed or beds of young vegetables.

'Rescuing' lost weeds

Later, the priority might be to pull out weeds that are about to be hidden by crops which are larger than the weeds, because if left, the weeds, far from being smothered, are more likely to continue developing and produce seeds, although not so many as they would if they had been able to grow to their full potential. It is a mistake to believe that any crop can smother weeds; the effect is never 100%. Even a small, spindly weed under a canopy of potato leaves can produce a few hundred seeds.

AN ALTERNATIVE STRATEGY: THE AREA APPROACH

Alternatively, you could adopt an area approach rather than the preceding 'subject' approach. The area approach is to start at one end of the garden and do everything that needs doing, bed by bed, plot by plot, regardless of priorities. For this to be successful you have to be disciplined and know that you will cover the whole garden before any problems become serious, e.g. weeds going to seed or weeds being covered by crops so that some are not found or damage is caused to the crop plants during the search. The advantage of this method is that when you have finished you know that everything is done and there is nothing to worry about. You can then start again!

HAND-WEEDING

Hand-weeding has a reputation for being boring and back-breaking. I can only relate my own experience of having a vegetable garden that proved just big enough to feed a growing family, provided it was managed intensively and efficiently. Ruthless weeding was a necessity in order to grow the amount we needed. Because it was a necessity to achieve that aim, weeding became a satisfying, even enjoyable activity. Again, I believe being methodical helps. The only time one needs to dart about in a seemingly random way is when, due to unavoidable neglect, there are individual weeds about to shed seed. Then the priority is to pull off the seed heads, as described above. At all other times I would say that it is more efficient, as well as more satisfying, to remove weeds completely from a particular area, according to the time available. Perhaps there is time to clear all the paths or hand-weed just one bed most in need of it. Then, to be able to stand back and see exactly what you have done is very satisfying.

Some people prefer to kneel or sit while weeding rather than bend or squat. To allow space to kneel or sit, the paths between beds would have to be much wider than has been recommended for optimum use of the ground. There would just be room to kneel in parallel to the beds but that would necessitate an awkward twisting position. In an intensive kitchen garden, bending and squatting are the only options. Both become uncomfortable after a few minutes but there are strategies to counter that.

Firstly, alternate between the two positions. Secondly, when standing and bending, rest one hand on a fork, which can be placed in the ground between rows. For this, it is more comfortable to use a fork which is shorter than the optimum length for digging. The advantage of a fork is that it does not compact the surface, but it could be injuring numerous creatures in the soil. I have not tried this but something like a shaft with a fork handle at both ends would probably be practical, or you could improvise something with a flat-bottomed block of wood at the end of a handle of whatever length suits. However, a fork might be needed anyway if some weeds need to be dug out. Thirdly, periodically, stand up (slowly, to avoid feeling faint due to loss of blood in the head), place both hands against your back at the waist, then slowly bend backwards, the neck and head also, keeping all muscles as relaxed as possible but with legs fully straightened. Repeat a few times, bending a little further each time. This prevents a build-up of strain and pain in the back.

When squatting, if it is not comfortable to bend both legs equally, alternate between which leg is bent most and takes most weight. Some support can still be provided by having a trowel in one hand and resting on that.

Particularly when weeding a bed of young vegetables that have become smothered by weeds it is very satisfying to start at one corner of the bed, work along to the other end, pulling out weeds as far as the middle line of the bed and then work back from the other side of the bed to clear the other half. To see the rows of young crop plants emerging from the jungle of weeds is an encouraging and pleasurable experience.

Having pulled up weeds, they can either be put into a bucket, which may then be emptied into a wheelbarrow or taken straight to the compost heap. Or, they can be left in piles along the path and collected later. No one will be *that* organized not to need two buckets or to make two sets of piles, one for weeds safe to be composted and the other for those that have gone to seed or have started to flower and will need to be burnt, drowned or deeply buried. However, if the weather is hot and you are confident of making a hot compost heap, all the weeds can go straight on to it. If seeding and flowering weeds are to be burnt, there is a problem of storing them until then, without the seeds dropping where they can grow or blowing around in the case of dandelion, sow thistle, etc. A paper sack is one option. It allows some drying out but, if the contents are compressed, remaining moisture dampens the 'fluffy' seeds to some extent, so that fewer of them blow away when the bag is emptied; or you could burn the sack along with its contents. If paper sacks are not available, make piles but try to keep fluffy seeding stuff covered by weeds that do not produce airborne seeds. Young weeds make ideal compost material. The soil sticking to the roots contains all the organisms necessary for decomposition and the soft, green material will heat up quickly. If the compost heap is enclosed and excludes light and if you expect it to get hot, perennial roots may be included. When the compost comes to be used, any roots found to be still living can be picked out and added to a new heap. Or, if you prefer and have the space, perennial roots can be spread out to dry before putting them on a heap. Otherwise, they can be put on to a pile of woody material waiting to be burnt. It is better to keep them off the ground to prevent them taking root again.

It will only be in the first year or two of a garden that has been neglected that a dense carpet of weeds will emerge. Provided that weeds are never allowed to go to seed, each year there will be fewer coming up. A graph of the decline in the number of weeds emerging each year would show a curve, with a rapid fall in numbers to begin with and a slower rate of decline from year to year. Alarming figures about how long weed seeds can remain dormant in the soil refer only to those that do survive. Each year a proportion will die naturally.

Research on frequently cultivated land growing vegetables, where weeds were not allowed to seed, revealed that each year the soil seed bank fell by about half, for one reason or another (Roberts, 1982: 116–7). So, after seven years the weed seed bank in the soil would be down to less than 1% of the original number. A very weedy field could have 75,000 viable weed seeds in each square metre of topsoil. If I have done my sums correctly, after seven years, halving the number each year, there would be 586 left. Cultivation brings some of the dormant seeds near enough to the surface to germinate. On average, of the total seed bank, only 5% will germinate each year, which means that in the seventh year there will be 29 weeds per square metre, which is about one every 18.5cm if in an even grid.

I used to wonder why, having pulled out every weed in a bed, a few weeks later there were what appeared to be just as many weeds there again. Two explanations come to mind. Both or neither might be correct:

1   Germination of weeds near enough to the surface to germinate is, for some reason, staggered over a period.

2   As you pull out a weed, some soil from throughout the rooting depth is pulled nearer to the surface. That soil will contain dormant weed seeds, and the soil that is shaken off the roots before the weed is taken away will also contain weed seeds.

HOEING

The Dutch hoe, used with a pushing action while walking backwards, is, in my view, far superior to the draw hoe. On the hard surface of the paths, the action of using a draw hoe requires more effort. If you progress backwards, you are continually covering weeds about to be hoed with weeds that have just been hoed. If you walk forwards, you will be treading on the weeds that have just been hoed. This does not matter much if they are going to be raked up and taken away but if you intend to leave them to dry out and die, unless conditions are very hot and dry, treading on weeds will enable some to take root again. In the compacted soil of the paths, the surface can be moist while the surface of the looser soil on the beds has dried out.

Some hoes are designed to cut with both forward and backward action. I have only used these in fields, where we were walking between widely-spaced rows, where the weeds were small and fairly sparse and where the soil was dry. In these conditions this type of hoe is very effective and fast. In a garden, with less room to manoeuvre between more closely-spaced rows and having to reach over to work from the paths, the more 'surgical' action of the push-only hoe is preferable, in my view.

When buying a Dutch hoe look for the narrowest width of blade and then, if the design allows, saw off as much as you can from each side to make it even narrower. This will enable you to get in between rows with less risk of damaging the plants. With the bed system, where the aim is optimum equidistant each way spacing of plants, there is limited opportunity for hoeing on the beds. It is only when plants are quite young that there is room to get a hoe between closely-spaced rows. Some will be too close from the start. Another advantage of a narrower blade is that for a given force of push there is more force exerted per centimetre of cutting edge, making it easier where weeds are dense or have been left too long and have become a little tough.

Some weeds thrive in the compacted soil of the paths. Annual meadow grass (*Poa annua*) and common pearlwort (*Sagina procumbens*) grew at an unbelievable rate on the paths in a garden I had for 19 years where, in spite of my determined efforts, I did not manage to eliminate either of them. Yet in every other garden I have worked in, these two species were not serious problems. The soil must have been particularly suitable in that one garden – and in the surrounding fields. I once spent a day pulling wild oats for the farmer. The effort of dragging my feet through a dense mat of annual meadow grass at the base of the barley resulted in a painful condition in the upper part of my feet for the next few days. If you have annual meadow grass on the paths it needs to be hoed more frequently than anything else, as it runs to seed very fast and will flower and seed all year round, provided the temperature is high enough to allow growth, i.e. above 5°C.

It is when hoeing the paths that you will appreciate the effort put in to raking up or picking off stones when the paths and beds were being laid out. Hoeing a stony path is hard work and will wear the hoe out much faster.

As well as the density of crops, another reason why hoeing opportunities on the beds are limited is the nature of the soil surface. Creating a fine, friable structure for sowing seeds and, subsequently, not treading on the soil leaves the surface layer fairly loose. If the hoe is not kept really sharp and if the weeds are a little too mature and tough, there is a tendency for them just to be pushed along rather than cut through. Then, if the soil is at all moist they will simply carry on growing. So, a sharp hoe and a fast action are required, which is a risky business between close rows of delicate young vegetables. Do not be surprised if there is never an opportunity to hoe the beds while crops are present.

Hoeing can be done with gusto when a bed has been cleared, after harvesting onions or garlic, for example, or when bean plants are cleared away. Then it is very satisfying to hoe and rake up the *few small weeds*, add them to the compost heap, go over the bed with the cultivator and sow something else, vegetable or cover crop.

I find hoeing a particularly pleasurable activity. It is usually done when the weather is warm and dry, it is done standing upright (bending should not be necessary), a satisfyingly useful job is being done, and it does not require much brain. You can think about other things at the same time. As with hand-weeding, it is as if a picture of the crop being hoed is keyed into the brain and everything else can be destroyed with little conscious thought, except if you come across a perennial weed, which should be pulled or dug out.

Sharpening a hoe

This should be done on the upper face of the blade only. The metal will wear away much more on the underside of the blade with use, especially from hoeing paths. As it wears, there is a tendency for the hoe to slide upwards, out of the soil. More and more downward pressure is then required to keep the blade slicing the weeds just below the soil surface. The aim should be to keep the underside of the blade flat right to its edge. It can be sharpened with a file, resting the hoe on a fence post or edge of a wall. Or, if there is a fine concrete surface, paving slab or flat stone available, provided you do not mind the mark it will leave, a hoe can be sharpened by turning it upside down, lowering the shaft until it is nearly parallel with the ground and, applying sufficient downward pressure, pushing it back and forth on the abrasive surface. If the angle of crank is right for hoeing, it will be about right for this method of sharpening.

The angle of crank

The angle of crank is critical. This refers to the angle between the shaft and the hoe blade. The optimum length of shaft is one that comes up to the eye level of the user, when the tip of the hoe rests on the ground. With this length of shaft, if the hoe is pushed from the end with one hand while the other merely acts as a guide, provided the blade has been sharpened on the upper face as recommended, it should slice through the soil horizontally, with no tendency to dig downwards or slip out of the soil. If there is not enough of a bend in the metal part, the blade will tend to dig downwards, or, to avoid that, you will need to bend down to lower the shaft to get the angle of the cutting part right. If there is too much of a bend, in order to make the hoe move horizontally through the soil, a very awkward action is required which is tiring on both arms.

I like to buy just the hoe head and make a handle to fit, either from a pole of hazel or holly or, better still, by rounding off a length of sawn hardwood, using a draw knife in either case.

OPTIMUM TIMING TO AVOID COMPETITION AND MINIMIZE EFFORT

Weeds compete with crops for water, nutrients and light. They also impede air flow, creating a damp microclimate favourable to fungal growth. The stage of growth when weeds begin to compete with crop plants depends on how close they are. If a vegetable seed and weed seed germinate right next to each other they will begin to compete almost straight away, but a weed growing midway between two rows will not compete until much later, perhaps weeks, depending on crop spacing, type of crop and weed, and growing conditions.

Weeding within/along the row has to be done by hand anyway, unless the crop is one sown in stations more than a hoe width apart. Even then, hand-weeding will be necessary next to each plant. The situation, described earlier, of a bed of seedling vegetables smothered by weeds, should not have been left to get to that stage. The weeds will already have had a detrimental effect on the crop plants. Roberts (1982) describes research with onions grown in separate trial beds. One bed was kept weed free while the others were weeded at different times and kept weed free thereafter. It was found that for each day of delay in weeding, the final yield was reduced by 4%. A delay of two weeks, therefore, reduced the yield by more than half. Onions are particularly vulnerable as their upright, tubular leaves offer little competition to weeds. Also, after a certain stage in their growth, onions do not make new leaves; so, they cannot compensate for earlier competition by making new growth. In the trial just described, by early June, the weight of weeds in a bed that had not been weeded was twenty times the weight of the crop.

Optimum timing of hand-weeding and hoeing can minimize detrimental competition and also minimize effort. The ideal strategy, therefore, is to hand-weed around each seedling vegetable, or along the whole row of close-spaced crops, at an early stage, as soon as there is appreciable germination of weeds. It is a matter of judgement as to when this will be. Too early and the weeds might be difficult to get hold of and there will be more to come in the next few days, requiring repetition. (There could be subsequent germination of weeds anyway due to the drawing up of seed-containing soil as described earlier.) Too late and competition will already have had some detrimental effect.

It is easiest to pull up weeds when the soil is just moist; it also seems to cause the least disturbance to the seedling crops. Then, later, the ground between the rows (and between plants of widely-spaced crops) can be hoed. Again, it is a matter of judgement when this will be. The weeds need to be still young enough to be easily cut through just below the surface, the soil should be slightly moist but drying, and the weather should be warm and sunny with no prospect of rain for at least 24 hours. Morning is the best time for hoeing. If there is not room to hoe, hand-weeding can be done, a little later if you wish. Pulling weeds is easiest to do when the soil is moist right to the surface.

Some gardeners go easy on the weeding towards the end of summer, saying that the crops are big enough to out-compete the weeds. That is true but the starved, dry little weeds struggling beneath the crops will still be making seeds by the tens and hundreds. Year-round vigilance is required if you wish to reduce the soil seed bank and make life easier each year. It is possible. The longest period I had one garden was 19 years. Perennials were eliminated in the first few years. Even seedling docks became rare, from being as dense as grass, in patches, in the first year. For the last ten years or more it was fairly easy to manage annual weeds on the beds but the paths remained a constant problem with the ubiquitous annual meadow grass and pearlwort. Every garden will have a different range of weeds that are most troublesome.

On land commercially cropped with vegetables for many years, it was found that there was much similarity in the species of seed in the soil bank; regardless of location or soil type. Annual meadow grass, annual nettle, chickweed, fat hen, field speedwell, groundsel and shepherd's purse were the most common species, comprising 70% of all the weed seeds found (Roberts, 1982, page 140). These seven species are the winners, the great survivors, wherever weeding is not done thoroughly.

WEEDS AS SOIL INDICATORS

When taking over a garden or allotment, particularly if it has been neglected for a couple of years or more, the predominating weeds could indicate the type and quality of soil, as well as some underlying problems.

▶ **Acid soil indicators:** Corn spurry (*Spergula arvensis*), indicates very acid soil. Knotgrass (*Polygonum aviculare*), grows well on acid, sandy soils. If there is a lot of plantain it could indicate an acid soil. Plantain also tolerates compacted soil. Horsetail (*Equisetum arvense*) indicates damp conditions, either from a high water table or poor drainage. It also prefers acid soil. Curiously, this genus has an affinity for gold in solution and can concentrate it more than any other plant, to a maximum of 0.25g per kg of tissue (Hyam and Pankhurst, 1995). It also accumulates potassium, phosphorous, silica, calcium and cobalt. It does, therefore, make a particularly useful contribution to the compost heap.

▶ **Alkaline soil indicators:** Field pansy (*Viola tricolor*; also known as heartsease); charlock (*Sinapis arvensis*), and wild poppy (*Papaver rhoeas*).

▶ **Fertile soil:** Stinging nettle, sow thistle, fumitory, dandelion, cleavers and groundsel, especially if they appear particularly large. I have seen nettles three metres high and sow thistles over two metres.

SOME PROS AND CONS OF WEEDS

These are just a few examples. There are many specialist books on the subject. See Recommended Reading.

	Pros	**Cons**
Annual meadow grass *Poa annua*	I have seen sparrows eating the seeds.	Flowers and seeds very fast, all year round. Thrives in compacted soil and dry places. Has surprisingly large ball of fine roots. Disturbs nearby seedling crops when pulled out.
Chickweed *Stellaria media*	Edible. Easy to hoe.	Attracts whitefly and red spider mite. Host to cucumber mosaic virus which can be carried in seed. Plant shows no symptoms. Host to viruses that affect lettuce.
Cleavers/Goosegrass *Galium aparine*	Edible. Very easy to pull out. Host to beneficial insects, e.g. predators of woolly aphis.	
Fat hen *Chenopodium album*	Edible. Contains oxalic avid, which blocks iron absorption. Amount increases with age. So, eat plants young. Quite easy to pull out.	Produces large number of seeds.
Ground elder *Aegopodium podagraria*	Young, shiny leaves good to eat. Available when there might be little else in the garden.	Spreads by roots, which easily break when being dug out.

	Pros	**Cons**
Groundsel *Senecio vulgaris*	Occasional host to cinnabar moth larvae.	Host to cucumber mosaic virus and beet western yellow virus, which can infect lettuce.
Hairy bittercress *Cardamine hirsuta*	Edible.	Produces seed very early in year. Seed explodes into your eyes if ripe pods are touched. Host to beet western yellow virus.
Horsetail *Equisetum arvense*	Shoots were eaten like asparagus. Accumulates Ca, Co, Fe, K, Mg, P, Si. Good for composting.	Very deep rooted and spreading.
Nettle, stinging (perennial) *Urtica dioica*	Top few pairs of leaves good to eat in spring. Very nutritious. Host to peacock butterfly.	It stings! produces large number of seeds.
Shepherd's purse *Capsella bursa-pastoris*	Edible. Easy to pull up.	Host to clubroot, beet western yellow virus and cauliflower mosaic virus.
Sowthistle *Sonchus oleraceus/ arvensis*	Edible. Pigs love it!	Large number of airborne seeds. Hydra-like regrowth of shoots if cut.

Summary

1 Dig out perennials thoroughly.

2 Never let any weeds go to seed.

3 Dig, pull or hoe at the optimum time a) to avoid competition with crops and b) to minimize effort.

4   Clear weeds in autumn to avoid 'bridging' effect of crop
    diseases from one season to the next. Use sown cover crop
    species to protect the soil.

5   It is better, in terms of saving time as well as crop yield, to
    manage a small garden that is kept free of weeds than to try
    to manage a garden that turns out to be too large for the
    weeds to be kept under control.

6   It is a myth that any crops or cover crops smother weeds.
    Crops just make weeds more difficult to find. Clear weeds
    before crops cover the ground.

Bonfires

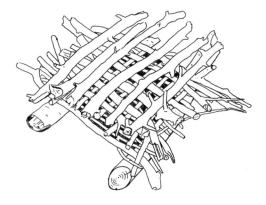

INTRODUCTION

It should be possible to manage a large vegetable garden
without ever needing to have a bonfire. However, most gardens
produce material which is most conveniently got rid of by
burning. There might be prunings from fruit trees and bushes,
and other trees and shrubs, hedge trimmings, diseased crops,
and weeds that have gone to seed. I think gardeners should take
responsibility for this sort of material from their own gardens,
rather than for it to be transported, which uses fossil fuel, and
then made into compost, which uses more fossil fuel in the
stacking and turning, followed by more fossil fuel to transport it
to customers, in bulk or worse, in plastic bags. An alternative is
to shred it yourself but that requires fossil fuel and the noise
would be annoying to neighbours. I have heard of someone
designing and making a hand-powered shredder but I have not
seen it. Another option is simply to stack pruned material until
it has rotted down enough to put on to compost heaps. That

could take years and occupy a lot of ground and it still would not take care of diseased crops or weed seeds.

Burning plant material is carbon neutral, it simply puts back into the atmosphere the CO_2 that was taken out during the period of growth. If the material were left to rot, the same amount of CO_2 would be released, although over a longer period. There are problems, of course, if you have neighbours. Bonfire smoke does contain some toxic compounds. *Never* burn anything other than natural plant and woody material; burning plastic produces very toxic compounds and a particularly unpleasant smell. I have to confess I have always liked the smell of burning wood and plant material but not everyone appreciates it. So, if you do have bonfires it is important to know how to manage them so that they burn fast and hot, with a minimum of smoke. This requires planning ahead and being organized – preparations that will also save you time, as the fire will be easy to light and burn efficiently at a rate under your control.

PREPARATION

It is possible to burn recently cut material, whether leafy or woody, but a larger fire of dry wood is needed underneath to sustain it and the large clouds of white 'smoke' (which will be mostly water vapour) make it look worse than it is. So, it is advisable to stack material to allow the moisture content to fall – how much is a matter of judgement and experience. The time required will depend on temperature and how much wind it has been exposed to. Fruit tree prunings cut in winter, when they contain less moisture anyway, will burn well after two or three months. The more moist summer prunings and hedge trimmings, as they will be drying in higher temperatures, will take about the same length of time.

How not to make a fire is to accumulate a single stack of material and then try to light it. It can take many repeated efforts and might end in failure or only a partial burn. Also, if it does burn, much wildlife will be incinerated: mostly invertebrates but there could be hibernating hedgehogs and even nesting birds, depending on the size of the heap and the type of material. The secret of success in starting and sustaining a bonfire is to begin with a hot fire of dry wood. Once that is burning well, anything could be burnt, however wet. So, keep any dead wood separate, in three piles – twigs to use for kindling, intermediate wood (2–4cm thick) and anything bigger. Before stacking, break or saw into lengths of about a metre. This will make neater, more compact piles and save time later. Also, cut to metre lengths the recently cut green wood. If any of the wood is particularly branchy and resistant to being compacted, lop it into shorter pieces. Seedy weeds and diseased vegetables are more of a problem. They should be kept isolated from the soil. A layer of non-seeding weeds could be laid on the ground first, or the material can be kept in sacks, preferably paper and preferably ones that can be spared to be burnt with their contents.

Before starting to accumulate piles of material for the bonfire, decide where exactly the fire will be sited and, if there is a prevailing wind direction, position the piles upwind, so that when feeding the fire you are not always standing in the smoke. In a built-up area, however, air movement is unpredictable and can often be in the opposite direction to the actual wind.

It should not be difficult to confine bonfires to two periods in the year, late spring for, mainly, winter prunings, and autumn for summer prunings, hedge trimmings, seedy weeds and diseased vegetables – onions and garlic with white rot, for example. During the ground-clearing stage when starting a garden, bonfires may be sited on areas yet to be cleared but in an intensively cultivated garden there might be no waste areas. In late spring and autumn, however, some beds can be made available, although perhaps not for as long as three months towards the autumn period. It might be necessary to move the stacks of material during the period of drying. This will help the drying process and also disperse the wildlife population in the stacked material. The super-efficient gardener will have catch crops growing in spring where tender crops will be planted out later but one or two of these beds would be available for storing bonfire material and for burning it just before planting out. In autumn there will be more choice of beds available, beginning with, in summer, where early potatoes or garlic have been harvested.

STARTING AND MANAGING THE FIRE

In a built-up area the general wind direction is of little relevance if you wish to avoid smoke blowing into neighbouring properties. Smoke tends to billow around in all directions. Experience of your own location will tell you if there is a least worst time to have a fire, with regard to strength and direction of wind. Choose a day when there have been several dry days previously, so that the fire is easy to start and burns with a minimum of water vapour, which makes the smoke appear worse than it is.

The most reliable method of starting a fire and maintaining it in a controlled way, so that, if necessary, it can be extinguished without having to soak all the material you wish to burn, is to start very small and build it up to a hot, fast burning fire before adding any damp material or recently pruned wood. Material can be added at a controlled rate; keeping the fire small if there are vulnerable plants, trees or a fence nearby, or piling it on if size is not a problem and you want to burn everything as quickly as possible.

Before starting the fire, break up the kindling to about 15cm lengths for the thinnest pieces and 25cm for slightly thicker twigs. Take two pieces of wood at least 3cm thick and lay them on the ground about 10cm apart and in line with the wind direction. Take a handful of the thinnest, driest pieces of kindling and place them across the two sticks. Then lay a few slightly thicker ones at right angles, then another layer the same way as the first lot. Add two more layers in alternating directions. Then set light to the first layer at the end where the wind is coming from. This should be possible to do with one match and no paper! However, if that does not work, use a small piece of paper, scrunched into a length, light one end and gradually push it under the kindling, keeping the flame in the same position. This allows more time for the kindling to light. Once the kindling is burning, add progressively thicker pieces of dead wood, laying them across in all directions. Purists might want to make a conical structure. The real purist will start with a very small cone of tiny twigs and use just one match but the previous method described is reliable and is probably easier if conditions are less than perfect.

When all the dead wood is flaming well there should be very little smoke. At this point start to add the other material, beginning with any dry weeds or the thinner pieces of prunings. The purpose of cutting pruned branchy, twiggy wood into shorter pieces will now become apparent. It can be compressed enough on the fire to keep it burning. If left uncut the gaps between the sticks are too great and they are very likely not to burn. If you are in a location where smoke will not be a problem to anyone and if you have a large volume of damp material to burn, the more you pile on the greater the build-up of heat and the easier it is to burn it. It is almost impossible to put a fire out by piling on a large volume of stuff. As long as there is the tiniest whiff of smoke, it will burn. It is best to go away and leave it; disturbing the fire *can* put it out.

When it has burnt out so that it resembles a smouldering volcano with a wide rim of unburned material, more can then be added. Before doing so, use a fork or the cultivator to rake around in the ashes. This has the effect of bringing to the surface lumps of charcoal that would otherwise be smothered by the fine ash. Exposed to the air they continue to burn and will keep the fire going. You can also spread them out if you want to maintain a certain size of fire. Otherwise there is a tendency for the area of the fire to shrink, because of the way that air is constantly being drawn in towards the centre of the fire. The rim of unburned sticks or herbage can be forked on to the fire before putting fresh stuff on or it can be left and added last of all.

When everything has been burnt, rake over the ashes again with a fork to bring lumps of charcoal to the surface. This is a good time to bake potatoes in the hot ashes. When the ash has completely cooled down it can be put into a paper sack and added to the compost heap, sprinkled on in layers, to recycle the minerals. There should not be anything in the ash that needs sieving out but, when clearing new ground there could be pieces of wire, lumps of iron, broken china and glass, or you might have had to burn old timbers with bolts, nails or screws in them. Choose a calm day for riddling ash, otherwise it is an unpleasant business. Small pieces of charcoal are fine to put in the compost and into the soil. It is thought to be beneficial, providing an enormous surface area for soil bacteria to live on. Furthermore, because charcoal will remain inert for many thousands of years, you will be sequestering carbon and making a tiny contribution to counteracting global warming.

Cover Crops and Green Manure

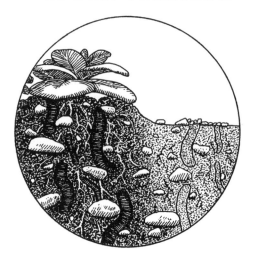

INTRODUCTION

A cover crop is one sown for the purpose of covering the ground between one season's crops and the next. A green manure is a cover crop that is actually dug or ploughed into the soil. The fertilizer value of a cover crop that is not incorporated is probably greater than one that is, for reasons explained below. In both cases the below ground part of the plant is retained in the soil. Up to the point when a green manure is incorporated, it provides the same benefits as a cover crop that is not. In this chapter, therefore, I shall simply use the term cover crop to refer to both.

Nature can be a useful guide when making decisions about gardening practice. Wherever soil and climate make vegetable growing possible, left to itself the ground would be covered by year-round vegetation. Anything less than that allows for the possibility of detrimental effects to the soil. The above ground parts of plants protect the soil surface from exposure to sun, wind and rain. Sun can dry the soil and wind can blow it away, but in temperate latitudes it is rain that is likely to cause most damage. Rain hitting the surface of bare soil can cause a hard crust called a surface seal or soil cap. This reduces subsequent percolation and drainage of water. If the surface is level it could flood but any slope will result in runoff; the steeper the gradient the greater the likelihood of soil erosion. In the small scale of most gardens this is unlikely to be a serious problem, as it is the combination of gradient and length of uninterrupted slope that determines the amount of erosion.

Soil is a highly diverse and complex environment and living plant roots are part of that interdependent ecosystem. If they are not present for a few months everything else suffers. Various compounds exuded from roots contribute to the formation of soil aggregates which maintain soil structure. The physical presence of roots also helps keep the soil 'open' and less likely to slump into a compacted state. The continuous process of root cell formation and sloughing off of dead cells provides food for bacteria in the rhizosphere, that part of the soil immediately next to plant roots. Sugary exudates from roots also provide food for bacteria. Soil bacteria are very important in the functioning of a healthy soil. For example, nitrogen-fixing bacteria are much more active and numerous in the rhizosphere, where there is more food to fuel this energy-intensive process. The complex interactions between soil, microbes and roots are beyond the scope of this book, (see Brady and Weil, 2002 and Gregory, 2006). Suffice it to say that the presence of living roots in the soil is highly desirable.

The tradition of digging in autumn and early winter seems to me to be merely imitating traditional agricultural practice. Before the era of tractors, ploughing took a long time. It was necessary to start in autumn to get it all done in time for spring sowing. On clay soil, exposure to frosts broke up the clods, making it easier to prepare a tilth later. On lighter land ploughing might not have been necessary to get an adequate tilth but no-till or low-till methods had not been thought of and simply burying weeds was one reason for ploughing. In a garden, once the initial clearing, digging and laying out of beds has been done, the fact that beds are never walked on and compacted, combined with the beneficial effects of additions of compost, will gradually result in improvements in soil structure, making digging, for its own sake, unnecessary. The planting and harvesting of potatoes when they come round in the rotation provides quite enough deep cultivation in a garden.

When soil is dug (or ploughed) an unnaturally high level of oxygen is incorporated into the soil matrix. This results in a rapid increase in the oxidation of organic matter through the activity of soil bacteria, whose populations are given a huge boost by the sudden influx of oxygen. Carbon is lost from the soil in the form of carbon dioxide and nitrate is released into the soil. There tends to be a natural peak in soil bacteria populations in late summer/early autumn, resulting from the combination of warmth built up over the summer and, usually, increasing moisture from rain, plus the fact that ripening crops are transpiring less water from their leaves and, with crops that have been removed, none at all. The best strategy at this point is to disturb the soil as little as possible so as not to add stimulus to soil bacteria, a) to conserve organic matter and b) to minimize release of nitrate. Unlike other plant 'foods' nitrate is not held by soil colloids (clay particles and humus) and tends to be leached out by the net downward movement of soil water over the winter period and when there is no growing crop to take up the nitrate. In summary, autumn cultivation promotes loss of carbon and nitrogen. The practice of autumn digging and spreading manure seems doubly perverse: most of the nitrogen in the manure will be lost through a combination of volatilization of ammonia and leaching of nitrate. It could be said that if digging were not done there would be no need for the manure – saving two jobs.

FUNCTION AND VALUE OF COVER CROPS

Vegetation is largely responsible for the creation of soil, from the first lichens that colonize bare rock, followed by mosses, grasses and trees; the natural situation for soil is for it to be covered by vegetation. Anything less than complete cover, therefore, has the potential for instability and damage to soil structure and quality. The most stable soils are to be found under natural woodland, followed closely by permanent pasture. Stable does not mean static; soil is a dynamic system that constantly replenishes itself. Soil in these two situations is self-sustaining. The ideal in gardening is to follow one crop with another, without a break. In practice, where there is a cool season with short day length, there are considerable constraints on this ideal. Just as effective, as far as the soil is concerned, is to grow whatever can be established in the autumn to cover the ground through the winter.

Cover crops serve a number of specific functions:

1 They intercept and break the force of raindrops falling on to the soil, greatly reducing the likelihood of soil capping and erosion.

2   They take up some of the available nitrogen in the soil, thus
    reducing pollution of groundwater and losses to the
    gardening system, as the crop will either be collected and
    composted or incorporated directly into the soil.

3   They add organic matter to the soil, from roots as well as
    above ground growth.

4   Exudates from the roots bind soil particles together to form
    aggregates or peds, which are important for soil structure.
    The existence of aggregates allows for concomitantly-sized
    pores which facilitate water movement, gas exchange
    (oxygen in, carbon dioxide out – necessary for root and
    fauna respiration) root growth, and movement of soil
    organisms.

An example of the last point, the beneficial effect on soil
structure, is the humble corn salad or lamb's lettuce,
Valerianella locusta. This may be sown in late summer to
provide pick-and-come-again salad leaves throughout the
winter. I once left a whole bed to flower and produce seed. It
does so quite early in the growing season and, therefore, will
not interfere with crop production, provided it is sown where
it can remain long enough to seed. It is easy to hoe off and
shake the seed out. I carefully dug up one or two roots to look
at them and was amazed by how large the root bowl was, and
how fine and closely packed the roots were. The soil structure
was already good in the garden but where the corn salad had
been it was as if the soil had just been cultivated or put through
a fine riddle.

PROBLEMS AND PRACTICALITIES

There are, unfortunately, some problems with growing cover crops. It is assumed throughout this book that the gardener wishes to maximize the production of edible crops. Some crops stand over winter but most are harvested in late summer or autumn. If a cover crop is sown after that I cannot think of any species that will grow enough to cover the soil surface or have much of a root system to provide significant benefit below the surface. If a crop is harvested early enough to allow a cover crop to get well established and provide good cover over the winter, then it is also early enough to sow another crop for eating. However, it is better to have small plants of cover crops than bare soil.

One way of getting round the problem of timing is to broadcast the cover crop seeds while the vegetable crops are still present, in July or August. This is known as under-sowing. The precise timing will depend on the type of crop and the weather. However, except for alliums, optimum densities of crops, when mature, will leave little or no soil visible from above. Not only will it be difficult, then, to sow the cover crop but there will be insufficient light or moisture at the soil surface for germination. If the cover crops are sown earlier, while there is still enough light reaching the soil, they will compete with the vegetable crops.

For a number of years I used oats as a cover crop, as I could get as much as I wanted from a neighbouring farmer in exchange for a bag of vegetables. At first I broadcast the grain and raked it in but some were not deep enough and got eaten by birds. So, after that I sowed in drills, nine per 1.2m wide bed. This was time-consuming enough but in the spring the top growth, if it were long enough, had to be scythed off and then the stubble, by then quite tough, had to be dug in and buried. Cereal varieties are bred to be vigorous. Unless it was thoroughly buried it would keep growing. I tried hoeing it off and raking it up for compost but that was even more laborious.

Grasses, including cereals, have good root systems for 'soaking up' available nitrogen and benefiting soil structure but they are not easy to get rid of. Hungarian grazing rye and annual ryegrass are commonly sold for green manures. The grazing rye will produce the most bulk of organic matter but is tough to dig in. Both, and also tares or vetch, when dug in have an allelopathic effect, that is, as they decay, chemicals are released into the soil which inhibit the germination of small seeds. Digging in should be done a month before any sowing.

The practice of digging in a cover crop is, in my view, a dubious one. Unless your soil is so compacted that it needs digging anyway, to make it suitable for growing crops, then the digging in of a cover crop is just a time-consuming job. The problems associated with cultivating in autumn, discussed earlier, will be less of a problem in spring, as the soil will be cooler, bacteria activity will be lower and nitrate released by their actions can begin to be taken up by the crops that will soon be growing. The amount of carbon released from the soil will also be lower than from autumn cultivation but the very act of digging does reduce, somewhat, the benefits of the cover crop – *some* soil organic matter will be oxidized and *some* nitrogen will be lost.

THE BEST WINTER COVER CROPS

What is needed is a crop that can be easily hoed off and

composted, leaving the roots in the ground with no danger of them growing again. Once or twice I have grown a bed of vetch after harvesting garlic. A huge amount of top growth was produced in the spring, it was easy to hoe off and vetch does not grow again from the roots. Loosening the surface with the cultivator was all that was required before sowing a vegetable crop. However, garlic is harvested early enough for a crop of beetroot, or even an early variety of carrots to be grown and there is plenty of time to sow winter-hardy salads – land cress, corn salad, miner's lettuce and rocket. In my experience vetch does not establish well unless it is sown while it is still summer and the weather and soil still warm.

However, perhaps I gave up too soon with vetch. In my garden diary for 25th September 1988 I wrote, 'Went slug hunting with a torch.' (And a sharp knife. It was the first time I had been out at night to look for slugs.) 'Killed over 400! mostly on the vetch. No wonder it has been disappearing, requiring repeated re-sowings.' The slugs were the small, pale grey, soft-bodied ones – field slugs, easily cut in two. My memory tells me that I went out the following night and killed another 400 but the next mention in the diary is for the 28th when 173 were killed. As I recall, over the winter I killed over 2000. For the next nine years I had that garden I had less of a slug problem.

The vetch had first been sown on the 24th August following a crop of onions. Presumably, if I had started slug hunting when it first came up, it would have grown well enough to cover the ground before winter. Vetch has quite a big seed and needs to be sown in drills to ensure good germination, unless the weather is very wet for several days, when broadcasting might be quite successful.

Corn salad, *Valerianella locusta*, has a much smaller seed, similar in size to those of cabbage and, therefore, requires less moisture to germinate. It is also easy to hoe off in the spring, before or after flowering, is soft and rots down well in the compost, and the roots do not re-grow. A little work with the cultivator produces a good seedbed. It is possible to scatter corn salad seed amongst soon-to-be-harvested crops in late summer and then disturb the soil with a fork to ensure some are buried. The above-mentioned problem of not being able even to see the soil is, in practice, not such a big problem. Where there are still maincrop potatoes there is no point sowing, as the ground will be dug in the coming weeks. Instead, grazing rye can be sown after harvest. Where winter and spring bassicas are there is less need of a cover crop, as the brassica leaves should be sufficiently extensive to intercept most of the rain and break its force. If you have a large area of winter squash, that is more of a problem but even there the leaves begin to die back in late summer. You just have to be generous when scattering the corn salad seeds.

You will need to experiment with the timing of this under-sowing to suit the conditions in your area. If they flower before winter, sowing was too early. If they do not grow to their full size, only 6–8cm across, before winter, sowing was too late. Sowing late enough to avoid flowering will ensure that they do not compete with the main crops.

Buying seed for cover crops can be quite expensive. I strongly recommend growing your own. Vetch and corn salad can be fitted in the rotation by sowing a bed or two after harvesting the earliest onions. The following year the plot will be mostly brassicas but after the seed is harvested there will be time to grow beetroot, a late crop of lettuce or possibly an early variety of carrots. Vetch and corn salad can also be sown after harvesting early or second early potatoes. As that plot will be planted with the tender crops the following year, there should just be time to harvest the seed before planting out the main crops. If not, those beds can be used for late salads, beetroot or carrots.

WINTER SALADS AS COVER CROPS

Cover crops that are also edible seem to me to be the best answer. The four that I have tried all need to be sown in late summer, before most main crops are harvested but because they are not just edible but very nutritious and valuable over the winter, it makes it worthwhile putting some time and effort into getting them established. You will need very carefully to loosen the soil around standing crops, scatter the seed or sow in drills if possible, then firm the soil to ensure good contact with the seed. If the soil is very dry it might be necessary to water a few hours before sowing to create ideal moist conditions.

On the morning of 10 January 1982 the temperature at Newport, Shropshire, was $-26°C$, the lowest on record for England. This was not so very far from our garden in north Herefordshire. My garden diary does not record whether I was growing winter salads but it does state, for 24th January, that the garlic shoots were coming up well. In most winters I grew corn salad (*Valerianella locusta*), land cress (*Barbarea verna*), rocket (*Eruca, E. vesicaria*), and occasionally, miner's lettuce (*Claytonia perfoliata*). Apart from some losses of rocket due to frost I cannot recall the other three ever succumbing in any winter. I could not say that corn salad has a particularly nice flavour but it is fine mixed with other salads or with bread and cheese and it has a high vitamin C content. Land cress is hot and tastes like water cress. Rocket is not so hot but has a unique savoury flavour and is high in vitamin C and potassium. Miner's lettuce has a pleasant, mild flavour and a nice texture and is also high in vitamin C.

All four of these salads are well worth growing for winter use. Land cress and rocket take quite a long time to produce ripe seeds in the summer but just a few plants will yield thousands of seeds. I would not recommended either as a cover crop, more than is needed for eating, as both have a tough central root that is difficult to hoe off, although they can be pulled up. Miner's lettuce seeds are not easy to collect as they tend to fall off the plant over a period of time but the plants are easy to hoe off.

Cooking Vegetables

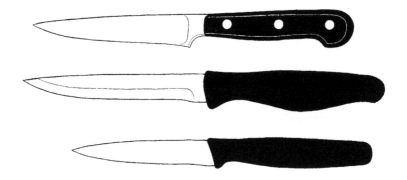

In Chapter 6 the problem of declining levels of minerals in all food was discussed. Growing your own vegetables and fruit, while endeavouring to improve the fertility of the soil, is likely to lead to an increase in mineral consumption. This will be especially true if, as a result of growing your own, you eat more vegetables and fruit because they taste so good and you do not want to waste any. Having devoted time and effort growing and harvesting, it makes sense to conserve as much as possible of the nutrients when cooking and also to maximize the body's absorption of nutrients when eating. The axiom, 'you are what you eat' is not quite true, rather, 'you are what you *absorb*'.

There are many different approaches to the art of cooking. I take the view that if you have fresh, high quality ingredients they need little preparation or cooking to produce tasty nutritious meals. This also means that a minimum of time and energy (for cooking) is required. What method of cooking can be done at minimum temperature and is convenient to do for short and variable periods of time? The answer is, boiling.

Boiling has acquired a bad reputation but the reasons for this are the way it was and still is done. In the last ten years I have shared kitchens with many people, mostly under 25 yeas old, in a number of places and countries. I was dismayed by two things: (1) their very low consumption of vegetables, (2) when they did cook vegetables by boiling, they submerged them in water which was poured down the sink after cooking. What remained was dry and tasteless. If food is deficient in nutrients to start with and if this is the usual method of boiling, it is not surprising that children are unenthusiastic about eating vegetables. Pouring down millions of plug holes vitamins and minerals from vegetables already low in these nutrients is tragic. Steaming is the method commonly recommended. It has always puzzled me that, if it is recognized that vegetables will cook in steam, why is it thought necessary to cover them in water when boiling and then to throw the water away? Perhaps cooks are either boilers or steamers and no one ever does both!

My method of cooking vegetables is, I believe, the best of all, for conserving nutrients, for energy efficiency and for the most pleasure of eating. Using an ordinary saucepan with lid (stainless steel or glass are safest – avoid aluminium or copper) simply boil, but in a minimum of water. Some experimentation might be needed to ascertain how much, or rather, how little, water is required. Nutrients will, of course, be leached into the water. You can decide whether to be left with just a few teaspoons of thick, sweet and incredibly tasty liquor or a little more to mash into potatoes or drink on its own. As a rough guide, if the pan is near full of vegetables to begin with, only a centimetre or two depth of water is needed. Most of the contents, therefore, are actually steamed rather then boiled. Some designs of pan lose more water vapour than others. So, check during cooking and add more water if necessary, to prevent burning.

Opinions will differ but I prefer to cook vegetables together. The different flavours are still distinguishable but they seem to enhance each other in the mixed flavours of the cooking water. Provided the vegetables are high in nutrients to begin with, this small volume of water is very flavoursome, whatever is being cooked. Even brassicas give a pleasant flavour if they are not over-cooked. There is no need to end up with soggy vegetables; they can be cooked for as short a time as you like. The shorter the cooking time, the less water is needed to start with but you will still end up with some tasty juice.

When I was young I was told that the water potatoes had boiled in was poisonous and that was why it was drained off. When potatoes are baked, nothing is taken away. Whatever is in the cooking water is also there in the baked potato. As with other vegetables, potatoes can be cooked in a minimum of water, which can then be used to mash them up in, so that no nutrients are lost. Potato varieties differ in the amount of water they contain. Some seem to absorb water while others seem to contribute to the cooking water. So, different amounts of water are needed depending on variety.

Potatoes should rarely need peeling. They can be scrubbed with a stiff brush or the outer thin skin scraped with a small knife. The knife needs to be sharp for this to be done easily and efficiently. Then any diseased bits may be cut out and also the flesh surrounding slug holes, as this has an unpleasant taste. You can smell this. So, you can smell when you have cut enough out.

Each type of vegetable can be added to the pan in order according to the cooking time needed. If the saucepan is big enough for the amount to be cooked, potatoes and vegetables can be cooked together – it saves energy and washing up. Potatoes, therefore, would normally go in first, unless Jerusalem artichokes or beetroot are to be cooked. Beetroot, peeled and diced will lose most of its flavour, unfortunately, but it is still all there in the cooking water and, if you just want a little for colour and variety, it is quicker than cooking it whole. Next in the pot would be other root vegetables, closely followed by onions. These should take no more than ten minutes, although swedes and parsnips might need to go in a few minutes earlier. Finally, with five minutes left of potato cooking time add any green vegetables. However, to my taste, the outer coarse green leaves of leeks and the solid red or white cabbages need as long as roots or onions. I have never noticed any unpleasant sulphurous smells or flavours resulting from this long cooking time of the hard types of cabbage. Salt may be added at the end of the cooking time so that it can dissolve and be mixed in. Otherwise, with coarse salt, it can be a bit like eating sand.

There has been much public health information urging people to eat less salt, but it is important not to take salt reduction too far. Sodium is necessary for many physiological processes. In my view, a rough indication that the right level of salt has been taken with a meal is that there is very little sensation of thirst between meals. One might wish to drink various liquids for other reasons but the need for water is minimal. This is assuming that the meal had a fairly high fluid content, as with porridge or potatoes and vegetables. If one does feel thirsty it could be because there was too much salt in the meal or too little. The first reason is well known, the second perhaps less so.

If too little salt is taken with a high fluid meal the salt in the blood becomes diluted to below the optimum level. The body then excretes fluid, in the form of urine, in an attempt to bring the salt concentration in the body back to what it should be. Then the fluid level in the body is below what it should be. So, one has a sensation of thirst. If one then drinks water, the process of salt dilution in the body is repeated. It is a thirst that cannot be quenched just by water. This was my experience when, many years ago, I tried to eliminate added salt from my diet. Plants have a lower requirement for sodium than mammals. So, plant foods do not supply us with adequate amounts. Fortunately I was still getting some salt from one source, cheese.

The sensation of thirst caused by too little salt is subtly different from that caused by too much; something I realized when I resumed eating salt. I have even noticed the low salt type of thirst when I tried using low sodium salt. The subject of salt is a fascinating one and I claim no expertise in it. Some people recommend ancient rock salts while others recommend sea salt. I use both. I recently came across Cornish sea salt, which is probably as clean a source as you will get from anywhere.

What size pieces should vegetables be cut into? To some extent the smaller the pieces the quicker they will cook and, potentially, the more leaching there will be, due to the greater surface area. Leaching only occurs for as long as there is a concentration gradient between vegetable and water. The smaller the volume of water the sooner equilibrium is reached, leaving the solution in the vegetable with the same concentration of nutrients as in the cooking water. If vegetables are cooked in a large volume of water equilibrium might not be reached, which means that right to the end of the cooking period nutrients are being drawn out.

Vegetables that have been drained will cool relatively quickly on the plate. If potatoes are mashed with cooking water not only can surface area be reduced but the extra water holds heat. With other vegetables, while it might be supposed that if left in large pieces they will cool slowly, in practice, a larger number of small pieces can form a single pile with relatively low surface area, or they can be pressed into the mashed potato and the small volume of tasty cooking water poured on top – yummy!

Many other ingredients can be added to a pot of basic vegetables, according to the season, gluts and personal tastes. In spring the young shiny leaves of ground elder are surprisingly pleasant and nettle tops are also good and very nutritious. They only need a couple of minutes' cooking. Many other leaves are edible. (See 'Recommended reading: Weeds'.) One year I had a glut of outdoor cucumbers. Sliced and added to the other vegetables, the cooking brought out some surprising and interesting flavours. I have known people who boil lettuce – well, you can eat more of anything if it is cooked. Unripe tomatoes add an interesting flavour and ripe ones are delicious mashed into potatoes. A few young leaves of lovage, or later, some seeds are excellent. Try whatever are your favourite herbs and spices. I used to be purist about vegetables but now confess to a weakness for adding a little dried fruit – tomatoes or apricots chopped up or raisins as they are. Their sweetness and fruitiness are an absolutely delicious complement to vegetables. It would be a shame to add fresh fruit to cooked vegetables but if you have a glut of apples they can add an interesting contrast of acidity and flavour.

The final complementary food to crown all of the above is a knob of butter. Fallon (2001: 20) states, 'use as much good quality butter as you like'; Richardson (2006) advises moderation; Harvey's (2006) chapter, 'In Praise of Yellow Butter' is an eloquent condemnation of modern, high-yield dairy farming and explains why organically-produced butter is better. Surely no one could continue to eat non-organic dairy produce after reading it.

Appendix I
Maintenance and
modification of tools

FORKS AND SPADES

Until a spade is many years old and has worn thin, it should be sharpened from time to time. They are not sold sharpened but it is hard work trying to push a blunt spade into hard soil or if you have to use one for lifting turf. The metal will probably be very hard. A file will soon become blunt on it. There are two other methods. Depending on the curvature of the blade it can be sharpened on a flat paving stone or fine concrete surface. Turn the spade over so that its concave or upper face is downwards. Only that side should be sharpened. The angle is not critical but should be less than 45°. The shaft will probably be near to horizontal while you sharpen. Push the spade back and forth with as much weight as can comfortably be applied. The other method is to use an electric bench-mounted grinding wheel. Great care must be taken not to over heat the metal. If it turns blue/black at the edge, it has got too hot and the hardness of the metal has been affected. So, apply little pressure and keep the spade moving from side to side. Forks are normally sharp enough and will become sharper with use, from abrasion with mineral grains in the soil.

The weak point on forks and spades is where the wooden (or worse, plastic) shaft meets the metal socket. The metal of the socket is stronger and less likely to bend or break than the shaft, therefore where they meet is a pivot point. Not only is the shaft thinned at this point, in order to make a flush joint but, with the wooden shaft tools, an unnecessarily thick rivet is put through socket and shaft just below the join. So, very close to the weakest point, where it is most at risk of breaking, about a third of the wood has been drilled away to take the rivet. This is a bad design. If you wish to make longer handles for spades and forks for people over the age of 12 the design can be greatly improved by using an iron splitting wedge to force the socket wider and making the shaft increase in diameter a few centimetres above the socket, so that it is stronger at this point. Also, drill new holes through the socket at least 3cm below the existing ones, so that this weakening of the shaft is further from the pivot point at the top of the socket. There is no need to have a rivet right through the shaft. Two short, round-headed screws put in from either side are adequate. The screws do not need to be opposite each other either. One can be further down so that the shaft is not weakened by two holes being drilled opposite each other.

THE CULTIVATOR

I suppose not many of these tools survive because it is a long time since they were required for their original purpose – they would have had heavy use and would have been liable to get broken. What is more likely to be obtainable is an old muck fork, which were the same design except not bent at right angles to the shaft. This is where a blacksmith is very useful. A muck fork can be bent and reinforced at the neck and a new shaft fitted. Modern muck forks are an unsuitable design to be adapted in this way. The prongs are too thick and tend to be slightly flattened towards the end, but in the wrong direction – the better to lift manure but not for pushing through the soil. My cultivator has prongs which are slightly flattened the opposite way – elliptical in parallel plane to each other, making them more streamlined in the soil. The shaft of the cultivator should be as long as the height of the user. Children can use an adult-sized cultivator, as the extra length of wooden shaft makes little difference to its overall weight. Children have no difficulty using this tool, as the prongs can be thinner than the modern muck fork, though it would be good to have the choice of a three-pronged version for children and for heavy soil.

Other uses are: raking up large amounts of coarse, cut weeds and pruned sticks and twigs at the site clearing stage and also for dragging from a pile of such pruned material, manageable amounts to put on to a bonfire.

Appendix II
Transplanting from pots

This description is for how the process comes naturally to a right-handed person. At the time of transplanting, the soil in the pot needs to be neither wet nor dry but damp, something like field capacity (see Glossary). This is so that the root ball slips out of the pot, holding together, without sticking to the sides or crumbling away and falling from the roots. Evening is the best time to transplant, or if it is actually raining, any time of day is fine, provided the weather is going to remain wet or overcast for the rest of the day. If the weather is wet and the plants have been hardening off outside, it might even be necessary to cover them to allow the pot soil to dry out a bit. If it is dry but cool, watering the day before planting might be appropriate but if the weather is hot and dry, watering just a few hours before planting might be needed. Ideally, the soil in the bed should be similarly damp. If it is wetter, there is not much you can do about it but if it is dry it will need watering, allowing time for it to drain to field capacity. For widely-spaced plants, such as squash and courgette, it is only necessary to water an area about five times the diameter of the pot, or the area that has had compost turned in for each plant, whichever is the greater.

I like to put the pots on the bed at their planting positions before starting to plant. It allows you to see if the spacing looks right, bearing in mind they are going to grow! You can also check that you have calculated correctly and have enough plants. Dig a hole, a little bigger than the pot, with a trowel. Turn the pot upside down in the left hand with the stem of the plant between the second and third finger, so that the fingers prevent soil falling out. Tap the tip of the trowel upwards against the rim of the pot. Two or three taps should be enough to make the soil drop out intact on to your fingers. Put the trowel down and use the freed hand to support the soil ball as you turn the plant upright and place it in the hole. Continue holding the stem lightly to keep it upright and use the trowel to fill in the gap around the pot soil, using the soil dug out earlier. Lightly firm the backfilled soil into the gap to eliminate large air pockets but do not compact the soil as this could slow down root penetration into the surrounding soil of the bed.

Appendix III
Useful knots

Whenever using string it is useful to tie a knot in each end before doing anything else. It will prevent the ends fraying and in some knots, square lashing for example, it enables you to keep the string taught, by grasping the knot in the end you have been working with, while tying it to the other end of the string.

REEF KNOT

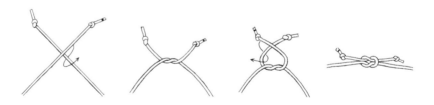

The reef knot is used for joining together two pieces of string or rope of equal thickness. It may also be used for joining the two ends of a piece of string to make a large loop with which to string up onions and garlic. It is easy to remember: left over right and under; right over left and under. Depending on the friction of the string and how tight you have pulled the knot, it can be undone by holding all four strands and pushing them towards each other.

BOWLINE

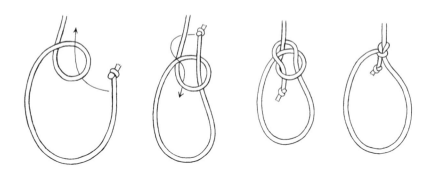

The bowline is used for making a non slip loop in the end of a piece of string or rope. Decide how large the loop is to be and allow enough string for that. 'Write' a figure 6 with the string. Thinking of it as writing helps to remember which part goes over which. It does not work if the upright part of the '6' is in front. Push the end of the string up through the loop from the back, then round the back of the upright going towards the left, then back through the loop from the front. To pull the knot tight, hold the short end and both sides of the loop in one hand and the upright in the other, and pull apart.

SQUARE LASHING

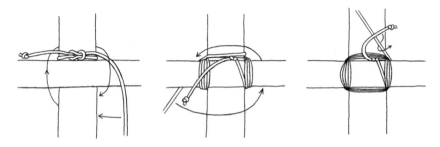

Square lashing is used to join two sticks or poles together at right angles. It is useful for attaching a horizontal stick to a row of upright bean poles. Natural fibre garden twine is best for this. It has a good friction property (explained below) and, when the bean poles are taken down, it is easily cut and can be left to rot, put on the compost heap or burned.

What length of string is needed depends on the diameter of the poles or canes. Stout hazel poles might need a metre but bamboo canes half that. The first thing to do is tie one end of the horizontal stick, temporarily, to the pole at one end of the row. Then lift the stick to see which pole it will reach. Lash it to that one first. Begin by tying one end of the string to the upright at a convenient height, about chest high, using a reef knot, but leave about 10cm of the short end for tying when the lashing is finished. With hazel, tie the knot just above the stump of a side shoot and with cane just above where it thickens at a node. When the long end is pulled to begin the lashing, the reef knot will change. This does not matter.

For a right handed person it seems natural to hold the working end of the string with the right hand and take it downwards in front of the horizontal stick towards the right, then behind the upright to the left. A left handed person might do the opposite. Whichever you do, try to keep the string taught all the time. Continuing with right hand instructions, bring the string to the front and take it up in front of the horizontal stick, then behind the upright in a right hand direction. Repeat this three, four or five times. Then when the string is brought to the front from behind the upright pole, *either* above the stick (to right of pole) or below the stick (left of pole), instead of taking it in front of the stick again, it is taken in front of the pole, behind the stick, in front of pole, behind the stick a few times. This squeezes and tightens the lashing previously done. When there is just enough of the working end of the string left still to allow it to be held taught, tie it to the short end left free at the start. Use the short end as the working end for a reef knot, putting it over and under the taught long end. Pull this 'half' knot tight. This is when the string's friction property comes in. You need two hands to take the short end over the long to complete the reef knot. Friction will keep the half knot tight while the second half is tied. Another half knot may be tied to make sure the knot stays in place.

Appendix IV
Wildlife gardening is bad for wildlife!

WHY GROWING FOOD IS BETTER FOR WILDLIFE THAN HAVING A WILDLIFE GARDEN

Suppose a family has a garden big enough to grow all the fruit and vegetables they need but choose not to grow food and instead have a wildlife garden, full of native species of grass and flowers, small trees, a pond, mosses, etc. A similar area of ground will be taken up elsewhere to grow the food the family requires. Some of that land will be in this country and the rest in other countries. That total area of land could, otherwise, be left for wildlife. Unless this commercial production is using organic techniques, the fields could be quite *un*friendly to wildlife. So far, then, there is no net benefit to wildlife from the wildlife garden. However, because the family's vegetables and fruit are having to come from other places, tens, hundreds or thousands of miles away, you need to add to the area of land actually required to grow the food, their share of all the roads, airports, sea ports, packing sheds, distribution depots, supermarkets and car parks that are required in order to get the food from the land where it is grown to their house. Also, a variety of pallets, crates, boxes, sacks, packets and bags are used in the process, which require land to grow the material or oil to make plastic, plus fossil fuel to manufacture and transport these things. So, one family's requirement of land to produce the food and get it to them is much greater than the size of the garden in which they could grow it all themselves. Therefore, having a wildlife garden results in a net loss of wildlife.

The value of land for wildlife is proportional to its size. The larger it is the greater the number of plant and animal species it can support. The greater the biodiversity the more stable and sustainable the whole system is. One wildlife garden is not big enough to support rabbits, hares, foxes, badgers, a range of rodents, owls, buzzards, hawks, snakes and deer, to name but a few animals. Nor is it big enough to have oaks, ash, limes, field maple, holly and pines, to name but a few native trees. Also, the wildlife garden will be surrounded by a combination of wildlife *un*friendly gardens, fences, houses and roads. All in all, the isolated wildlife garden is of limited value. If, though, it is a choice between a neat lawn and a wildlife garden then the latter is, of course, preferable but the family who wishes to fill their garden with a diverse range of vegetables, fruit, herbs and, of course, some flowers, should not feel that they are being unfriendly to wildlife, quite the reverse. It is better to have large areas of countryside left uncultivated than a fragmented patchwork of wildlife gardens in urban areas.

An intensively productive kitchen garden does actually support a large range of wildlife. While writing this I have just gone into the garden and looked at one plant, a marjoram which is in flower. On it was a female gatekeeper butterfly (recently I have often seen several there together), two honey bees, several small spiders, other unidentifiable 'creepy crawlies' and two beautiful tiny moths also which I could not identify. So, on one plant at one time of day several species were 'making a living' one way or another. I would, however, concede that some of these creatures probably also depend upon neighbouring neglected and ornamental gardens. Gardeners also know that gardens support a variety of aphids, slugs, snails, caterpillars, worms, beetles, and birds that feed on some of these creatures.

Glossary

Adsorbtion The attachment of an ion, molecule or compound to the charged surface of a particle. For example, positively charged ions of calcium, magnesium, sodium and potassium are adsorbed on to negatively charged surfaces of clay and humus colloids.

Biennial A plant that lives for two years, producing flowers and seed in the second year.

Bolt, bolting Applied to a plant that flowers earlier than expected. For example, a biennial plant flowering in its first year. In vegetable growing the term is also used when environmental conditions of heat and drought stimulate flowering earlier than is usual.

Brickearth Fine-grained silty deposit occurring in south eastern England, of complex origin; probably resulted from the reworking of loess, either by hillslope washing or by redeposition in standing water. (*Oxford Dictionary of Earth Sciences.*)

Capping Surface compaction of soil caused by rain. Rain washes the fine particles of soil to fill up soil pores between larger grains, causing a high density surface layer, known as a surface seal or soil cap. When dry this becomes a hard crust which can impede or prevent the emergence of seedling shoots. Sandy and, especially, silty soils are prone to this condition.

Catch crop A fast growing crop grown before, after or in between a main crop.

Cation A positively charged ion.

Cation exchange capacity The capacity of a soil to adsorb cations. This has a positive correlation to the soil's potential fertility.

Clamp Potatoes or other root crops placed in a pile for the purpose of storage and covered with soil. Traditionally, the crop would be covered with straw before adding on the soil.

Colloids In soils, refers to very small particles, of clay or humus, typically, one thousandth to one millionth of a mm. The characteristic quality is high surface area to volume ratio.

Earthing up The practice of drawing soil up around a plant or row of crop plants: to blanch the crop, as with leeks and celery; to support the plant physically, perhaps through stimulating further root growth, as with bassicas; or to stimulate further tuber growth in potatoes and prevent light from turning the tubers green.

Field capacity Soil moisture content after drainage (from *transmission pores*) under gravity has ceased, following saturation. Depending on soil texture and structure, this might take two or three days. A well-draining soil – a good loam or sandy loam – will drain in a much shorter time. What remains is what is held by surface tension (suction) around soil particles and within *storage pores.* Plant roots can draw on this water until the *permanent wilting point* is reached.

Friable Refers to soil consistency where the soil may easily be crumbled.

Frost pocket Area of land that is low lying relative to its surroundings and, usually, sheltered, where frost is particularly prone to form.

Haulms The stems of crops after harvest; usually applied to beans, peas and potatoes.

Honeydew is the sweet, sticky excretory material from aphids and whitefly.

Ions Atoms, groups of atoms or compounds that have lost electrons and are positively charged – cations – or atoms that have gained electrons and are negatively charged – anions.

Loess Unconsolidated, wind-deposited sediment composed largely of silt-sized quartz particles.

Mycorrhiza Literally, 'fungus root.' A close physical, usually symbiotic, relationship between a plant root and a fungus. A mycorrhizal root has greater access to water and nutrients via the fine and extensive hyphae of the fungus than do uninfected roots. The fungus obtains sugars from the plant.

Ped Unit of soil structure, e.g. aggregate, crumb, granule, prism or block formed by natural processes, in contrast to a clod, which is a compact lump of soil produced by digging or ploughing

Permanent wilting point The moisture content of the soil at which plants can no longer draw in water because the suction exerted by the plant is equal to that exerted by the surface tension of the remaining soil moisture held in *residual pores*. Plants permanently wilt.

Quartz Crystalline silica – silicon dioxide, SiO_2.

Residual pores Soil pores smaller than 0.2 μm (one micrometre = 10^{-6} metre or one thousandth of a mm). Plants are unable to draw water from these pores.

Spit Spade-depth of earth (*Concise Oxford Dictionary*). In the text the width of a spit is referred to. This refers to the distance from the forward face of the fork or spade, when pushed into the soil, to the edge of the soil about to be dug, i.e. to the cut made by the previous line of digging.

Stale bed A vegetable bed that is cultivated and prepared for sowing seeds but then left for a period to allow for the germination of weeds, which can then be removed before crop seeds are sown. There are, subsequently, fewer weeds to compete with the crop than there would have been. Stale beds are also effective in avoiding the bean seed fly. See pests and diseases of French and haricot beans on page 163.

Storage pores Soil pores 50–0.2μm (one micrometre is one thousandth of a millimetre, which is 10^{-6} metre).

Tiller As a noun, refers to a shoot growing from the base of the stem. As a verb, to produce such shoots. Usually applied to crops producing multi-stems, stimulated by the cold period of winter, e.g. cereals and broad beans.

Tilth The physical condition of the soil with respect to its structure, size of peds, friability and ease of cultivation. A good tilth is friable and a fine tilth is desirable for sowing seeds.

Transmission pores Soil pores larger than 50μm.

References

Bleasdale, J.K.A. (1979) 'Space to grow', in Salter, P.J., Bleasdale, J.K.A., Burchill, R.T., Cleaver, T.J., Gray, D. and Wheatley, G.A. *Know and Grow Vegetables*. Oxford: Oxford University Press.

Brady, N.C. and Weil, R.R. (2002) *The Nature and Properties of Soils* (13th edn). Harlow: Prentice Hall.

Burchill, R.T. (1979) 'Diseases of Vegetables', in Salter, P.J., Bleasdale, J.K.A., Burchill, R.T., Cleaver, T.J., Gray, D. and Wheatley, G.A. *Know and Grow Vegetables*. Oxford: Oxford University Press.

Campbell, S. (1996) *Charleston Kedding. A History of Kitchen Gardening*. London: Ebury Press.

Chinery, M. (1986) *Collins Guide to the Insects of Britain and Western Europe*. London: Collins.

Fallon, S. (2001) *Nourishing Traditions. The Cookbook that Challenges Politically Correct Nutrition and the Diet Dictocrats*. Winona Lake, IN: New Trends Publishing, Inc.

Goldman, A. (2004) *The Compleat Squash. A Passionate Grower's Guide to Pumpkins, Squashes & Gourds*. New York: Artisan.

Gregory, P.J. (2006) *Plant Roots. Growth, Activity and Interaction with Soils. Oxford:* Blackwell Publishing.

Halley, R.J. and Soffe, R.J. (eds) (1988) *The Agricultural Notebook* (18th edn). London: Butterworths, p.15.

Harvey, G. (2006) *We Want Real Food. Why our Food is Deficient in Minerals and Nutrients – and What We Can Do About It*. London: Constable.

HDRA (2001) *The Organic Way* **165,** Autumn 2001, p. 13.

Hessayon, D.G. (2006) *The Vegetable and Herb Expert*. London: Transworld Publishers.

Hibberd, S. (1863) *Profitable Gardening: A Practical Guide to the Culture of Vegetables, Fruits* . . . Quoted in Davies, J. (1987) *The Victorian Kitchen Garden*. London: BBC Books.

Hills, L.D. (1971) *Grow Your Own Fruit and Vegetables*. London: Faber & Faber Ltd.

Hyam, R. and Pankhurst, R. (1995) *Plants and their Names. A Concise Dictionary*. Oxford: Oxford University Press.

Ingram, D.S., Vince-Prue, D. and Gregory, P.J. (2008) *Science and the Garden. The Scientific Basis of Horticultural Practice* (2nd edn) Published for the Royal Horticultural Society by Blackwell Publishing.

Jönsson, H., Stinzing, A.R., Vennerås, B. and Salomon, E. (2004) *Guidelines on the Use of Urine and Faeces in Crop Production*. Stockholm: EcoSanRes Programme, Stockholm Environment Institute.

Kollerstrom, N. (Published annually) *Gardening and Planting by the Moon*. London: Quantum.

Phillips, R. and Rix, M. (1995) *Vegetables*. Basingstoke: Macmillan.

Pickup, J. (2002) *Potato cyst nematodes – a technical overview for Scotland*, Scottish Agricultural Science Agency (adapted from an overview for England and Wales by Dr Sue Hockland).

Pollock, M. (ed.) (2002) *Fruit and Vegetable Gardening. The Royal Horticultural Society*. London: Dorling Kindersley.

Richardson, A. (2006) *They are What you Feed Them. How Food can Improve your Child's Behaviour, Mood and Learning*. London: Harper Thorsons.

Roberts, H.A. (1982) 'Weeds and weed control', in Bleasdale, J.K.A. and Salter, P.J. (eds) *Know and Grow Vegetables 2*. Oxford: Oxford University Press.

Salter, P.J. (1979) 'Watering Vegetable Crops', in Salter, P.J., Bleasdale, J.K.A., Burchill, R.T., Cleaver, T.J., Gray, D. and Wheatley, G.A. *Know and Grow Vegetables*. Oxford: Oxford University Press, p. 106.

Small, F.L. (1974) *The Influent and the Effluent. The History of Urban*

Water Supply and Sanitation. Winnipeg: Underwood McLellan.

Steinfeld, C. (2004) *Liquid Gold. The Lore and Logic of Using Urine to Grow Plants.* Totnes: Green Books.

Sumption, P., Nunis, T., Rosenfeld, A. and Davies, G. (2005) 'Vegetable Crops for Organic Production', in Davies, G. and Lennartsson, M. (eds) *Organic Vegetable Production. A Complete Guide.* Marlborough: The Crowood Press.

Thomas, D. (2003) 'A study on the mineral depletion of the foods available to us as a nation over the period 1940 to 1991' *Nutrition and Health*, **17**: 85–115. (Accessed online 14.9.07. Data compiled from McCance, R.A. and Widdowson, E.M. *The Chemical Composition of Foods* (1940, 1946, 1960) Medical Research Council; *The Composition of Foods,* (1978, 1991) Royal Society of Chemistry/Ministry of Agriculture, Fisheries and Food).

Tucker, W.G. (1982) 'Storing Vegetables', in Bleasdale, J.K.A., Salter, P.J., Innes, N.L., Robert, H.A., Stone, D.A. and Tucker, W.G. *Know and Grow Vegetables 2.* Oxford: Oxford University Press. p. 103.

Wheatley, G.A. (1979) 'Insect Pests', in Salter, P.J., Bleasdale, J.K.A., Birchill, R.T., Cleaver, T.J., Gray, D. and Wheatley, G.A. *Know and Grow Vegetables.* Oxford: Oxford University Press, p. 30.

Zachar, D. (1982) *Soil Erosion.* Amsterdam: Elsevier. Cited in Morgan, R.P.C. (2005) *Soil Erosion and Conservation* (3rd edn). Oxford: Blackwell Publishing.

Recommended Reading

SOILS AND GROWING

Brady, N.C. and Weil, R. (2002) *The Nature and Properties of Soils* (13th edn). Harlow: Prentice Hall. (Contains more than the title suggests. If you want one book on soil science, buy the current edition of this.)

Gregory, P.J., (2006) *Plant Roots. Growth, Activity and Interaction with Soils.* Oxford: Blackwell Publishing.

Hessayon, D.G. (2006) *The Vegetable and Herb Expert.* London: Transworld Publishers. (Highly recommended for pest and disease identification.)

Hills, L.D. (1971) *Grow Your Own Fruit and Vegetables.* London: Faber & Faber Ltd. (A classic. Still worth reading.)

Ingram, D.S., Vince-Prue, D. and Gregory, P.J., (eds) (2008) *Science and the Garden. The Scientific Basis of Horticultural Practice* (2nd edn). Oxford: Blackwell Publishing.

Pollock, M. (ed.) (2002). *Fruit and Vegetable Gardening.* The Royal Horticultural Society. London: Dorling Kindersley.

NUTRIENTS, HEALTH AND CHILDREN

Clayton, P. (2004) *Health Defence. How you can Combine the Most Protective Nutrients from the World's Healthiest Diets to Slow Down Ageing and Achieve Optimum Health* (2nd edn). Aylesbury: Accelerated Learning Systems.

Fallon, S. (2001) *Nourishing Traditions. The Cookbook that Challenges Politically Correct Nutrition and the Diet Dictocrats.* Winona Lake, IN: New Trends Publishing, Inc.

(A cornucopia of information on food and health. The Introduction is a book in itself.)

Harvey, G. (2006) *We Want Real Food. Why our Food is Deficient in Minerals and Nnutrients – and What We Can Do About It.* Constable, London. (Very readable.)

Harvey, G. (2008) *The Carbon Fields.* Bridgewater: GrassRoots.

Myhill, S. www.drmyhill.co.uk (Nutrition, vitamins, minerals and diets.)

Palmer, S. (2006) *Toxic Childhood.* London: Orion Books.

Richardson, A. (2006) *They are What you Feed Them. How Food can Improve your Child's Behaviour, Mood and Learning.* London: Harper Thorsons.

(The above six books contain copious interesting references.)

COMPOST TOILETS, ETC.

Esrey, S.A., et al. (1999) *Environmental Sanitation.* Stockholm: SIDA.

Harper, P. (1994) *Fertility Waste: Managing your Domestic Sewage.* Machynlleth, Powys: The Centre for Alternative Technology.

Harper, P. and Halestrap, L. (1999) *Lifting the Lid: Ecological Approach to Toilet Systems.* Machynlleth, Powys: Centre for Alternative Technology.

Jenkins, J. (2006) *The Humanure Handbook.* Grove City, PA: Jenkins Publishing.

King, F.H. (1911) *Farmers of Forty Centuries, or, Permanent Agriculture in China, Korea and Japan.* Reprinted by Rodale Press, Inc. Emmaus, Pennsylvania. (No date.)

Pickford, J. (1995) *Low Cost Sanitation: A Survey of Practical Experience.* London: Practical Action Publishing.

SAVING SEED

Cherfas, J., Fanton, J. and Fanton, M. (1996) *The Seed Savers' Handbook.* Grover Books.

Stickland, S. (2001) *Back Garden Seed Saving. Keeping our Vegetable*

Heritage Alive. Bristol: Eco-logic Books.

WEEDS

Etkin, N.L. (1994) *Eating on the Wild Side.* Tucson: University of Arizona Press.

Grieve, M. (1977) *A Modern Herbal.* London: Penguin Books.

Mabey, R. (1975) *Food for Free.* London: Fontana/Collins.

Mears, R. (2008) *Wild Food.* London: Hodder and Stoughton.

Phillips, R. (1983) *Wild Food.* London: Pan Books.

Ryrie, C. (2001) *Weeds.* London: Gaia Books.

Weise, V. (2004) *Cooking Weeds.* Totnes: Prospect Books.

Index

Note: individual pests, diseases and mineral deficiencies for each crop are not indexed. See relevant crop section in Chapter 7.